To Alan and Barbara our good and
close friends from Falmouth.

John and Gillian 31st March 1985

This book is dedicated to my mother,
Ida,
daughter of A. W. Martyn,
who like her parents, grandparents and great grandparents
has been selfless, compassionate and generous to all.
"Never thinking it a virtue on her part."

The Best

The Best

a history of

H. H. MARTYN & Co.

Carvers in wood, stone and marble.
Modellers of decorative plaster enrichments.
Sculptors, architectural carvers and craftsmen.
Artists in wrought iron and stained glass.
Casters in bronze and other metals.
Cabinet makers and joiners.
Creators of memorials in stone, bronze and glass.
Decorations in ships ~ trains ~ palaces ~ cathedrals ~
churches ~ stately homes and public buildings.

Also including the founding of the

GLOSTER AIRCRAFT Co.

Researched and written by John Whitaker

Foreword Sir Hugh Casson CH KCVO
Drawings and design Gillean Whitaker

Whitaker, John
The best : a history of H.H. Martyn & Co. : carvers in wood, stone and marble.
1. H.H. Martyn & Co. — History
I. Title
338.7'61729 NA3547.6.H5

ISBN 0-9510252-0-1

Published by the author, Old School House, Southam, Cheltenham, Gloucestershire GL52 3NR.
Printed by Cornwall Lithographic Printers Ltd., Cardrew, Redruth, Cornwall.
Bound by R. Booth, Carnstead, Mabe Burnthouse, Penryn, Cornwall.

CONTENTS

LIST OF ILLUSTRATIONS

ACKNOWLEDGEMENTS

In compiling the information for this book over a period of six years, I have received help from so many people that it would be impossible to thank them all. Also unacknowledged, are the many craftsmen who in the pages of this book go unmentioned in spite of their immense contributions to the company and the world of visual artistry, but who are no less a part of the story and the success of Martyns. I hope these people will know that they have contributed, however indirectly, to this record.

I must mention some without whose help and encouragement I would not have started the book or having started would soon have lost heart.

It was the enthusiasm of Ken Brookes which gave me the impetus to start. His help in obtaining many photographs and contacting ex-employees of the company and his incredible memory for names and details of work, from art work to aircraft, have been invaluable.

Thanks also to Stan Lodge, who copied photographs for me in the early stages until I was able to do my own processing, and to Derek James for permission to quote from his book 'The Gloster Aircraft Co. since 1917', and help with editing the chapter on Glosters.

S.F. Scorey is thanked for the gift of the wonderful photographic sequences acknowledged in the book and for his advice on photography.

I count it a privilege to have enjoyed the help and advice of Hugh Burroughes, who at 94 years gave me the benefit of his amazing memory.

Thanks also to:

Miss Edwards, for saving so many photographs of foundry work by her father and granting patient loan of them.

Keith Bawden, whose enthusiasm spurred me on at the right moment, for saving some of the older carvings and moulds from destruction.

David Perkins, for saving the writings of H.H. Martyn and granting me use of them.

Dr. Steven Blake, Mary Greenstead and the staff of the Cheltenham Art Gallery Museum and Library for frequent patient help.

Amanda Chatwin, for permission to quote from her book, "Cheltenham's Ornamental Ironwork".

Graham Grinnell, for showing me what to look for in carvings so as to recognise excellence and genius.

Chris Prouse, a good friend who typed from my carelessly formed writing and said she enjoyed doing it! And repeated the process at each stage.

John Heapey of Schindler Lifts Ltd., for rescuing a box of old records at Sunningend.

Russell Adams, F.R.P.S. for his air-to-air photographs of Gloster aircraft.

A.D. Ingram for his help with information on the foundry, castings and library searches.

Pamela Lewis, librarian of Cheltenham College of Art, for the loan of over 80 superb photographs of work and for help in searching the Architectural Review.

M. Meddick, for information on the surgical appliances and other inventions of her father.

Mary Paget, for help with research on Cheltenham Ladies' College.

Mary Martyn, for information on her father's carving and for the only 1905 brochure to come to light, which she willingly loaned.

David Longden, for his help with some of the history of his father.

F.G. Taylor, for his considerable help with information on metal work contracts.

Victor Yates, Selfridge's archivist, for his willing searches and helpful information.

P. Dodds, Cheltenham Ladies' College archivist, for help with photographic work at the college.

G. Syed, for help with old records of church work in the Cheltenham area.

A.H. Nottingham, for considerable information about the foundry.

F. Hopkins, for information on foundry work.

L. Timms, for information on woodcarving and plasterwork.

A. Merrett, for information concerned with the welding of castings.

F. Payne, for information on the Cheltenham Manufacturing Co.

T.A. Miller, an ex-director of Maple-Martyn, for information on the closing years.

Jack Booy, Polishing Shop, for his friendly help.

Jack Claridge, for information and gift of photographs of plasterwork. Also thanks to his wife for her firsthand description of women at work on aircraft production.

Ted Clifford, for help on furniture and for photographs covering many aspects of the company's activities.

Bernard Arnold, who at over 90 was the sole source of information on stained glass manufacture.

Harry Constable, carver and modeller from 1920s era, for his helpful information and old photographs.

L.T.P. Banbury, retired Dowty Equipment director who helped with information on Dowtys.

Robin Paul, for showing me the whereabouts of Martyn and Emms work in Cheltenham Cemetery.

G.T.L. Summer, for information on joinery and H.H. Martyn (Aircraft) Ltd.

D.L. Peach for information on Hursley Park Winchester.

G. Dennis, for considerable help and assistance on a variety of quests.

My thanks for permission for the reproduction of the sequence of the casting of Robert the Bruce which was kindly given by the Trustees of the late C.d'O. Pilkington Jackson, A.R.S.A., F.R.B.S., F.R.S.A.

My special thanks must be expressed to Edward Welby, a long-time and true friend of mine and all the family, who worked diligently with expert attention to detail to ensure that perfection might be attained in the presentation of this book. His painstaking work and special skills are gratefully and sincerely acknowledged by myself and all the family.

Particular thanks to:

The Governor and Company of the Bank of England for permission to use the photograph of Ariel.

The publication Architectural Review, which was a source of invaluable information and photographs.

The staff of Cornwall Lithographic Printers for their willing help and genuine interest in the endeavour to produce a book to match the subject.

Finally, heartfelt thanks to my wife, Gillean, for her patience and good humour despite living for six years surrounded by an ever increasing litter of manuscript which spread itself from room to room, on table and floor; for her invaluable help in repeated copy checking, illustrating great-grandfather's writings, design work and not least for her unfailing support and belief in me.

My unbounded gratitude to Sir Hugh Casson for linking his eminent name and lifetime experience in the arts to this book, thereby giving the craftsmen and artists of the company a resounding accolade.

Keystone, something on which associated things depend for support. Webster.

Foreword

SIR HUGH CASSON CH KCVO

"THE BEST" — A splendid title for a splendid and indeed moving story . . . the story in text and pictures of a remarkable man, H.H. Martyn, of the remarkable enterprise he founded and drove to success and of the hundreds of gifted craftsmen — hitherto unknown — who dedicated their skills and loyalty to establishing the firm's reputation. "*What I ask of my fellow workers*" he wrote "*is the best that is in them to do . . .*" and in the following pages we can look at and enjoy the work — "*their best*" — that these craftsmen created in response to that challenge.

The beginning chapters of the story, as narrated by Martyn himself, are as gripping as a Dickensian serial. After a childhood of appalling squalor and poverty and a brief period (aged 13) as an art student, he became in his teens an errand boy, a button polisher, a photographer's assistant and a railway clerk — but always keeping his interest in the arts. In his twenties he became a self-employed monumental mason and by the age of 40 he was Chairman of the great firm that bore his name. Like all the best Victorian employers he believed in self-improvement and individual dignity, and a warm social conscience inspired him to provide classes in art, elocution, history and music for his workers. Over the next sixty years Martyns grew and prospered, expanding into every field of architectural enrichment. Just look at the pictures. Palaces and shops, civic centres and cathedrals, cinemas and ocean liners, national monuments and memorials, bronze lamp standards, plaster reliefs, silver wash basins and stained glass — even the House of Commons Despatch Boxes. This flood of ornament — carved, cast or modelled — was interrupted only during the two great wars when with characteristic enterprise and public spirit, Martyns launched into the design and production of aircraft. Characteristically too the products were spectacularly advanced in design and performance.

But the story ends sadly. In the austere post-war years of the fifties there was little money or demand for richness of form or delicacy of ornament. There were virtually no war-memorials this time. Nobody wanted new town halls or cinemas. Architects had lost their taste for enrichment — and indeed as well their ability to design it. In 1934 Martyns became the victim of a take-over and unbelievably in 1971 it was closed down. The craftsmen were dispersed, their skills scattered. The name of Martyns began to slide into the past. Anyone who has seen a great ocean liner being towed to a scrap-yard will recognise the poignancy of this moment. Luckily however, all over the world **"The Best"** still remains for us to look at and admire — luckily too, thanks to the careful and affectionate researches of the author of this book, we have recorded for us, the names of many of these modest and dedicated master craftsmen who too often — particularly in this country — go unrecognised and are therefore unjustly unknown.

I welcome this fascinating book therefore not just as a history of a great enterprise but as a symbolic roll of honour of those craftsmen who gave of **"the best"** that was in them to do. I hope it will be widely read — particularly by those in my own profession of architecture.

INTRODUCTION

H.H. Martyn & Co. was founded in 1888 as stone, marble and wood carvers, much of the work being gravestones, memorials and ecclesiastical decoration. Before the turn of the century the company had extended its activities to include decorative plaster work, joinery, cabinet making, wrought iron and small castings in bronze and gun metal. Royalty had already used the company's services by the 1890s and so outstanding was the work that other prestigious orders followed world wide.

By 1909 the fitting out of luxury liners had begun and this was to become a mainstay of the company business, over one hundred vessels being worked on. Many Cunarders, including the great Queen liners, had their finest First Class quarters fitted out by Martyns. In 1909 very large scale casting in all metals had begun. In 1914 important sub-contract work on aircraft was started and in 1917 a new company was born from Martyns: The Gloucestershire Aircraft Co.

The skilled workforce of Martyns, despite depletion through military service, was soon producing 45 aircraft a week. In 1919 yet another skill was added, stained glass work. Pressed steel work followed soon after.

The company's fine artistic workmanship in stone and wood, wrought and cast metal work, decorative plaster work, joinery, furniture and stained glass was put to the service of top designers, architects and clients in palaces, ships, trains, government buildings and houses all over the world — important works of art which will last through the centuries and be spoken of with respect by the art historians of future years. However, the reputation quickly won by the company for the finest work carried out in this country at the turn of the century tended to eclipse the individual artists and craftsmen they employed. The growth of the company was rapid and in 1900, just over a decade after its inception, over 200 men were employed, most of them outstanding craftsmen and artists.

The noted sculptor and designer Walter Gilbert expressed in 1926 the very sentiments which prompted the writing of this book; the largely unappreciated role of the art craftsman.

"I have used the word 'self-denying' in reference to the artist, and I will venture to suggest that I am entitled to do this, for what are the rewards held out for the long study vital to sound craftsmanship?

It is necessary for the craftsman, the artist, to look this aspect courageously in the face, for the rewards are not many.

Money? Few of those who pass their lives in the sincere love for the industrial arts do more than keep the wolf from the door.

Honours? How many artists, how many craftsmen in this country reap the honours which from time to time crown the achievements of the architectural profession? In this country, for a craftsman to hope for such recognition of his work as is so freely given in France, seems to be as futile a wish as one could express.

What, then, can the architectural profession do for the craftsman?

1. Give the artist credit for his share in the joint task, and explain the craftsman's point of view to the client; if possible take the craftsman to the client that he may explain his scheme in person.

2. Do not let price be the determining factor in awarding the commission, but give preference to the imagination and skill which come from long and arduous study.

With these two rewards of recognition generously given, the architect may rely upon the content, the goodwill and the unbounded generosity of the artist and the craftsman with their imagination and their skill."

On January 8th 1916 the Cheltenham Looker-On carried the following announcement:

THE KING has been graciously pleased to grant a Warrant of Appointment to Messrs Martyn & Company Limited of Sunningend Works, St Marks, Cheltenham as Architectural Decorators to His Majesty. This in consequence upon considerable decorations this firm has recently carried out in connection with the new Picture Gallery at Buckingham Palace, and also at Windsor Castle.

This space is left for the individual who had a father, husband, brother or indeed mother, sister or wife who worked at Martyns, to enter their name, so that posterity will know of their part in this extraordinarily gifted and special company.

Name ....

Address ....

....

....

....

Department ....

Dates employed ....

Martyns had become the largest employer in the Cheltenham area and continued to be so for decades. Men came to find work from far and wide and would speak with pride of the fact that they worked at Martyns. The pay was always better than elsewhere in the town, though the skills demanded were paramount. Men did not last long if their work was not up to the high standard demanded; even their peers would be intolerant if the side might be let down. Only the exceptional craftsman lasted but last they did, many throughout their working lives, and with great pride and affection for the company.

Orders increased rapidly year by year, generated by the high quality of the work. The company expanded and diversified until by 1920 over a thousand men were employed. The company name was further enhanced and firmly established, individuals of extraordinary personal talent selflessly submerging their personal reputations in the greater name of Martyns. I hope that this book will redress the balance a little in favour of the many men who by their work and dedication made H.H. Martyn & Co. pre-eminent in its field. Out of the several thousand men who were employed over the years I can mention only a few by name, but I hope that the many photographs will serve as a testimonial to all the men who put devotion to the company and dedication to perfection first in everything they made at Martyns.

It has not been possible to mention more than a fraction of the work or the venues in which work now resides. It can be estimated that the output of upwards of 1000 men over a period from 1888 to 1971 — 83 years or 80,000 man years or 160,000,000 hours of work — would require many volumes to do it justice.

In writing the history of Martyns and the chapter on Gloster Aircraft I am painfully aware of my lack of technical knowledge of the arts and sciences of the many aspects of their work. I am also aware that individuals who worked for the company will probably be even more horrified at what is left out. I myself will wish printing had been delayed as new exciting information comes to light in the course of time. However, within the limits set by time and the space between the covers of this book I hope some justice will be seen to be done to redress the void which existed unreasonably before.

Having discovered details of Mr. H.H. Martyn's life written by him in 1912 at 80 years of age, I feel he should have the first say and I have therefore devoted much of the first chapter to his own written words. Readers may find his style old fashioned, as indeed he was, in today's terms. However, his description of his early life and struggles is too vivid and poignant not to be included as fully as possible in his own style. By great good fortune his writings were discovered intact in the cellar of Wysham, London Road, Cheltenham, where they had lain for 60 years, successive owners feeling they belonged to the house. Mr. David Perkins, the present owner, kindly let me use them. The house once belonged to the company secretary, Mr. C.H. Denley.

H.H. Martyn aged 71 and his wife Fanny in 1913.

Chapter 1

THE PRINCIPALS

The founder: H.H. Martyn.

Herbert Henry Martyn was born in 1842 of very poor parents in Litch Street, Worcester. His father was a second hand clothes dealer and glover and life was very hard. In extreme old age he recalled his beginnings in these words:

> *No doubt, judged by the standard of living today, [1912!] the state of the poor in the middle of last century would be considered deplorable, and indeed it was so. Our next-door neighbour was an agricultural labourer, with a family of several children. This man's wages were about six or seven shillings a week and God only knows how they managed to exist; mostly on potatoes, for bread, bad at any price, was dear, so the menu was changed from swedes to turnips or potatoes, with occasionally buttermilk for sauce and perhaps, about once a month, a scrap of meat, for this, as also bacon, was cheap.*
>
> *It is little wonder then that I, like many of the children, grew into a dwarfed and sickly child and upon one occasion, when my mother carried me to the doctor, he pityingly covered my face with her apron and told her to take me home and let me die in peace. That was some eighty odd years ago.*
>
> *Indeed, the present-day more highly-paid labourer can form little idea of the discomfort and want endured in those days; but please don't run away with the idea that even want banished happiness: it was not so: people were more content and making the best of things had in a measure that which seems to be lost to-day — PEACE.*
>
> *Yet the want was often cruel, and I recall a scene which sadly illustrates this. On a stormy winter's night as my mother and I sat in our wretched kitchen* **Home**, *with its damp stone floor, while down the discoloured walls moisture stole in little streams from ceiling to floor, the wet and wind driving round the ill-fitting door and curtainless window, a large grate at the end of the room was fireless. On a broken table a rushlight gave the little glow which but increased the gloom. Nearby my mother sat deep in thought, her strong face sorely marked with trouble.*
>
> *Hers had been a life of hardship, borne ever bravely, but for once she was feeling the chill of hopelessness, work being difficult to get.*
>
> *In those young days, though not seldom hungry I was generally happy for I seemed to be living in a world of my own, even when at school, though I assure you it was* **not** *a boarding school or even a board school. It was situated in one of the poorest streets of Worcester, which street led from the Cathedral precincts down to the river, hence many of its residents were fishermen, bargemen, or general labourers. The school was in close contiguity to a factory, although the employees therein were mostly 'too respectable', or thought they were, to dwell in such a low quarter. This was the school in which at about the age of six years I was duly received by the headmaster who, I soon discovered, was in his own estimation a humorist and given to express himself in rhyme; these gifts, enforced by the aid of a long cane to point his jokes and enforce respect for his poetical genius, were generally successful in making the wise laugh and the injudicious howl.*
>
> *At about the mature age of eight years I was delivered from the immediate sphere of his cane somewhat, by being made a salaried* **teacher** *to the so-called infants, the appointment bringing me a wage of seven shillings per quarter* **plus** *evening lessons by the second master 'when convenient' to him. It was, indeed, a proud lad who took to his mother the first quarter's pay and, like the noble woman she was, she at once haled me out to the nearest book-shop and made me happy by spending a shilling in the purchase of my own first book, which, by the way, was Mrs. Stowe's 'Uncle Tom's Cabin', chosen on the recommendation of the elderly shop-lady whose grey side curls seemed to convince me of her literary judgement.*
>
> *You may smile at my onerous duties at this school, but seeing that some of the pupils under my control were stout, well-fed children while their teacher was but a puny*

On a broken table a rushlight gave a little glow which but increased the gloom. Nearby my mother sat deep in thought, her strong face sorely marked with trouble.

sample of humanity, you may realise that often my dignity was touched by promises of what would happen after school-hours if they caught me alone; but threats of the master's cane, if not of his rhyming, were sufficient to keep the peace.

This tuition cost the parents twopence per week which, in my case, some good soul paid, or my early education would have been supplied in that wider school, the street, or in the Church Sunday School which I and the others were expected to attend. To me it was more joyful than to many of the 'scholars' for, having a good memory, I was generally successful in getting the prize of a few coppers offered weekly by my not very brilliant teacher to the lad who best learnt to recite certain texts, collects, etc, and cheap it was at the price, for it filled up the lesson time and entailed scant preparation by the teacher.

'So to school most regularly' — as an infant Pepys might have said. After an hour we were duly marched through the High Street to the grim Parish Church, for in those good old days before the powers that be had evolved the practice of 'cleanliness being next to godliness', the church was as grim as the undisturbed dust of half a century could make it.

Heading our procession was our portly superintendent, a most respectable draper, who waddled along bearing the symbol of authority, viz:- a long wand or cane, which latter, I may say, was often heard by the congregation and felt by some unlucky boy during the tedious service, this favoured boy generally responding with a disturbing howl, for very often it flopped on to the head of one who was innocent enough.

The ancient house to which we had moved from our kitchen home was in the centre of a street much shunned by respectable citizens, though but a few years earlier its cobble-stones were rattled over by the coaches which daily passed to and from the City, the local story being that Charles, the King, there met his advisers previous to his flight from 'The Faithful City'. Its rugged rafters and beams, its uneven floors, all dark with time and foul with the soiling of many years, dim with the scant light from thick, rough glass in the diamond paned windows, its many nooks and corners with ghostly shadows — all combined to make the house a source of mystery and wonder to me, yet in my mundane moments I must have realized that it was a home of sheer poverty.

The front room, dignified by the name of 'shop', had many years before been doubtless whitewashed between its dark oak beams and over the ruggedly plastered walls; but in my time it was seasoned to a variety of tones from drab to deep grey; the box-like counter and the window-boards were strewn with stock, some of which, during the day, was hung at the doorway, the whole presenting the appearance of a vile rag cemetery wherein were stored the hopelessly patched and cast-away coverings of man and woman. Some of it had probably been worn with pride, when the earth was younger, by the well-to-do, and then descended faithfully to serve the poor, for shoddy was then unknown; ultimately, threadbare, bepatched, to be bought for a song by the very poor.

Indeed our short street was full of both comedy and tragedy, for it seems to me to have been peopled with odds and ends of humanity. There was the old soldier who mended our shoes until they were beyond even his skill. I can see him 'in my mind's eye, Horatio', seated in his little shop with his wonderful leather apron and paper skull-cap, plying his awl or hammer or, indeed, sometimes his strap on the teasing children, when caught, who would push open the lower half of the front door, (the top part being generally open), to make the little bell hanging thereon ring. This cobbler was a devout believer in the Constitution as exemplified by 'The Great Juke' under whom he had served; but the point of interest to us boys was his belief that the ghosts of his old regimental band had taken their anything but resting place in his head, for he declared that they practised therein night and day, 'down 'em', gin being the only remedy he had found to stay their 'Dog's-holiday'.

There were at least five other emporiums for the restoring and selling of decayed boots and shoes, and these were intermixed with shops dealing in old clothes, pubs and tramp lodging-houses, hucksters' shops and a baker's, where, on Sunday, those neighbours who were sufficiently prosperous took their dinners to be cooked at a charge of one penny per dish.

Nearly opposite to the Bakehouse was our Public Library, kept by one of the restorers of foot-wear who had found it useful in supplementing his meagre earnings. There, at the cost of a penny for the week, he supplied a volume of the current literature bound roughly by himself, and there being in those days no censor, his collection was very mixed. Each volume consisted of about half a dozen weekly numbers, such as 'The London Journal', which was wholesome reading; but not so much can be said of 'The Mysteries of Paris and London' and even viler publications, which to-day would be rightly banned. Nor did he lack customers from amongst the factory people, who were mostly girls.

In our street the folk practised one of the teachings of Positivism: they 'lived openly' and it was no unusual occurence for the various families to wash their not over-clean linen in public, when the sympathetic neighbours would be regaled as they stood or sat in their doorways with 'spicy' information about each other's domestic affairs, varied with numerous events in their life's history, the whole conveyed in anything but classical language. Not seldom this ended in their husbands lending a hand or two, until a cry would arise from the outskirts of the fray-'Peeler!' Which cry acted swiftly as a restorative of seeming order and innocence.

Occasionally our street became a meeting-place of magisterial squires, law-making lords and sporting gentry generally, for our street and the whole City were the proud possessors of another boot-mender, born and reared therein, whose fame went out to the ends of the land as a champion light-weight. Sometimes he held a levee and displayed his form in a match held in a building at the back of his father's 'Black Horse' Inn, which at ordinary times could scarcely be thought of as fashionable; such seemed to be the intellectual joys of eighty years ago.*

It was in such surroundings that my early childhood was lived, seeing, yet not understanding, like most of the children, for I am under the impression that eighty years ago the rising generation was not so precocious as to-day; certainly I was not unhappy, though a wan and sickly child whose one reality amidst my dream-life was the mutual love between my mother and myself. She was a woman who cheerfully toiled with a spirit of noble independence, rugged and unlettered, maybe, but self-denying and willing at all times to help others. I have known her, after a long day of labour, sit up through the night with a poor, ill or dying neighbour's child, not occasionally but often, and think it no special virtue on her part. Certainly she had a splendid physique and possessed not only a strong will, but a keen intellect; disliked by her mother because she was not a boy, she, as a child, was made a drudge and while her sisters were educated she was not, and when a child of twelve she left her home to enter service. Not long afterwards, finding work at glove-making, she taught herself to read and, as she was a poor hand with her needle, often read to the other girls while they helped her with her work. At the age of fifteen she married my father who may have been a year older, but of him the picture films are not pleasant. A clever man with many opportunities to attain success in life, he wasted all, including life, in pursuit of so-called pleasure, following, indeed, in the footsteps of his father.

They were well-connected, and my father in his poverty was visited by a gentleman who explained that he had searched for him and at the same time arranged to take him the following day to claim an estate. The man

* This was George Mantle, of Lowessmore.

gave my father a few sovereigns to obtain necessary clothes and promised to bring a post-chaise for the journey on the following day. When the time and man arrived my father, who had had a glorious day with his friends, was found in a state of log-like bliss. The disgusted gentleman remarked, 'Wealth would be a great curse to such a man,' and departed never again to be heard of.

At this time my mother was the only wage-earner, for my father had broken completely down and for a long period had been paying the penalty of his unwisdom. The time came when she found life unbearable and after a violent scene, they parted. She left, taking me with her, though at that period my mother's niece, who had married a farmer, would have adopted me, as she was childless. With them I spent two or three days in what, doubtless, was comparative luxury; but they were glad to send me home for I would not be comforted, and I can remember the joy with which I greeted my mother upon my return, laden with fruit and cake, and a bright silver coin in my hand proudly to give my loved one.

The new residence my mother had secured was one room, over a shop in the same street. It was as quaint as the one we had left; the floor as uneven, the walls as grimy, for it was very ancient: its one virtue was its cheapness, the rent paid being about one shilling weekly.

At the age of eleven or twelve I became a 'student' at the Art School held in connection with South Kensington, or 'School of Design', as it was then called, for my proud mother had shown to one of the ladies at whose houses she worked, a drawing I had made on a scrap of paper from a bit of broken china, and coloured by the aid of a toy box of paints. The result was that this lady undertook to get me into the school, for I was considerably under the age at which students were taken, and also to pay the fees.

What a poor knowledge she must have had of 'Art', but I would here record my gratitude to her, for this event was to colour my life's destinies and I would wish to believe that from the other side of the veil she has seen that her kindness to a poor lad resulted in his earning a respectable name among his fellow-craftsmen.

The students at this school were all older than myself, some few being middle-aged, and were all of them in a better social position and better educated than I, but they were mostly kind or tolerant to me. One student became a well known Royal Academician, who on one occasion expressed in not very flattering terms his poor opinion of myself. Being some years my senior and a highly respectable youth, he doubtless was justified in objecting to my running in his wake on the way to the school, and so, calling me a little ragamuffin, he threatened dire punishment if I persisted in following him. I was too abashed to reply, though, indeed, it was my simple way of showing adoration for one who to my childish mind seemed a being of higher order than my poor self. I do not wonder now that a smartly-dressed, fine youth should have been irritated at such rude behaviour from a small boy, clad too often in a dirty pinafore or 'smock', which, worn half the week on its right side, was turned inside out and worn for the remaining days, topped with a cap of sorts, and round the neck a muffler, generally ragged to match.

This artist's brother, who was also a student at the school, and who in mature life was knighted for a great engineering work, was far more tolerant. These gentlemen, being successful, doubtless became wealthy. I am more, for I want neither wealth or fame to make me fairly happy, and I had no thought of such things in those early days, when I lived in a joy-dream, my hunger often stayed by a crust of bread, for I felt the gladness of simply living, and sang songs of my own without rhyme or conscious reason as I fairly danced or skipped on my way. Sometimes I developed a wild desire to fly, arms extended over the heads of slow-going mortals, with, occasionally, rather disastrous results to hats and bonnets; nor did I wait to see my astonished victims retrieve their head-gear but really "flew".

Our School of Art was an excellent one and several well known artists received their early inspiration and helpful encouragement from the kindly headmaster who, natheless my untidy appearance and restless ways, was unvaryingly gracious to me.

It was about the mature age of thirteen years that I made the acquaintance of my future wife and it was a case of calf-love at once — on my part anyway — and finding that by leaving school at eight o'clock in the evening I could generally see her, my art efforts were made subservient to 'love's young dream'. Anyway I see a pleasing picture of my child love, standing hoop in hand, clothed in a short calico dress, shyly smiling from under a sun-bonnet, with her frilled drawers, white stockings and sandaled shoes. A fair sight indeed, at least I thought so and at once expressed my determination to be her husband and which some eleven years later I was happy to become, and for fifty three years we enjoyed the ups and downs of life together to the accompaniment of eight children.

About this period of my life my mother thought it necessary to take me to 'see the Doctor', or, rather, that he should see me. After the usual perfunctory examination he decided that I was not strong enough to attend both night and day schools and that one must be given up. Needless to say which I was most in favour of, and so for a short time I became a loafer, to the envy of the other boys. One day, meeting the headmaster of another school, I was stopped by him and

I see a pleasing picture of my child love, standing hoop in hand, clothed in a short calico dress, shyly smiling from under a sun-bonnet, with her frilled drawers, white stockings and sandaled shoes.

asked why I was not at school: upon my explanation being given he inquired if I should like to be at work and, not without qualms, I replied, 'Yes, sir.' A few weeks before that, on the recommendation of my art master and immediately on leaving the day school, I had found work at a well-known china factory, and something like a week spent in its gilding department had been more than sufficient to make me suspicious of workshops. Being poorly dressed, small and shy, the other and older lads engaged in the gilding department found me an easy prey for their cruel fun which culminated when, one day, they asked me if I should like one of the nuts they seemed to be enjoying; naturally I replied, 'Yes', and they gave me the largest, which I at once put into my mouth and cracked. Then the 'fun' began, but not *for me. The taste and smell of the rancid oil with which they had filled it 'haunts my memory still'; thereupon I retired as gracefully as I could, considering my sudden* sickness, *and with a lasting disgust for their 'art'fulness.*

Now for a few of your 'ifs', my friend. 'If' those boys had not offered me that nut, or 'if' I had had sense enough to refuse or not to crack it with my teeth, and possibly other 'ifs', I might have passed my long life edging cups and saucers with the chocolate-coloured paint that, when taken from the kiln, becomes gold. But, taking my friendly schoolmaster's recommendation, I at once proceeded to the Bookshop, and there secured a dignified position as errand-boy with the large wage of two shillings per week. Among my various duties was that of devoting my spare time to dusting stacks of second-hand books stored in rooms over the shop. This was a joy to me for I loved reading though, until then, my acquaintance had mostly been with 'The London Journal' class of literature. Now, when one day I opened one of the volumes I entered a strange new world entitled 'Gulliver's Travels', every word of which was true to my poor, untrained mind, and indeed was a wonderland where even hunger was forgotten.

As errand-lad I stayed until, at the age of fourteen, I left to be apprenticed to the trade one of my brothers had learned who was at this time working at the same shop as a fully-fledged workman, having completed his seven years' apprenticeship. He was now married and, having a family, lived in another part of the town. The trade was that of picture-frame making, though bearing the more dignified name of 'Carving and Gilding'; the carving had become a thing of the past and had declined to casting from wood or sulphur moulds, 'compo' decorations which were glued on to the frame mouldings, while the gilding was reserved for the more experienced workmen.

The apprenticeship term was for seven years and the wage, starting at one shilling per week, increased by a similar amount through each of the seven years. The hours of labour were from six in the morning until eight in the evening, excepting Saturday, when we left at six o'clock. Half an hour was allowed for breakfast, a few minutes for tea, and one hour between one and two o'clock for dinner, which latter was all too long for my scanty meal. This often consisted of an apple baked in dough and was not over-sustaining, but my mother's earnings of one shilling per day had to keep our home.

At about the age of 16 my mother despairing and being strongly urged gave up our rooms and took work about 20 miles away at a farm where her niece and her husband lived. So I became homeless, and hearing that a newly opened Working Men's Institute took in lodgers, I applied, and though being under the age of 16 at which members were admitted I was allotted part of a double-bedded room at a charge of 2/- (10p) per week. There were six or eight other lodgers, mostly artisans, and 100 or 200 members.*

It was at this Working Men's Institute that I gained considerable experience and a little education, of sorts, by joining a class or two and becoming acquainted with other odds and ends of the great human family.

Our Institute was a many-roomed building quaint enough in its interior arrangements, for it was ancient and, I believe, had once been a school. Besides the rooms occupied by the caretaker, his wife and maid and also about eight lodgers, there was ample room for smoking, reading, refreshment and games, as well as class-rooms. Outside, the large grounds supplied space for a giant's stride, bowling alley, wash-houses and a large hall for meetings, concerts, dances, etc; in fact, the whole formed a workman's club and was well managed by a committee of its members. Its custodians, both old servants, were a childless couple, kindly-hearted and capable, who, with the aid of a maid, kept the place very clean and comfortable.

Though seventy years have passed, I can see the prim housekeeper, with her dangling curls on each side hanging like spirals from her scalp, sometimes to be shaken a little angrily before her easy-going and occasionally self-indulgent husband, a man who loved a joke and did not despise a pot of something stronger than tea, when his 'Mary' was not about — good souls both.

For some months I found work in staining and polishing leather buttons under my brother's direction, for he had discovered a new method to do this kind of work although occupied mostly himself in his photographic studio. Owing to domestic troubles, he suddenly determined to leave the town and disposed of the studio to a man who was under the impression that he could run the business after a few hours' instruction and who promised to pay for the stock at some future time. After about a week this promising *purchaser repented of his bargain, sought me out and, declaring that he was not cut out for artistic work, asked me to take over the 'going' concern and offered to teach me the little that he had learnt. Being out of work and penniless, I accepted and after an hour or so's instruction, behold me, at the age of sixteen, a fullfledged photographer. Very soon my professional troubles began; my first client, a lady with two or three children, required a family group to be taken and, after arranging the group to my own satisfaction, I prepared and exposed my first plate — in fact, a round dozen of them in succession, with most consistent results. Where the charming picture should have been was a good representation of a thick London fog, and after an hour or so, the sitters became fidgetty. It had not taken that time to make* me *more so, and we were all relieved (they less than I, probably), when, at last, the lady's husband turned up to inquire for his missing family. We at once held a committee meeting and this gentleman, knowing more about photography than I, advised me to rectify the silver bath used at that period for 'positive' pictures, and, collecting his patient property, retired, leaving me rather sick. Mercifully he abstained from asking compensation for his family's wasted afternoon.*

Ah me! Half the misery of life seems due to disappointments through sheer incompetence, but, possessing the confidence of ignorance, I struggled on until, by chance more than design, I was able to produce the necessary pictures for the few customers who, induced by my show-case exhibited at the entrance of the yard where the studio stood, came to seek my artistic services. In those days money was not so plentiful as it is today and that, combined with the out-of-the-way position of my studio, kept me in a chronic state of seediness. Some weeks I would do fairly well and others deplorably; a worse evil than poverty following from lack of customers, being the enforced idleness which made the days seem long and dreary, petrifying body, soul and spirit into stony hopelessness.

Occasionally I had curious visitors and listened to their strange ideas of the mysteries attached to my profession. One day a couple of country women came to be photographed; evidently they believed the whole process was magical, for I heard them discussing if 'the devil who drawd *them was hid in the little box (camera), or in the dark room;' anyway it was highly suspicious. Why was it not done straightforwardly in the day-light? It was uncanny; and they shook their heads*

* Ribbesford, near Bewdley, Worcs.

until the picture was produced when their pleasure at seeing themselves represented on the plate was amazing.

In those early days of photography, before dry plates and paper pictures had been evolved, the work was done by the aid of collodion film on glass, the results, when completed and dried, could be painted on and one was generally able to get extra pay for colouring the face, ribbons, etc., or adding rings, brooches and chains by the use of gold paint.

Bad times grew worse, and soon to my studio, empty and forlorn, I bade adieu without a tear, and as 'nothing will come of nothing' I soon was like the Prodigal Son 'an-hungered', and looking doubtingly at my other investment viz, a brass or gold chain.

Alas, there were no buyers although I offered it at the price of a week's rent. How well I remember the Sunday following; a crust of bread for breakfast, and though I knew of friends who would graciously give me a dinner, my gorge rose at the thought, so making the excuse of being out for the day I wandered into the country — in the company that I least liked, my own.

In such circumstances the beauties of nature appealed in vain to charm; hopeless and weary I at length sat on a stile, and I fear, shed a few tears in the miserable cause of self-pity. Anyway it was an experience, I soon realised its weakness and futility, and with a small glimmering of hope, I determined to pay a visit, on the morrow, to the poor man's 'uncle' and see if it were possible to soften his hard heart and realise a few shillings on my last asset, to wit, the brass chain.

The next morning I, with palpitating heart, sought the residence of my, until then, unknown relation. Presenting the chain I tremblingly stood, muttering, 'What will you lend me on this?' Taking it in his hand I saw him apply some clear liquid, and after a few moments he sternly asked, 'Where did you get this gold chain, young man?'

I tried to explain, but he seemed suspicious, and tossing it to the counter remarked, "I decline having anything to do with it". This was long before the era of the telephone, or I might have been detained pending enquiries, and so I retired, not slothfully, cheered by his golden opinion. Hastening with some confidence to a jeweller's shop I asked the jeweller its value; having tested it, the man offered me thirty shillings; though far less than its value, as I realised afterwards. I felt like embracing that dealer; visions of a good meal quickened my poor wit, and I accepted the offer on condition that he gave me the much ornamented key that was attached.

This was handed to me together with thirty shillings and I afterwards disposed of the key for twelve shillings.

But being unemployed made this period of my life a wretched one, not only because of its poverty or actual want, but the objectless loafing, the dreary feeling of hopelessness, leading to helpless despair. But soon one of my more practical young friends, who was employed as a clerk at the local railway station, procured for me a small beginning as a clerk in the goods department at the princely remuneration of seven shillings per week, and in a few days, I was duly installed in the office as coal invoice clerk. The chief of my office, a fine fellow physically, was given to boast that he had little to learn from old 'Nick' or his minions, which soon seemed to me to be the only truth he was capable of uttering. His confessions made me, a simple youth, believe that he was a veritable Mephistopheles from the time when, as a child, he was entrusted by his father, a sober church-warden, with half a crown to place on the church collection plate and he substituted a penny-piece, until that day some thirty years later.*

This life, according to his showing, had been a long prostitution of gifts and opportunities, and of adventures which a modern Boccacio would blush to record. In all the office the fellows, like Falstaff's gang, seemed to be 'pickers-up of unconsidered trifles', and most of the desks were filled at the season with choicest fruits, or, indeed, with articles which the fellows deemed desirable, and which came to or through the station — from the chief to the porters all seemed to me to be tarred with the same brush.

I must plead a little guilty, if only as an occasional receiver of fruit; but the temptation to an always hungry lad when offered apples, pears or plums by the others who were eating them may plead for me.

Out of my weekly stipend of seven shillings, two shillings and sixpence went in lodgings and laundry, and the remainder left for food, etc., made but ill living; although the payment I received may have been extravagant for the work I was able to do, as coal invoice clerk, and the ignorance which I displayed in trying to accomplish it. Of course the consequences ought to have been foreseen, for the system upon which I had to work was not a little complicated, or so it seemed to me, being quite untrained in office work. For instance, some of the coal from certain districts had what was called preferential rates to the large dealers, who obtained their goods through at rates from thirty to forty per cent less than did the small dealers, this doubtless being done to help the small man to develop patience and perseverance.

It was no wonder then that my results in keeping accounts got mixed, and a special clerk was sent to put things right; I may add, however, that victory was with me, for the 'special' soon gave up the job as hopeless and, in language more pointed than refined, declared that 'Old Nick' himself could make

* Thomas Cook, pioneer of the modern travel industry.

nothing of it. The consequence was that the Company, being unwilling to part with such an unique assistant, promoted me to the desk and duties of 'Claims Clerk', which consisted of examining into claims made for damage to goods or for loss in transit; the main thing being, after long delay, if the matter was not vigorously pressed by claimants, to ignore it or, if the customer were persistent, to get the claim reduced and, in the end, to settle it for the lowest sum possible.

This work made me very miserable, although I honestly strove to do it well; nevertheless, when away from the office, I was fairly happy for I had made many friends at the Institute where I lived and spent my wages so as to dodge hunger, but after Mondays it was largely a case of dry — very dry — bread.

These were indeed hard times (1856) throughout the country during which it was no unusual sight to see gangs of men, starved miserable looking creatures wandering from town to town begging from people almost as poor as themselves. A great number of workless homeless men crying as they passed through the streets, "We are starving! Give us bread!" Those in employment were paid such a low wage that it was a perpetual fight against hunger and its consequence, disease.

After these years of intermittent work and unemployment and quite considerable hardship a job was offered H.H. Martyn which was his real turning point. James Forsyth, an architectural carver, offered him seven shillings a week (35p) to work for him as a journeyman carver. He resigned his job as claims clerk, a position to which he had risen on the railway, and started without delay. He rejoined his evening class at the art school and to his delight was awarded a bronze medal for his sculpture of the head of St. Jerome. This was in 1861 at 19 years of age.

Thus did I step on the way to becoming a craftsman, a step I never regretted and which led in 1916 to the company I formed being appointed Architectural Decorators to His Majesty King George V.

*In December 1861 I was sent by James Forsyth into the country to carve in the Great Hall of Eastnor Castle. For the sum of eighteen pence per week (7½p) I was accommodated with a small bedroom, attendance, cooking, kitchen room, and stories — vitriolised for the neighbours disliked by the old lady who kept the establishment and sold sweets, cotton, tape and a small assortment of other harmless objects. One Sunday at the castle and when Nature had covered itself in white robes, two friends came to visit me from Worcester and brought the sad news of the death of Queen Victoria's Consort. While I was carving in the Hall at Eastnor Castle some eminent visitors passed through the Hall where I was working; among them was the great painter Watts, the explorer Nineveh Leyard and the quaint artist Doyle, designer of the cover of Punch and painter of fairies, gnomes etc.**

One of James Forsyth's amusements was to get some of us into a cellar under the castle and have a bout of boxing; only once was I persuaded to patronise these performances, and as I quickly retired, was convinced by my sore nose that my gifts lay in quite an opposite direction.

Soon after my return to the City, I entered upon my second year of service, and consequently my wage was doubled, but as work was slack and my employer had the opportunity to get a younger and cheaper assistant, things were made so unpleasant for me that, after some words, we parted.

I was much troubled at the prospect before me, being nigh penniless and conscious of the fact that my knowledge of the craft was nearly negligible, but summing up courage I paid a visit to another master,† who had recently been appointed to restoration work at the Cathedral, and to carry out this and his other commissions had built a temporary structure or studio at the back of his residence.

Of course this man was one who knew his business and had a considerable reputation all over the country amongst leading architects. Having listened to my application for work, and making no objection to the wage I asked, which was thirty shillings a week, he at once engaged me, but the sense of my ignorance was forced on me as I saw the work done in that studio, dulling the happiness which I felt at this prosperous opening.

The work I was put to do was simple and within my experience, and gave satisfaction, especially to me. For my first job he asked me to take piece work, and very readily accepted the price I named; the job was wood carving of a rough kind which I did in a portion of the studio curtained off from the stone shop.

So I saw nothing of him until leaving off time when he came to look at my work; this he said would do nicely and asked if I had done a dozen paterae, so called, which would amount to less that the stipulated wage, and I can see his astonished face and hear his expletives now when I told him that I had completed forty-eight, earning nearly three times the ordinary wage.

Under these circumstances I started and, by working very hard, did fairly well, but alas! when I was put into the other shop to carve stone I soon had excess of humiliation, for I found that even the young apprentices could do better work; still I struggled on with set teeth, often tears on my cheeks, and being not altogether a dullard I rapidly improved.

* Watts was a friend of the Earl and Countess Somers and was a frequent visitor to Eastnor Castle.

† R.L. Boulton.

If some of my working hours gave me pain, my evenings brought me pleasure, for as I before intimated I loved a lass, for 'the child with the hoop' of my boyish days had grown to womanhood.

Piecework on wood carving brought better than the thirty shillings (£1.50) a week normal pay and at 23 H.H. Martyn married Fanny Clissold, the girl he first met at 13 years old. They married at Ribbesford Church, near Bewdley. His mother was working at the time as housekeeper for her cousin at the farm adjoining the church and H.H. Martyn arranged for the banns to be read on impulse one day, telling Fanny on his return.

She tried to say angry words, ending up of course by forgiving me.

At length the wedding day arrived, (30th March 1865) and after an early breakfast the wedding party, excluding myself, departed for the 15 mile drive to the farm house, while I going by train arrived in time to receive and introduce them to my mother and cousin. The ceremony with just a handful of friends began late when the parson eventually turned up. The service was raced through in order to end before midday. Thus it seemed to me not a very serious performance, for the bare empty church, the hurrying clergyman and the yokel of a clerk all helped to make the ceremony seem unreal."

They were married for 53 years and had five sons and three daughters, five of whom survived childhood. The children who died young were Harry Homer, Harvey and Gertrude. The surviving children were Alfred Willie, Frank, George, Nell and Jessy. George became a professor and through his experiments with X-rays lost his fingers. He also discovered how to prevent the harmful effect of acetone on workers employed in applying dope to the canvas of aircraft by using the regular consumption of milk as an antidote. He presented the details to the government free.

I did not remain long in Worcester, and being sent to work at various places in the country my wife generally accompanied me; one such place was at Torquay where I was sent to carve at St. Mary Magdalene Church, Upton, for Sir Giles Gilbert Scott, and had a very unpleasant experience.

One morning while at the studio a message was brought to me which called me to the governor, who, for it was early, was still in bed; he at once instructed me to proceed by the first train, taking my tools, to this town some two hundred miles away, and while he lay in bed he made a sketch of the sort of design I was to work out, this being necessary as at that time my knowledge was small, adding certain instructions which to emphasise he wrote across the paper.

Behold me then on a scaffold inside the chancel trying my best to carry out the instructions given.

Unthinkingly, or rather ignorantly, I placed my coat and tool bag on the undraped altar table, and a few days later was startled to see a gentlemen enter, who perceiving my lack of reverence for things holy, ran up the aisle and with a savage sweep cleared the table, then ascending the scaffold with, I am afraid, a swear word, demanded to know what instructions I was acting on. Feeling horribly nervous I foolishly handed him the paper containing same, across which was written, 'use plenty of fake.' Now 'faking' was a process by which labour was saved and cheap effects obtained, and I fairly trembled as I watched the effect that sentence caused to the gentleman. He blurted out several well known words, then hoped he would be forgiven (as by the way did I) then seeing me as limp as I expect I should be facing a roaring lion, he became more merciful saying, 'I cannot altogether blame you, young man, but your employer is a blank, blank, blank, and now let me warn you that if ever you work on my jobs again and I find you using 'fake', I shall at once have you ignominiously turned away', though he did not use quite that language, and I believe the letter he favoured my employer with was painfully brief and pointed.

Having completed the work I returned home somewhat nervously, but the master said but little about it to me although a few years later, while carving at a convent for one of the ablest Gothic architects of that time, he stood smilingly by whilst I was being slated by the mad architect, and though he knew that I was blameless in the matter said softly, "Now I have paid you back for showing my instructions to Scott in Torquay."

This last scene was a curious exhibition of the architect's waywardness; I was sent to do this work and told that I was to please the Reverend Father, and this Reverend gentleman had ideas of his own. Having written some homilies on the Saints he desired to illustrate his themes by my carving various flowers and fruits of the different countries where the saints had lived.

Many of these natural products I was unacquainted with so the Father supplied me with pictures of them, and although I knew that this architect hated the sort of thing, in this dilemma I carried out my instructions and tried, and in fact succeeded in pleasing his Reverence.

Other venues where H.H. Martyn almost certainly worked for Mr Boulton include the reredos of Holy Trinity Church at Shrub Hill, Worcester, James Forsyth his previous employer executing the font, both works being completed in the period 1863-1865 (Pevsner). St. Phillip's and St James' Church, Hallow, Worcester, Reredos by Boultons, Font by Forsyth 1867 (Pevsner). Also work on the chancel and Lady Chapel of Worcester Cathedral where in the spandrells is sculpture of foliage and animals and many religious scenes by Boultons. (Pevsner).

About this time, (1866—67), my employer having completed his restorative work at the Cathedral in my native city, removed his studio to Cheltenham, where considerable church building was in progress; thither, I with my bag and baggage, which included my wife and one babe, settled into apartments near the new studio.

Our first apartments in this town were over a small shoe shop, the proprietor and landlord being a white-headed, fine old man, whose yarns were many and to me interesting. He related with glee how when a young man he was sent one morning early to measure a young lady for some boots, and found that she had not risen; by her directions he was taken to her bedside and there, displaying her comely foot, she desired him to take the measure and get them completed in time for her to wear that evening at the theatre, where she was taking the part of Lady Teazle. *This was the actress who afterwards became wife to the great banker and brewer, and later married the Duke of St. Albans.*

Of the generous donor of the fine, new Gothic Church nearby, which I was then adorning, my landlord had many stories to relate: of his whimsicalities — how this bachelor squire would take his lunch, if his maids were busy, sitting under a hedge enjoying his bread and cheese, sometimes he would send a new pair of shoes back with the request that they should be lengthened at the heels, or toes; so also his wearing apparel would be sent back to be altered for odd reasons, never disputing the charges made, if five per cent was allowed off.

One day, years later, he inquired from me if I could tell him where he might purchase a 'secondhand tombstone;' poor old gentleman! One wonders if, today, he fidgets over the fit of his wings.

But to return to my shoe-maker, who at this time was a high-spirited youth of seventy odd, who loved whist moistened by gin, taking enough of both each night excepting Sundays when, after patronising the evening Church Service, he was content with the gin in the company of his friends at their favourite inn, discussing the evident decadence of the times.

It does seem strange to note how one's memories are linked with past generations, and in a humble way with the men famous or notorious who are now but names, as in the case of the landlord and his wife who, later, let us apartments for some months before we settled into a home of our own. Both the landlord and his wife had interesting histories, the man claiming that, in his youth, he was valet to Beau Brummel, the one-time, friend or boon companion to the Prince, who afterwards ruled as King George IV while the landlord's wife, Mary, dear good soul, ruled him, if not with a rod of iron, at least with a powerful tongue; she had been head-nurse in her time to the children of the great Duke of Wellington's heir. Many were the stories she told us of those days; how, for instance — one day she was told to dress the children nicely, as the Duke was coming and would see them — He arrived in the nursery in due course and, after greeting, he caused dismay in the nurse's heart by going to the fire-place, getting some soot therefrom, and carefully daubing the white dresses of the little ones, telling the horrified nurse that 'he came to see children, not dolls.'

My friend was very proud of a present she received from the then young Queen Victoria who acted as god-mother to one of the babies she nursed later. Then for some thirteen years she was in Germany as nurse to the child of a German aristocrat, where she saw, amongst many visitors, the young Bismarck, afterwards Prince. She was treated well and most generously while there, and until she died many years later regularly corresponded with her former nurseling, whose letters to her were always those of a son. I know, for I was the scribe who answered his letters and, in each, had to express her wish to hear of his getting married.

About this period I became a proud rate-payer, being able to leave apartments and start a home of our own, for, on completing some profitable 'piece-work', I had a considerable balance to draw. Well can I remember the joy I felt as I watched my grudging employer doling out the separate coins, grumbling as each sovereign fell into my nervous hand, with his "Tut-tut! sixteen!" — a scratch of his head, "seventeen, tut, what a lot!" and so on, until, with a deep sigh of relief, he fumbled out the last sovereign.*

Surely no spendthrift ever had the joy in distributing other's earnings than I and the wife received in disbursing my hard earnings in furniture for our new home.

About two years later,† being annoyed with the injustice of my employer, I suddenly determined to leave him and commence business for myself. For some time he had been in the habit of putting young apprentices to do work for an architect who often referred appreciatively to my work and if the boys' work came in for condemnation he would openly say that it was mine; on one occasion he sent some photographs of special work designed and executed by myself to South Kensington, and on their application for the name of the craftsman who had executed it, replied by sending, with mine, several other names of youths who had not even seen the work. These things did not cause me much annoyance, but more serious injustice did.

Thus I came to leave a studio where I had some years of pleasure in hard work and where, I admit, I had learned a great deal, to start afresh with about as much capital as I had married on. I think the step I was taking was more due to ignorance than

* 32 Keynsham Street.

† 1874.

courage; some good folk would call it madness, for at that time I had other possessions, to wit, two or three children, my wife and my dear old mother.

When my late employer, who had been away, heard of the step I had taken, he came to me and finding me firm in my intention, gave me this advice: "Don't you go seeking orders — let them come to you," and I assured him that I fully intended to secure all the commissions I could.

The day I retired from Boulton's employment I met one of the ordinary workmen, a clever stonemason, who, hearing of my intention, at once offered to join me in the venture, and I accepted his offer.*

Borrowing the small sum of thirty pounds from a friend, this being supplemented by seventy pounds from my better-to-do partner, with our hundred pounds banked, we looked about for a suitable place whereon to build our wooden studio, and at once proceeded to purchase materials and to exhibit a sign, etc., etc.

While this was proceeding I visited my native city in hope of getting commissions of some sort from architects and builders, and was lucky enough on the first day to secure a (to us then), considerable order for carving to seats for the nave of the Cathedral, which, though not quite art work, realized for us at once profitable work.

The agreement between Mr Emms and myself was for a term of seven, fourteen or twenty-one years, but, at the end of fourteen years, we separated; meanwhile those years were fairly prosperous and were filled by a crowd of interests other than the business, for I became acquainted, and in some cases made friends, with all sorts and conditions of people. In the making of friends I was much blessed all through my life, and am grateful indeed for this blessing; I delighted to be with young people and, for a short time, conducted a chapel Bible Class. My house was open, especially on Sundays, to whomever chose to come, and my good wife was happy in doing her utmost to help entertain them with creature comforts.

One day a lady, who was a stranger to me, called to inquire if I could send to her any young man who was anxious to be taught, as she desired to be of use in her day and generation and, being herself highly trained, could undertake to help in many subjects. That lady is alive as I write and many middle-aged men to-day in various parts of the world and in many positions may well be grateful for the affectionate help they received from her.

Following this, as the number of applicants increased, I was induced to start a class for elocution, and for reading the works of Shakespeare: for this purpose a well-known architect who had offices in the town, on being asked, most kindly granted us the free use of his office on one night a week, and there we commenced, reading for our first play **'The Merchant of Venice.'**

The reader may reasonably inquire what were my qualifications for taking such a class. Well, firstly, as a venture, we knew no able one willing to make a beginning, and it seemed better for a fool to rush in where educational angels feared to tread, than that the thing should not be attempted. Secondly, I at least **loved** *the subject and had great enthusiasm for it, which latter enabled me to be what a piece of string is to a bunch of flowers, keeping the boys together, so with the courage of ignorance I took up the work.*

Another lady came along and desired to help by starting a singing class and by teaching the boys glees and so on, upon another evening; for this purpose we obtained from our architect friend permission to use the office for a second evening. It soon became a considerable success, for this lady was both accomplished and clever, with a charm of manner which appealed to the roughest lad; she was no frigid teacher and there was, at times, much amusement, for the youngsters were free to talk and air their wit between the glees, but they quickly found that the lady's wit was more than equal to the best of them. She always selected one of the class to accompany her home after the meeting, which seemed to give the favoured one much pleasure.

This lady was a member of a family well known in University circles; at that time she was one of the leaders of society in the town, an amateur actress, authoress, artist, almost a professional tennis player, a carpenter who made her own book cases, and prouder of being a good cook than of her many other acquirements. She possessed a keen sense of humour which may be illustrated by the story she told me — that, when a lass visiting her brother who was a Dean she was introduced to Tennyson who was the centre of an adoring group of ladies; expecting to hear words of beauty or wisdom from his mouth, she was surprised to hear nothing but a catalogue of his aches and pains; suddenly she remarked — "You must feel very like the whale did after he swallowed Jonah!" The effect was at least remarkable.

These small attempts to interest young men prospered so that other good friends came forward with offers of help; especially keen were a couple of clergymen, teachers who for years not only gave their best in the way of brains but also liberally with their means. A committee was formed and suitable rooms over a book shop in 16 Clarence Street were secured. Later we moved to no. 3 Liverpool Place. The new venture was announced under the rather flamboyant title of 'Working Men's College'.

So started the Working Men's College, whereat, for a fee of eighteenpence each term of six months, any youth from about sixteen

* E.A. Emms.

years of age could become a member, joining as many classes as he chose, attend all entertainment, join in the chess club, be a member of the debating society, or apply for and receive special lessons in nearly any subject, from multiplication to higher mathematics; from the English language to Greek, Latin or French, modelling, etc., science, art, literature and musical teaching from violin to banjo.

The teachers were not paid, although several were professionals from the two local colleges; over the debating society presided a clever Master of Arts, who seemed a little out of harmony with the untrained members, or with those who differed from his views, notwithstanding that some of the boys were fair speakers, though working men, porters, postmen, mechanics and coal heavers. The rooms were sufficiently furnished, even to a good piano for use at entertainments.

Nor was that good forgotten, for today, thirty odd years after the closing of the College, some of the old members record their gratitude; but a few months ago one of them called to see me; he was by now a man of means for he came in his own car on the way back to London from a tour with his wife. He talked about those long ago happy days and warmly expressed his gratitude for the help received at the College. Another of the boys recently sent me a splendid photograph of himself, showing him as an important member of the public life in one of Britain's greatest cities, and gave thanks for the useful training he had received.

These two are but samples of many, and may illustrate the mark made on a host of young lives, although not necessarily leading to so-called success, for comparatively few in any class attain that which character more than knowledge wins. It took a lot of that forty years ago to enable a youth to stick it.

Please, reader, do not think our College lacked pleasant diversions; for during the terms members were sometimes welcomed at the homes of our patrons, to give readings, or otherwise to display the varied abilities of the lads or their teachers. On one such occasion we spent an evening at the then called Ladies' College where we read 'Henry the Eighth'.

The headmistress kindly offered to read the part of Queen Katharine, and I was amused, when during the reading, a lady teacher of elocution whispered to me, "and **she** *is supposed to teach girls how to read!" Of course I had to look demure, but I could have laughed, for the lady's reading justified, in a small way, the King's desire for a divorce.*

The lady however also justified herself with the boys by giving them a bountiful supply of refreshing tea, cocoa, cake, etc., etc. About this time we had been successful in starting a Working Mens College Magazine, the first number containing a special essay by the above mentioned lady principal.

Example of Martyn and Emms work, Cheltenham Cemetery 1882.

H.H. Martyn & Co., Sunningend, 439 High Street, Cheltenham was formed as an association of Art Craftsmen on 11th February 1888. H.H. Martyn was aided in the enterprise by a relative, Thomas Weston Whiteman, and by Henry William Hooper. The indenture mentions Holly Cottage (Sunningend) 29 High Street (bounded by the Old Swan Inn), Stirling Cottage, Stirling Lodge and adjoining land situated at the east end of High Street, Cheltenham, all of which formed the workshops for the new company.

An early report on the Company also mentions other works premises at Sherborne Place and that H.H. Martyn was both agent and manufacturer of J. Hopkins Esq. patent removeable wooden church "which is no doubt the best temporary structure yet invented." E.A. Emms continued in business independently as monumental masons without great expansion, but in fact survived as a company for some twenty years longer than Martyns. Many gravestones and cattle troughs can be found with lead letters 'MARTYN AND EMMS' from their partnership days.

After ten years on his own, on 24th September 1898, H.H. Martyn took two partners into the business, his son A.W. Martyn and Henry Arthur Dutton, all three being described in the documents as sculptors. The two newcomers paid £1,000 each for a quarter share in the partnership, H.H. Martyn retaining 50 per cent. The property in the Schedule of Partnership was Sunningend, previously known as Holly Cottage, 59 High Street, the land adjoining the buildings and Stirling Cottage and Stirling Lodge. H.H. Martyn was by now an accomplished carver in wood and stone. The Ladies' College in Cheltenham had "Twelve Patriotic Women" carved for them, commenting in their archives that "the statues do great credit to Mr. Martyn." 'Building News' of July 5th 1889 shows the new reredos of St. Philips and St. James Church, Cheltenham — "Mr. Martyn, Sculptor" , a work on which he must have been engaged at the time he formed his company.

From an early age H.H. Martyn had many other interests — reading, the theatre, singing, writing, painting, the study of Shakespeare, bible classes — even politics. He was a Liberal and in 1870 helped Samuelson in his election campaign locally, but later lost interest in politics altogether.

He met a host of notable people during his long and active life, many of them artists or writers. These included Rodin, whom he met in Paris; leading contemporary artists like Watts and Swain; the author Frederick Myers, Professor Barrat, scientist, and Swan, inventor of the incandescent lamp. He was a close friend of Gustav Holst, who lived in Cheltenham at that time.

H.H. Martyn also had a driving conviction that the opportunity to learn artistic, academic or manual skills should be available to people at any age or stage in life. From its very beginning H.H. Martyn & Co. had an apprenticeship scheme which endured and proved so successful that in 1925 four employees became Royal Academicians. H.H. Martyn himself taught in the company's school for the apprentices helping to develop the gifts of many youngsters, "*some few of whom have far eclipsed their old, so-called master*," he remarked. He also felt that working men should be given the opportunity to improve their academic skills out of working hours. That is why he founded his Working Men's College, which opened in 1883 with premises over a bookshop in 16 Clarence Street, Cheltenham, two teachers from the Ladies' College, Miss Hemming and Miss Sawyer, giving their services free. The Ladies' College strongly supported the venture, allowing plays to be performed on their premises. H.H. Martyn was ably helped in the early stages of the College by the Rev. James Owen and the Rev. John Mugglestone. A leading Cheltenham politician, Mr. Agg Gardner, was also much to the fore in the enterprise as were two masters from the Gentlemen's College, who gave their services free. The Working Men's College lasted for 17 years and helped many working men to greater success than would otherwise have been their fortune.

H.H. Martyn says:

> *The opening night of our new Working Men's College was a brilliant success . . . the Principal of the Ladies' College (Miss Beale) painted a rosy picture of extension when the joint Colleges would form a centre from where the town would become famous as a University.*

Another speaker, less sanguine, commented "Such institutions, starting with trumpets and generally flourishing for the first year, decline in the next and with the close of the third comes the sad ceremony of burial." Neither of the speeches was accurate in the event.

H.H. Martyn was a man with an active social conscience and in 1870, with the support of the Rev. James Owen, formed a mission in Rutland Street, (now renamed Charles Street), situated in the Lower High Street area, where the local poor were provided with tea and coffee, sandwiches, outings to the country, organised dancing and singing, concerts and church services. Temperance was encouraged but was not allowed to dampen the pleasures. The mission was supported enthusiastically by the wives of the principals and by many other volunteer helpers.

To explain the need for such work, the creation of an oasis in what was a human desert, H.H. Martyn's own words serve best.

> *Truly the neighbourhood had long been a plague spot, well known, where drunken brawls were frequent and police were shy of interfering, especially after one of the force, more brave than wise, tried to stop a fight. He was suddenly decorated by having a cottage shutter for a collar which though proving the thickness of his skull, gave him scant comfort; anyway, it proved the necessity for police to go there in couples.*
>
> *The state of many homes in that neighbourhood was terrible, and at that time it seemed useless to call the attention of the authorities to it; as the Town Surveyor once told me, "It's very bad but what can we do? A lot of the property is owned by members of the council; if we make a stir we can do little good and make for ourselves unpleasantness." Certainly, if a pig had any self respect it would pity itself in such homes. Mr. Owen told me that in an experience of London slums for many years he had seen nothing worse. Can you realise a house, one room down, and one up, each about nine feet by seven or eight, the lower floor of which was composed of well worn bricks, mildew on the walls and damp everywhere? We visited such to find sickness rampant and misery such that Dante would shudder to describe . . . . One could fill a volume with such cases, and this in one of the wealthiest and most religious towns in our land, few would believe it possible, for fewer went to see it.*
>
> *I have known some labourers who came with the idea of jeering who really turned out to be our staunchest helpers. One such and his wife, who when the coffee tavern was started, were placed in charge, both of them being strong characters, and as, before his charge he had been a leader for ill, now became in a small way, leader of his companions to better things. His more capable, stronger willed wife, though she could swear on occasions, became a good angel, if rough, to many homes. I heard her talking to a great*

H.H. Martyn and his wife in 1918.

hulking labourer one night, who had sheepishly come to ask her to see his poor wife whom he had been beating while in drink, and in no measured terms she rated him. Poor she was, but never too poor to help those in greater need; uncultured — yes but with a heart of gold. Her husband, giving up drink, became a very useful member and was largely instrumental in getting his companions to join the Temperance Society which we also started and which, to the disgust of the neighbouring publicans, flourished for a long time.

Those involved in the Mission, Coffee Tavern and Temperance Society with H.H. Martyn admitted that if they had been required to live in such conditions they would be gin drinkers too!

"*Can you realise what a little loving cheer meant to these helpless derelicts?*" he asks. It was certainly selfless work carried out by all involved. The success may have been due to the right measure of help mixed with small doses of prayer, fun, food and equality. H.H. Martyn's early experience of poverty himself gave him the unpatronising and acceptable attitude which put the people at their ease.

The room they used was converted from a labourer's cottage which they purchased. A rostrom was made at one end and a gallery added opposite. A piano and harmonium provided the music for hymns, dancing and singing and for the concerts on Sunday afternoons. Plenty of light and pictures on the coloured walls made it a cheerful place for people to spend a few hours, especially in the winter when a good stove was kept burning.

H.H. Martyn founded the company of H.H. Martyn & Co. on the basis of his desire to produce **'the best'** and pride in its achievement. He stated in his writings: "*I have done little personally beyond inciting far more clever craftsmen to, at any cost, do* **the best** *that was in them to do.*" This philosophy persisted to the end, the last apprentices in the 1960's still maintaining the tradition of doing **'the best** that was in them to do' and possessing a loyalty, pride and love for the company, its past, its achievement of **'the best'** and its special aura which is very unusual to hear expressed today by anyone.

When H.H. Martyn reached the age of 58 years, he handed most of the responsiblity to his brilliant son Alfred Willie, who though only 30 years old was already a man with great skill in business. It was on 28th May 1900 that the partnership of H.H. & A.W. Martyn and H.A. Dutton was reformed and incorporated as a limited company with registered share capital of £18,500, the large sum showing the success of the former partnership. A.W. Martyn was made managing director, Fanny Martyn (wife of H.H.) was secretary, H.H. Martyn no doubt would have been chairman and Mr. Dutton the other director. The stamp duty on the transfer of the properties from the partnership was £2,000. There were 6,500 preference shares of £1, entitling the holder to a cumulative dividend of 6% per annum and 12,000 ordinary shares, such share capital issued subject to an original debenture issue of £8,000 in debenture bonds of £50 each, bearing interest at 5% to be redeemable at par on three months' notice.

The Company continued to grow rapidly and prosper, taking on more and more skilled craftsmen. In 1902 'B' debentures at £50 each were issued to raise £2,000, all being taken up and issued.

On November 22nd 1904 'B' debentures were increased to £5,000 and 'in view of the continued prosperity of the Company and the large increase in the assets' the first debenture issue was increased from the sum of £8,000 to £15,000 secured by 300 bonds of £50 each at 5% interest per annum. The trustees of the debenture holders were Walter Gerald Gurney, solicitor, John Haddon, mercer and Charles Williams, warehouseman. In 1908 a major expansion was undertaken when the company moved into a five acre site at Lansdown, the old William Letheren works known as the Vulcan Iron Works. A.W. Martyn took his daughter, Ida, still in socks at only ten years old, to see the premises. At the age of 86 she still remembered walking over plank bridges and builders making considerable alterations to the works.

On 26th June 1923 Sunningend, High Street, was let to William George Tibbles of the Crescent Coach & Motor Works, then of St. George's Place, Cheltenham at a rent of £100 per annum, the move from High Street being completed after 35 years on the premises.

H.H. Martyn remained a director but lived in Weston-Super-Mare for a time and took less and less part in the business, though he did return to more active work for a year or two during World

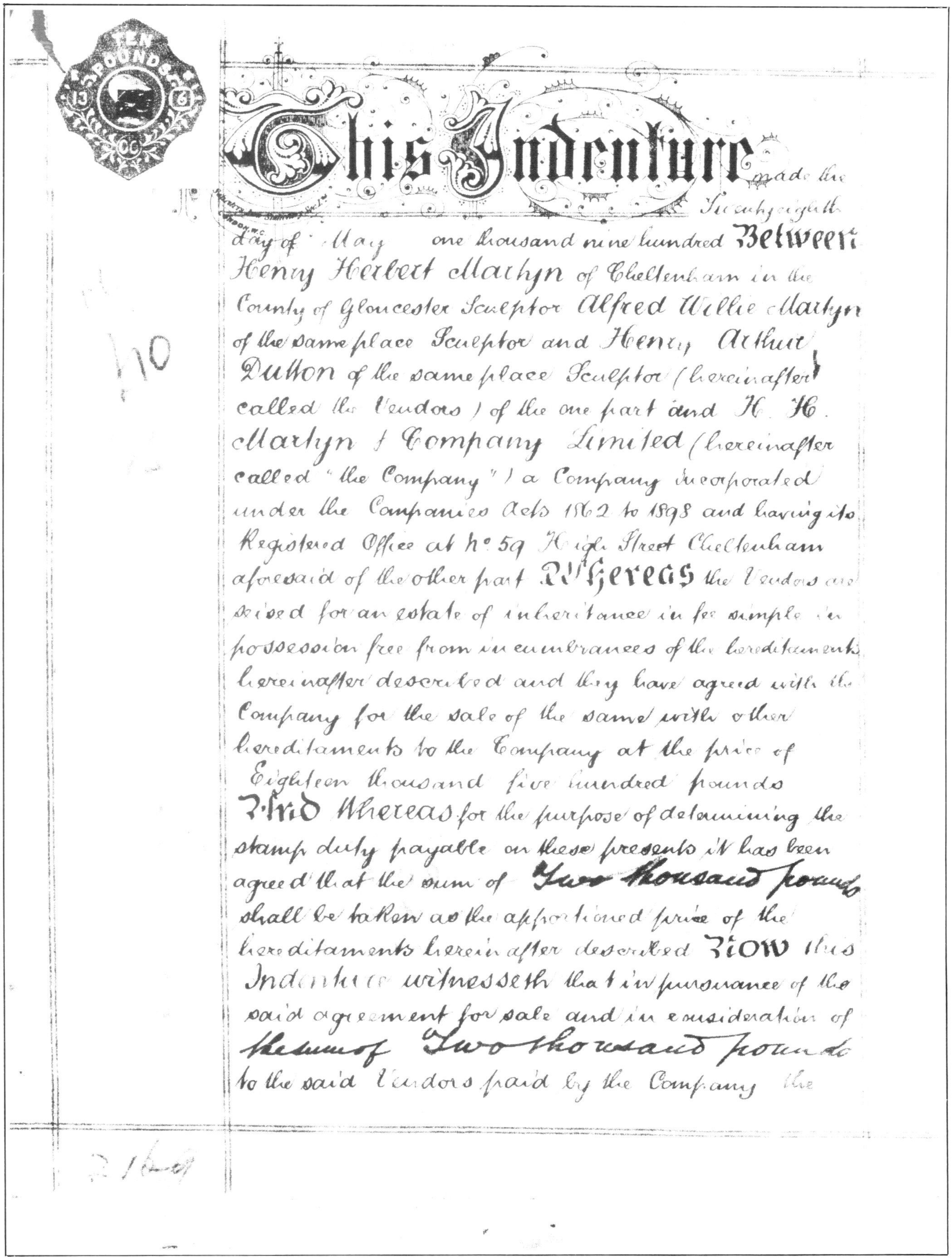
This Indenture made the Twentyeighth day of May one thousand nine hundred Between Henry Herbert Martyn of Cheltenham in the County of Gloucester Sculptor Alfred Willie Martyn of the same place Sculptor and Henry Arthur Dutton of the same place Sculptor (hereinafter called the Vendors) of the one part and H. H. Martyn & Company Limited (hereinafter called "the Company") a Company incorporated under the Companies Acts 1862 to 1898 and having its Registered Office at No. 59 High Street Cheltenham aforesaid of the other part Whereas the Vendors are seised for an estate of inheritance in fee simple in possession free from incumbrances of the hereditaments hereinafter described and they have agreed with the Company for the sale of the same with other hereditaments to the Company at the price of Eighteen thousand five hundred pounds And Whereas for the purpose of determining the stamp duty payable on these presents it has been agreed that the sum of Two thousand pounds shall be taken as the apportioned price of the hereditaments hereinafter described Now this Indenture witnesseth that in pursuance of the said agreement for sale and in consideration of the sum of Two thousand pounds to the said Vendors paid by the Company the

Document dated May 1900 describing the partners as sculptors and the value of the company as eighteen thousand, five hundred pounds.

War One. A proud honour for him was his appointment as an Honorary Member of the Society of Architects in 1912.

He wrote a number of books which were privately published. These were 'Doom' (1927), 'Temptation' and 'Dream of Eternity' (1929) and a document written in youth while in Worcester and 60 years later revised and renamed 'Visions'. His best novel was 'Broken on the Wheel' a work based on his own life. He also wrote 'Shapes of Clay' and lastly 'Grippy & Sons', all three written before 1914.

H.H. Martyn lived an active life, leaving for posterity many fine carvings done in his own hand. Most of them still testify to his skill as a craftsman though unidentifiable as his own by us now as records are few or lost. A man of powerful social conscience, he did much to help his fellow men, particularly in the field of further education. He also made a great contribution to the prosperity of his town of residence and business, Cheltenham. His desire to produce **'the best'**, his vision, hard work and success, brought extensive employment to the town. Martyns employed thousands over the years and many spent all their working lives with the company. The expansion of Martyns acted like a magnet, drawing business into the area and stimulating trade. One could add to H.H. Martyn's list of 'ifs'. If he had not worked hard to build his company in the early days, if he had not been fortunate in having a son to maintain its growth and venture into further areas of opportunity, Cheltenham's strong industrial base might never have developed. As a direct result of H.H. Martyn's vision enterprise and drive this rural corner of the West Midlands become a major centre of advanced engineering, the home of companies like Gloster Aircraft and Dowtys whose contribution to the nation's prosperity in peacetime and security in time of war it is difficult to exaggerate.

H.H. Martyn died in 1937 at the great age of 95, living to experience the rewards of success after an austere and challenging youth. His obituary in the local paper described him as a social worker and artist. His monuments in Britain and all over the world are legion.

Dinner on February 1st, 1913 for 200 employees of H.H. Martyn and Co. Left to right on the top table, Charles Denley, Henry Dutton, David Longdon, A.W. Martyn, H.H. Martyn, J.T. Agg Gardner. A presentation of silver plate was made to Mr. H.H. Martyn.

Cheltenham Chronicle picture of A.W. Martyn 1905 (Aged 35).

A.W. Martyn

'A.W.', as he was later to be known, was born at 32 Keynsham Street, Cheltenham, in 1870, four years before his father started in business with E.A. Emms. He was destined for a memorable career. As chairman and managing director he gave dynamic impetus to H.H. Martyn & Co., from 1898 to 1927, The Gloster Aircraft Co., of which he the Founder, from 1917 to 1927, and finally Dowty Equipment, from 1937 to 1947. He was also involved in education, local government and public assistance work. A.W.'s early years were spent in a small school at either St. John's or Holy Apostles, Cheltenham, where, like his father, he assimilated knowledge easily and was also made 'monitor' and taught the younger children when 11 years old; but at the age of 14 his formal schooling ended and he started work with Martyn & Emms doing basic stone cutting to be finished by the stonemasons. He worked at what was to him an arduous and boring task for some years but eventually became a stonecarver himself — early documents referring to him as a sculptor. The job took him to London for a long period when the partnership, Martyn & Emms, was working stone for the front of an unidentified London store. He spoke of lodging in London and having breakfast of bread and bacon and tea for 6d. (2½p).

It seems probable that A.W. would have availed himself of the facilities of his father's Working Men's College at some stage as he would have been eligible at sixteen when the College still had fourteen years to run. A.W. was adept at debate and mathematics, both of which he could have studied at the College.

At the age of 25, A.W. married Ada Newman, daughter of A.E. Newman, basket maker of Maisemore, Gloucester. Ada was employed in the gowns department as an apprentice at Brunswick House, (now Cheltenham's world famous department store Cavendish House), when they met. After their marriage they lived over the Sunningend Works in the High Street/College Road premises and later at York Lodge, St. George's Road, the house where their three children were born, Madeline (Watson), 1897, Ida (Whitaker), 1898 and Cyril, 1900. In 1918 they moved to The Hearne, Charlton Kings, where they lived until the house was requisitioned by the Government in 1939. A.W. and his wife were kind and generous parents, and their one great grief, particularly for A.W., was that owing to disability his son was unable to follow on in the business. This may have been the cause of his selling out at a comparatively early stage.

A.W.'s interest was in the management side of H.H. Martyn rather than sculptural stone cutting. He showed such extraordinary business ability that in 1900, at 30 years of age, he was made managing director by his father. He had by then already helped to expand and modernise the company, mechanising the basic work and launching the company into decorative plaster work and iron work, with plans for casting in bronze on a large scale. His goal for Martyns was to provide a complete service for architects, with all their decorative requirements available from a single source. No other company before or since could rival the range of services and quality offered by Martyns.

When H.H. Martyn & Co. moved into the new premises at Lansdown, a site with buildings covering five acres, the large-scale casting of bronze soon became a reality. About this time A.W. won the order to make elaborate gates and railings for Marble Arch, London.

In 1914 the Company opened its London office and showrooms at No. 5 Grafton Street, off Bond Street, in London's fashionable Mayfair — a perfect site to show off the Company's expertise and present the fabrics, antiques and carpets which were now also offered to clients as part of a complete interior decorating service. A document dated 25th December 1913 reveals the lease of 5 Grafton Street as being from Lord Byron, with a duration of 54¾ years. Sales offices were subsequently opened in Glasgow, Liverpool, Manchester, Newcastle and other major population centres.

Both A.W. and H.H. Martyn had the same great gift for recognising talent, expertise and drive in a man and then employing and encouraging those talents in the most constructive way. Under A.W. Martyn's guidance, combining business management skills and a flair for marketing, company fortunes improved. However, even Martyns was affected from time to time by business recessions, particularly during the period spanning the start of the 1914-1918 war, when cash flow problems were severe. At a time of great uncertainty the company was rescued by a contract placed in 1913 through the architect Walter Brierley to renew the decorative plaster work and panelling at Sledmere House, Yorkshire.

The new plaster work was to be to the original design by Joseph Rose, produced for Sledmere in 1790. Martyns craftsmen faithfully copied and reproduced the plaster work so that today it looks as fine as the original. Sledmere House had been damaged by fire and though the furniture was saved the ceilings and panelling were so severely damaged that some were beyond recognition and had to be copied from original drawings. The work took several years to complete and lasted through to 1916.

The war was a catastrophe for a business like Martyns, since demand for artistic and decorative work almost ceased. Martyns was severely hit in spite of the good contract for Sledmere. However, ammunition boxes in great quantity were produced following a war office contract in 1914, which helped to keep the wheels turning.

Throughout this period early in the war, A.W. was searching for work to keep the company going. His efforts were rewarded when he was approached by Hugh Burroughes, then of the Aircraft Manufacturing Company of Hendon. Burroughes was seeking a woodworking company to sub-contract

H.H. Martyn and Co. Ltd. Sunningend, Lansdown, from the air, about 1920.

Night scene, Marble Arch gates, 1934.

the manufacture of wings and fuselages for De Havilland and Maurice Farman aircraft. A meeting was arranged early in 1915 at the Royal Aeronautical Club in London at which A.W. Martyn, Percy Mott and S.J. Waring (who later became Lord Waring), all three leaders of high class woodworking companies, were interviewed.

As a result of this meeting and a later inspection of the premises, Hugh Burroughes chose H.H. Martyn & Co. from the several other woodworking companies he inspected. His reasons were the obvious capability of A.W. and the company's ability to handle the contract with a skilled workforce and modern machinery ready and available.

The first contract for Maurice Farman wings was quickly completed, standing up to searching inspections, with the result that many more useful contracts followed. This efficient and smooth switch from decorative woodworking to aircraft manufacture was supervised by Mr. Davidson, who was the highly efficient general manager whose task it was to organise the change. However, he could not have succeeded without skilled craftsmen who adapted quickly to the new task without sacrificing their normal high standards of work, skill and perfection.

At the end of 1916, after about 18 months of contract work on De Havilland and Maurice Farman airframes, A.W. Martyn conceived a plan which was to ensure work for the staff of Martyns and for an even larger workforce in due time. He decided to design and build the company's own aircraft at Cheltenham, to lead in aircraft production rather than follow as a subcontractor. He approached Hugh Burroughes with the proposition that a new company should be formed called The Gloucestershire Aircraft Company, the Aircraft Manufacturing Co. and the directors of Martyns each holding 50% of the shares. Martyns would lease work space and its skilled workforce to the new company, which in addition to building its own products would take over some of the existing contracts of the Aircraft Manufacturing Company. This bold and far-sighted plan guaranteed employment for the large labour force and launched a company which contributed greatly to the development of high speed flight through its Schneider Trophy entries and pioneering design projects and to the defence of this country in the 1914-1918 and 1939-1945 wars.

Little time elapsed between the idea and its implementation. The employement of a good designer was of paramount importance to achieve success. Typically A.W. secured the eminent talents of H.P. Folland, one of the most brilliant designers this country has produced.

Within a short time of turning over to war production, A.W. was forced to go into reverse. With the Armistice, orders for military aircraft came to an abrupt halt, and the slow return to traditional activities caused acute financial difficulties. However, A.W. was fortunate in being a close friend of Bernard Triggs, F.R.I.B.A., a gifted architect working in India. The Martyn family had provided a second home for Mr. Triggs' daughter as the Indian climate did not suit her. Bernard Triggs was involved soon after the war in designing a new palace for the Holkar of Indore and Martyns was given the contract to supply panelling, bronze work, decorative plaster, stone work and furniture for the entire palace, a massive contract and a challenging one. Work commenced in about 1920 and the following letters show a little of the financial arrangements up to completion date and with the tidying up of a few loose ends in 1927.

TELEGRAMS. SUNNINGEND, LONDON.

CODE 5TH EDIT. A.B.C.

TELEPHONE. 1148 & 1149 REGENT.

BY SPECIAL APPOINTMENT TO H.M. THE KING.

H. H. MARTYN & Co. LTD.
Sculptors & Architectural Decorators.

5, Grafton Street, Old Bond Street, W. 1.

CONFIDENTIAL

HJP/MW.

30th May 1921.

Dear Mr.Martyn,

I herewith enclose for your information only, copies of correspondence Mr.Bernard Triggs has had with the State of Indore. This is in respect of the first payment to be made to us on the signing of the contract. Please keep these very carefully and return them to me on Thursday when we visit Cheltenham. These copies have been made in the Office here when the originals were copied for transmission to His Highness in Paris.

Will you please let me know per return if any arrangement has been made for the transportation of Mr.Bernard Triggs and myself to Cheltenham on Thursday by Car, or whether we shall go by train.

Yours faithfully,

H.J. Parker

Lal Bagh,

INDORE. C. I.

23rd April 1921.

Mashir-us-Dowlah,
Govindrao Mysore., B.A., LL.B.
Chief Minister Holkar State,
INDORE. C. I.

- LAL BAGH PALACE -

- FINANCE -

Sir,

I have the honour to state that, in company with Lala Shree Man Singh, Huzur Secretary, I intend calling at the National Bank of India Ltd., Bombay, next Friday the 29th inst. to open the account styled Lal Bagh Palace Indore Account.

I shall inform the Manager that you will be paying them the sum of Rs.2,40,000/- on or before the 7th June,1921, for Telegraphic Transfer to the National Bank of India Head Office London, to the credit of a similar account which, on arrival in London, Lala Shree Man Singh and I shall open with them.

We, (that is Lala Shree Man Singh and I), will give the Manager in Bombay our specimen Signatures, so that, with His Highness' permission, we may jointly operate the Account in London; thereafter on my return to India, other arrangements will be made as may please His Highness.

I have the honour to be,
Sir,
Yours faithfully,

COPIES TO:

Narain Mangesh Sherlakar Esq.,B.A.
Finance Secretary Holkar Government.

and

Major J.S.Barker, M.V.O., R.E.
Chief Engineer Holkar State P.W.D.

for information.

DL/RP. 24th November, 1927.

Bernard Triggs, Esq.,
The Arts Club,
40, Dover Street,
LONDON. W.1.

Dear Sir,

LAL BACH PALACE, INDORE.
FINAL SETTLEMENT OF THE GENERAL CONTRACT
AND ITEMS EXTRA ON CONTRACT.

Following up our conversation in London on Thursday, the 3rd instant, I am of the opinion that the simplest method of coming to a final settlement is to ask you, on your return to India, to adjust the following:-

Work to Barber's Saloon and Electric Fittings.

You will, before returning to India, meet the account for the special carpets made as surrounds to Their Highnesses' beds.

On your arrival at Indore, provided the Throne draperies have been delivered safely, you will send us a further payment on account in the sum of £500. (Five hundred pounds) the balance of £400. (Four hundred pounds) to be paid after completion of the various items.

We on our part shall be pleased to meet your professional fee for the services which we are expecting you to render us, for the above work.

Yours faithfully,
H. H. MARTYN & COMPANY, LIMITED.

MANAGING DIRECTOR.

After the final leg of the journey from Sunningend, Cheltenham, packing cases of decorative work arriving on ox carts at the rear of the Lal Bagh Palace.

Anteroom of the Lal Bagh Palace, Indore, India. Designed by Bernard Triggs, F.R.I.B.A. All the decorative work and furniture by Martyns, throughout the palace.

The Lal Bagh Palace.

Above - Council Chamber.
Left - Cast Nickel silver washbasin.
Opposite page, top - The Throne Room.
Opposite page, below - Indian Drawing Room.

The Porte Cochere of the Lal Bagh Palace, Indore, India.

Cast nickel silver beadstead and mosquito net posts for the Holkar of Indore, Lal Bagh Palace, India.

A.W. Martyn resigned from the board of both H.H. Martyn and Gloster Aircraft in 1927 at the age of 57 following acute difference of opinion with several of the board members, including Hugh Burroughes and David Longden, to whom he sold his entire shareholding. A.W.'s daughter Ida recalls that his interests tended to lie with the H.H. Martyn organisation, whilst the other directors were keener to promote Gloster Aircraft and the engineering interests. He decided to give the young men the field by retiring from it.

Ida also recalls that on the day he left there was nothing to mark his departure, no word or gift; he just packed up his desk and left as if it was any other day. However, some time later he received a gold cigarette case engraved: 'A.W. Martyn, a token of esteem and affection from his boys — H.J. PARKER, C.H. DENLEY, G.F. TURNER'. It was a small compensation for his abrupt and unceremonial departure from the business to which he had dedicated himself for so long; he used it constantly and greatly valued it.

David Longden's agreement shows that for £6,500 he purchased 375 ordinary £1 shares in the Gloster Aircraft Co. Ltd., and 172 Ordinary £1shares and 35 Preference shares in H.H. Martyn & Co. Ltd., in June 1927, agreeing to payment by instalments. On A.W. Martyn's part it was a reluctant and sad parting, particularly as he was an active man and enthusiastic about the future of both companies. Many of the workforce greatly regretted his departure, feeling that Martyns lost something of its soul from that day. Within seven years (in 1934) H.H. Martyn & Co. was sold to Maples of London.

For the next ten years A.W. Martyn committed himself to public service and was elected a County Councillor. He also carried on his interests in education. Since 1920 he had been an advisory member of the North Gloucestershire Technical College and in 1934 he was elected chairman of the Governors, a position he held until his death in 1947. He also took an active advisory role in the Cheltenham School of Arts and Crafts. This keen interest in further education sprang probably from his own father's idea of the Working Men's College almost 50 years before, which must have made a lasting impression on him. Public assistance work was much to the fore, and he regularly visited Holm Hospital at Tewkesbury and St. Paul's Hospital in Cheltenham.

A.W. Martyn was a shrewd and tough man of business. He did not suffer fools gladly and could be scathing and ruthless, particularly with colleagues whom he thought were inefficient or weak. In some he inspired fear, though most respected, admired and got on well with him. However, he was also a kind man, considerate to his employees, friends and family in the widest sense, and exceedingly generous, looking after many relatives less well off, setting them up in a home and supporting them financially. He was often prompted by his wife in these matters but would willingly agree with her. His chauffeur of many years, Fred Winter, for whom he had great respeet, has often referred to his fine qualities and also to his great sense of humour.

One particular trait which was later to give him a renewed interest was his pleasure in helping young people to make a start on the business ladder. A good idea well researched and backed by enthusiasm was sure to meet with his approval and financial backing; quite a number of people can vouch for this and were helped both financially and with good counsel.

In 1935 A.W. was approached by George Dowty, a young engineer with ambitions to produce hydraulic aircraft components. A.W. instantly recognised George Dowty's qualities, which he described as a combination of engineering, design, and inventive skills coupled with a brilliant business brain such as is rarely found in one man.

As soon as George Dowty informed A.W. of his financial needs, prompt action took place. This must have been a pleasant surprise, as Dowty had sought finance for several years, trying all avenues, including Dunlop and the London finance houses, for backing. Firstly A.W. guaranteed an overdraft with a debenture of £2,000 to ensure that the company could carry on its day-to-day activities. Later in the same year, frustrated by the refusal of building consent for a factory on the outskirts of the town, A.W. Martyn again financially aided the company. The capital was increased to £30,000, enabling the purchase of Arle Court with eight cottages, outbuildings and nearly 100 acres for £6,500. The outbuildings were soon occupied by the plant and machinery which were moved, in one weekend, by the workforce of just 45. Robert Hunt drove one of the trucks, little knowing at that time that his destiny was to be chairman of the company, and also to be knighted. Following the large increase in capital, A.W. became the company's first chairman and remained so until his death in 1947.

In spite of what would seem to be substantial financial backing, cash was still a problem and finance had to be raised by going public, a step regretted by George Dowty for the rest of his life. He and A.W. received little for their part in the establishment of the company.

It was fortunate for the war effort and for the thousands of aircrew who depended on the tough Dowty aircraft landing gear, George Dowty and A.W. Martyn raced ahead with development and thwarted the potentially disastrous delaying tactics of the bureaucrats. Over 90,000 undercarriages and over 1,000,000 hydraulic units were delivered.

George Dowty, who was honoured with a Knighthood in 1956, is quoted by L.T.C. Rolt in his history of Dowty Equipment Ltd:

"A.W. Martyn had just the kind of business experience which the company lacked and an unbounded faith in its future based on a shrewd appreciation of the contribution we could make to the development of the British Aircraft Industry.

Early Dowty Board of Directors. Seated left G.H. Dowty, seated right A.W. Martyn (Chairman), standing left to right R. Bound, F.L. Blow, E. Glanville, M. Blackburn (secretary).

In fact, looking back, it is plain that A.W. Martyn by his confidence and optimism no less than by his financial aid gave the enterprise a vital shot in the arm at precisely the moment when it was most needed."

Hugh Burroughes gives this account of a meeting in 1936:

"George Dowty had been in charge of a section of the Gloucester Aircraft Company drawing office dealing with undercarriages and landing gear. Having resigned and started his own business, by 1936 he had spent not only his own savings, but those of his wife and sister, plus a £10,000 loan from Barclays Bank guaranteed by A.W.. Dowty was at the end of his financial tether when I was invited by Frank McKenna to meet him and Dowty for lunch at the Plough in Cheltenham. At this meeting Dowty told me he had been in touch with Dunlops to secure some more finance, but although an offer had been made he was reluctant to accept it because he would have to surrender control.

"My reply was that I was prepared to help him financially for at least a year, by which time I thought we could raise enough capital from sources in the City of London, where I had some influence. I was also prepared to liquidate the loan which A.W. had arranged on Dowty's behalf and put up £10,000 there and then to enable him to carry on. But, and this is important, I stipulated that Dowty should put these facts before A.W. because A.W. must be in agreement with my proposal. In other words I was not prepared to proceed unless A.W. endorsed my view. In the event A.W. found the extra cash himself, helped Dowty to overcome the crisis and got Dowty's company off the ground."

A.W. Martyn became chairman of Dowtys in 1936, when the company had just £5,000 worth of orders and 59 men on the payroll, and helped keep it on course through a decade of continuous and headlong growth. Within four years it had £10,000,000 worth of contracts on the books and had opened factories in Canada and the United States employing thousands of men; a vast world-wide organisation with developments in new technologies and dozens of factories.

Characteristically, A.W. started and was responsible for the apprentice scheme at Dowtys which he formed at the very beginning of his involvement. To him the vitality and future of a company were rooted in its apprentice scheme, as he had already demonstrated in the case of H.H. Martyn and Gloster Aircraft. His faith was vindicated by the outstanding and continuing success of Dowtys after 50 years, chaired at the time of writing by Sir Robert Hunt, himself one of the company's first apprentices.

A.W. Martyn could have made a considerable fortune by taking advantage of his indispensable financial support in 1936 but he chose a more generous course, preferring to set up his younger colleagues with a strong equity stake; he retained only 15%.

In 1980, Dowtys had grown to 44 companies with 17,000 employees pioneering in many fields, creating new products and materials, using precision production techniques and developing advanced technology in aerospace, defence, mining, industrial hydraulics, machine tools, electronics, automotive production and offshore work.

A.W. Martyn was referred to by many local businessmen as the father of industry in the area. As chairman, he certainly gave direction and impetus to three major companies in their formative years, Martyns, Glosters and Dowtys, which employed thousands directly and provided work and income for many thousands more who were employed by suppliers and sub-contractors. His companies were a magnet which drew other industries to the area, guaranteeing prosperity for the towns of Gloucester and Cheltenham, even down to the local corner shop. These enterprises overshadowed Mr. Skillicorn's discovery and promotion of the waters of Cheltenham Spa. The Martyns, father and son, turned two country towns into a thriving industrial centre.

Another enterprise which owed its existence to A.W. Martyn was less dramatic perhaps than Dowtys, lasting only as long as the life of its principal but of vital importance at the time to the nation and to many individuals. John Edgar Chandler's Gloucestershire Surgical Appliances Company, 1 Belle Vue Lawn, Cheltenham, came into being in 1915 with the financial support of the Gloster Aircraft Co. on A.W.'s recommendation. John Chandler was a brilliant art metal worker who had a forge in Cheltenham almost opposite Pittville Gates, the top section of which he made himself. He was employed later at Martyns for several years in the metal department. An example of his incredible artistic skill with metal, donated by his daughter Mrs Meddick, can be seen in Cheltenham Art Gallery. He had a fertile and inventive brain and during the first world war was inspired by the plight of the war wounded to develop special metal splints which were far superior to the crude devices then in use. He was encouraged by Dr Grace Billings to specialise in this field, and as a result of A.W.'s help his inventive skill was put to its best use aiding disabled servicemen.

Chandler had previously invented a development of the periscope and a revolutionary rifle sight, but

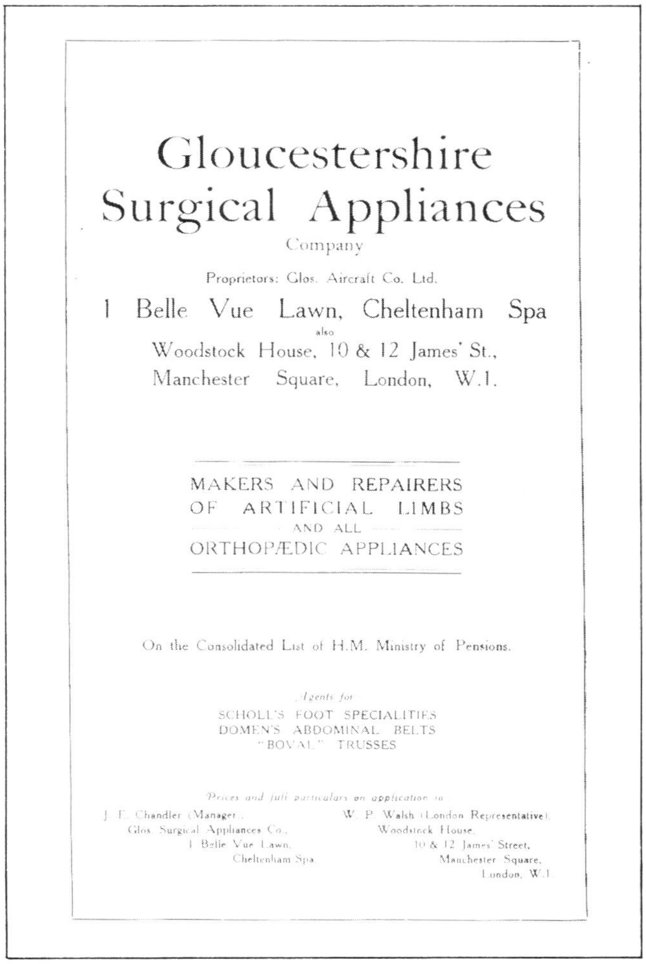
Gloucestershire
Surgical Appliances
Company

Proprietors: Glos. Aircraft Co. Ltd.

1 Belle Vue Lawn, Cheltenham Spa
also
Woodstock House, 10 & 12 James' St.,
Manchester Square, London, W.1.

MAKERS AND REPAIRERS
OF ARTIFICIAL LIMBS
AND ALL
ORTHOPÆDIC APPLIANCES

On the Consolidated List of H.M. Ministry of Pensions.

Agents for
SCHOLL'S FOOT SPECIALITIES
DOMEN'S ABDOMINAL BELTS
"BOVAL" TRUSSES

Prices and full particulars on application to:
J. E. Chandler (Manager), Glos. Surgical Appliances Co., 1 Belle Vue Lawn, Cheltenham Spa.
W. P. Walsh (London Representative), Woodstock House, 10 & 12 James' Street, Manchester Square, London, W.1.

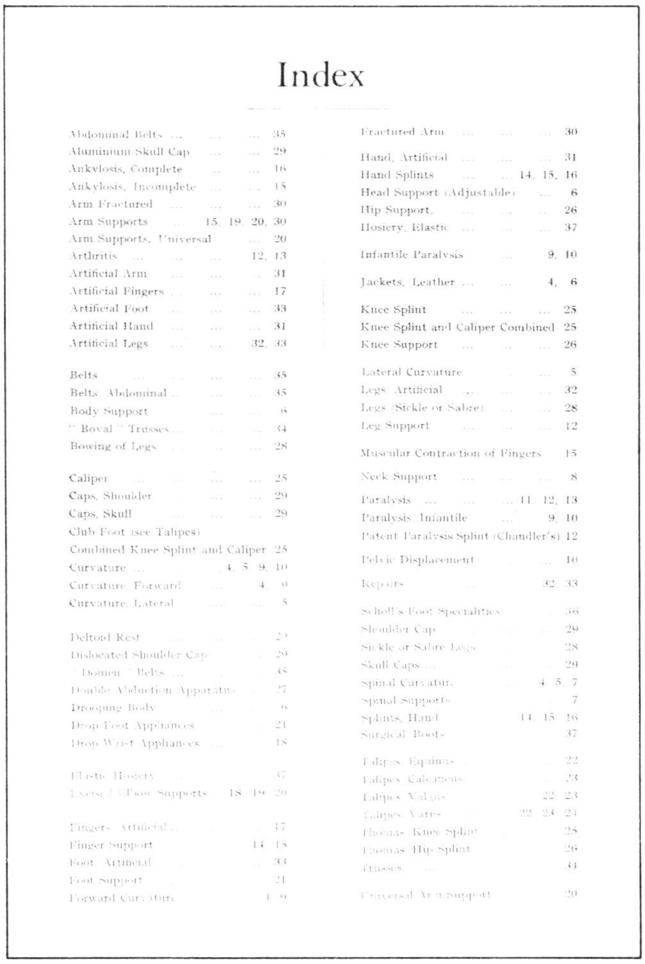
Index

Abdominal Belts 35
Aluminium Skull Cap 29
Ankylosis, Complete 16
Ankylosis, Incomplete 15
Arm Fractured 30
Arm Supports ... 15, 19, 20, 30
Arm Supports, Universal ... 20
Arthritis 12, 13
Artificial Arm 31
Artificial Fingers 17
Artificial Foot 33
Artificial Hand 31
Artificial Legs 32, 33

Belts 35
Belts, Abdominal 35
Body Support 6
"Boval" Trusses 34
Bowing of Legs 28

Caliper 25
Caps, Shoulder 29
Caps, Skull 29
Club Foot (see Talipes)
Combined Knee Splint and Caliper 25
Curvature 4, 5, 9, 10
Curvature, Forward ... 4, 9
Curvature, Lateral 5

Deltoid Rest ... ... [illegible]
Dislocated Shoulder Cap ... 29
"Domen" Belts 35
Double Abduction Apparatus ... 27
Drooping Body 6
Drop Foot Appliances ... 21
Drop Wrist Appliances ... 18

Elastic Hosiery ... 37
[illegible] Elbow Supports 18, 19, 20

Fingers, Artificial 17
Finger Support ... 14, 15
Foot, Artificial 33
Foot Support ... 21
Forward Curvature ... 4, 9

Fractured Arm 30

Hand, Artificial 31
Hand Splints 14, 15, 16
Head Support (Adjustable) ... 6
Hip Support 26
Hosiery, Elastic 37

Infantile Paralysis ... 9, 10

Jackets, Leather 4, 6

Knee Splint 25
Knee Splint and Caliper Combined 25
Knee Support 26

Lateral Curvature 5
Legs, Artificial 32
Legs (Sickle or Sabre) 28
Leg Support 12

Muscular Contraction of Fingers 15

Neck Support 8

Paralysis 11, 12, 13
Paralysis, Infantile ... 9, 10
Patent Paralysis Splint (Chandler's) 12

Pelvic Displacement 10

Repairs 32, 33

Scholl's Foot Specialities ... 36
Shoulder Cap 29
Sickle or Sabre Legs ... 28
Skull Caps 29
Spinal Curvature ... 4, 5, 7
Spinal Supports ... 7
Splints, Hand ... 14, 15, 16
Surgical Boots ... 37

Talipes, Equinus 22
Talipes, Calcaneus ... 23
Talipes, Valgus ... 22, 23
Talipes, Varus ... 22, 23, 24
Thomas' Knee Splint ... 25
Thomas' Hip Splint ... 26
Trusses 34

Universal Arm Support ... 20

Pages from the Gloucestershire Surgical Appliances Company brochure.

as a pacifist he baulked at profiting from it and discontinued the work. The reflective rifle sight came about because of his eccentric nature; believing that he was being mocked by people in the street behind him he fitted a small mirror to his glasses to enable him to see over his shoulder.

After managing the surgical company throughout the war he bought control from Gloster Aircraft in 1919. Mrs Meddick recalls his great regard for A.W. and his gratitude to him for setting up the business and eventually giving him the opportunity to take it over; help which he said enriched and fulfilled his life. Many of John Chandler's surgical appliances designs are used today, almost unchanged after 60 years.

Charles Denley

Charles H. Denley was associated with both Martyns and Gloster Aircraft as a most able company secretary, whose special efficiency was of inestimable value to both companies. He was a close friend of the Martyn family. In addition to his duties as secretary, he was a director of the Cheltenham Manufacturing Co., a subsidary of H.H. Martyn & Co., formed for the principal work of furniture manufacture. He retired on 20th March 1940, with £1,000, equal to one year's salary, plus £200 compensation. Apart from his other work he was also General Manager of H.H. Martyn from 1938 until his retirement.

David Longden

In pursuance of the Company's policy of recruiting men of exceptional talent, David Longden was approached during 1910 by A.W. Martyn. He was an architect, having qualified in 1907, and was employed as an assistant in the office of James Miller at 15 Blythewood Square, Glasgow. He was 25 years old in 1911 when he joined H.H. Martyn on 1st January to be manager of the drawing office of the ship decoration department. Ship decoration had been undertaken since 1909 when the contract for the Orvieto, the company's first ship, had been obtained.

David Longden 'was to be paid £238.0s.0d. per year in monthly payments with no deductions whatsoever.' He was also to receive 5% of the net profits derived from the ship decoration business but such allowance to be accumulated in the hands of the company until it reached the sum of £1,000 when it would be paid over to him. A further document shows an agreement by H.H. Martyn and A.W. Martyn to sell at market price to David Longden when his allowance reached £1,000 such ordinary or preference shares as the money would buy, and subject to election by the shareholders, to permit him to apply for a directorship, both H.H. and A.W. Martyn agreeing to 'use their best endeavours to obtain the appointment for him'. He was soon to become a director of the company as agreed, and a firm friendship grew

For Paralysis, Arthritis, Etc.

Fig. 18 is a single leg instrument of similar design with the addition of a dropfoot attachment.

This attachment is fixed to the sole of the boot, connected with a lever arm to which an accumulator spring is attached, for the purpose of raising the foot ; this is also detachable at the ankle.

In cases where it is necessary to lower the foot instead of raising it, the lever arm is reversed.

From a Patient :
Weston-super-Mare.

"I am letting you know how I am getting on, after all your kind patience with me.

"I have been able to walk much more comfortably.

"I intend returning to Cheltenham when you will be able to judge for yourself what a blessing it is to me."

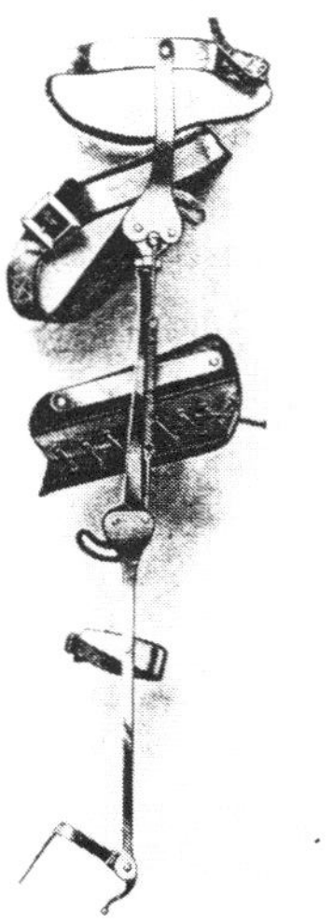

Fig. 18.

Devonshire.

Dear Sir

"I am sending you my splint to be repaired.

"I am sure it will interest you to know what a help this instrument has been to me.

"**The splint entirely corrects the inversion** and keeps my foot at the proper angle."

Yours faithfully.

From Doctor ——— Bridgnorth.

"I have much pleasure in testifying to the **efficiency and comfort of the support** you made me in July.

"When first I began to wear it **I found it far more comfortable and a much better aid to my paralysed leg** (and two months constant use has confirmed that opinion) **than the one I had been wearing for a number of years, which was made by a firm who specialised in these instruments.**

"Wishing you the success your skill merits."

"LOUD IN THEIR PRAISE."

From "One of the Old Contemptibles." Brighton.

"I am ——— who was at the ——— Hospital, 1918.

You made a leg splint for me with waist band, steel springs and shoe with drop springs.

"They have all been loud in their praise of your splint and want one made similar to mine.

"It is very comfortable and easy.

"I wrote this to let you know.

I am

"One of the Old Contemptibles."

Leg Supports

(Patented)

The unique construction of these appliances (see Figs. 16, 17, 18), which are protected by H.M. Letters Patent, **gives stability and support not found in any other similar appliances.**

Highly recommended for **paralysis, arthritis, and all kindred complaints**, in which the legs are unable to support the weight of the body.

Provision is made for flexion, abduction, and rotation of the leg and foot. Accumulator springs operate above the thigh and knee joints, assisting flexion.

The boot is detachable at the ankle joint.

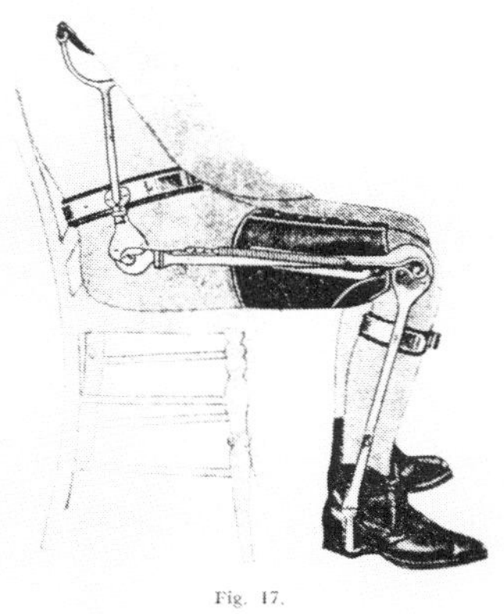

Fig. 17.

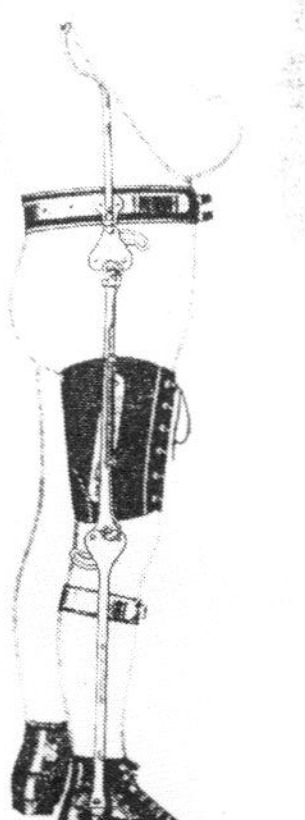

Fig. 16.

Fig. 17 shows patient in a sitting position fitted with same appliance.

Patent Paralysis Splint, see Fig. 16.

Cheltenham.

"You will remember that my doctor called you in to see me some two years ago. I was **then practically helpless** through the absorbation of the head of the left femur, resulting in a considerable shortening of the left leg, as shown in the X ray photo now in your possession.

"I wore your appliance for two years, and, as a result of the weight being taken off the leg, the femur has ossified as shown in the last X ray photo I sent you.

"I am now able to walk without any appliance, although for safety I wear it occasionally.

"I am most grateful to you for your skill and attention, which has saved me from a bed-ridden existence, and I hope many sufferers from arthritis may get to know of your good work."

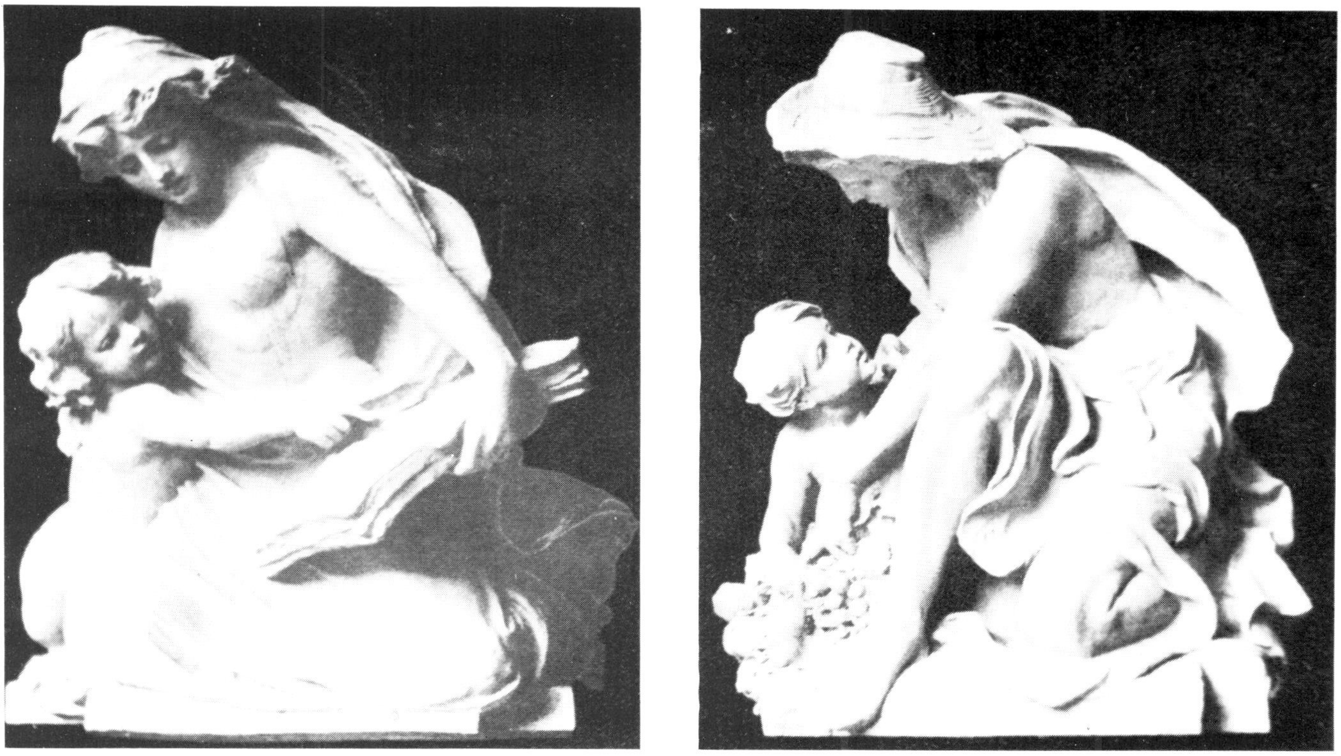

Two of several groups of statuary carved in Carrara marble by Robert Lindsey Clark R.S.B.S. for the Queen Victoria Memorial, Calcutta, India.

between the Martyn family and his own. David Longden was to be the principal motivator in advancing Martyns in the ship interior work for which it became so famous.

When David Longden was in Glasgow he met and became a close friend of Alexander McInnes Gardner, who during the 1920's was responsible for numerous ship interior designs including the Queen and the Monarch of Bermuda, Canadian Pacific ships like the Empress of Britain, the Aorangi Tiki and the Aorangi Tata for the New Zealand run, and many others. It can be no coincidence that Martyns received the contracts to carry out many of his designs. Unfortunately none survive, enemy action and the breaker's yard having taken their toll.

H.A. Dutton

H.A. Dutton was one of the founding directors of Martyns who aided A.W. in the days when the company became a limited company at the turn of the century. Dutton's wide experience of business and craft work was found of great value. As with the other members of the board, documents refer to him as a sculptor.

Robert Lindsey Clark R.S.B.S.

Robert Lindsey Clark was one of the key figures in the success of Martyns. He was the son of a well known Worcester ironmonger, J.D. Clark, and probably known to H.H. Martyn from his Worcester days. Robert Lindsey Clark joined Martyns in the early 1900's as an apprentice sculptor and quickly showed an incredible talent. He parted from the company for a time to study at the Lambeth Schools, returning to Martyns as head sculptor and art director. Work designed and executed by Robert Lindsey Clark for the company still exists in many parts of the world.

Robert Lindsey Clark exhibited at the Royal Academy on many occasions and in 1911 the Royal Society of British Sculptors added his name to its elite membership of only 200. He is known for his 'Cupid', a statuette, and 'Fortuna, Psyche and Eros', a marble relief, but his finest work which received universal acclaim was a bronze, 'The Broken Limber', intricately sculptured and cast in the Martyns foundry and exhibited at the Royal Academy in 1924. He and his friends regarded this as his most successful work. He was awarded the first prize in the open competition for a design for the Liverpool Queen Victoria monument shortly after her death.

On behalf of Martyns, Robert Lindsey Clark spent a considerable time at the marble quarries of Carrara in Italy while working on the memorial to Queen Victoria for Calcutta. Apart from his sculpture he was an excellent water colour artist and sportsman. Both his son and grandson followed his traditions and have become noted sculptors.

Malvern College, chapel reredos and altar.

Chapter 2

CARVING IN STONE AND MARBLE

Five of the Twelve Patriotic Women, carved by Mr. H.H. Martyn for Cheltenham Ladies College.

At one time it was thought necessary, if very fine carving or casting was required in England, to employ French, Italian, German or other Continental craftsmen to carry out the work. Many stately homes boast of such foreign expertise in their decor. This accepted tradition was dealt a lasting rebuff as Martyns craftsmen proved it false. The skill and virtuosity of the British artist were proved second to none. Buckingham Palace testified in a statement to this fact following work carried out there, and the Royal favour led to commissions from the owners of many other palaces and stately homes for carved adornments, decorative plaster ceilings, wood carving, wood panelling, bronze, wrought iron and metal work for doors, balustrades and ornaments.

In the early years, stone carving was still a thriving business, particularly as ornamented gravestones were popular with the Victorians and Edwardians. E.A. Emms and H.H. Martyn were involved in carving gravestones together, and even after dissolving the partnership both continued in that trade. This is illustrated in an 1890 photograph of the premises of H.H. Martyn & Co. at the corner of College Road, the forecourt of which is full of headstones on display. E.A. Emms continued with this work almost exclusively until the 1970's, their last foreman Mr. Paul still keeping the tradition going today with his own company.

As the company grew, extending its premises to works adjoining the Belle Vue Hotel and installing the latest machines to speed the basic cutting and ground work both of stone and wood, extensive contracts were placed by architects for more elaborate work of an architectural nature. As a result, the gravestones side of the business gradually declined.

Of 200 men employed in about 1905 the majority were talented carvers occupied in artistic work. At this time the fine reredos for Malvern College Chapel was carved in stone from a similar design to that of Truro Cathedral, to the designs of Sir A. Blomfield, R.A. In 1883 twelve statues were carved by H.H. Martyn himself for Cheltenham Ladies' College to depict famous women in history. Set in double niches in the quadrangle, they were Miriam and Deborah — Carmelia and Boadicea — Bathildis and St. Hilda — Elizabeth of Hungary and

The first premises of H.H. Martyn and Co. at the corner of College Road and High Street, Cheltenham, about 1890.

Blanche of Carlise — Joan of Arc and Catherine of Sienna — Louise of Russia and Chand Bebee. These statues were unveiled on April 16th 1883 and H.H. Martyn was personally credited in a local paper as having carved them. The Ladies' College Guide of the period states: 'The statues are a credit to Mr. Martyn'. Unfortunately the carvings were removed during 1939-1945 and have been lost.

Middleton, Prothero & Philpot, architects to Cheltenham Ladies' College, show in their records that between February and October 1883 Mr. Martyn was paid £490 for carvings for the New Wing. It is likely that as well as the twelve patriotic women, he carved the statues in Montpellier Street in niches of the New Wing. They are three great teachers, St. Paul, Socrates and Alcuin. He certainly carved the statue of Hope with Anchor in a niche on the east side. Mr. Martyn's personal connections with the College through his Working Men's College and stage productions there would have ensured him the contracts and committed him personally to their execution.

On February 22nd 1884 Mr. Martyn was paid by the above architects £7.0s.0d. for 'carving and altering Miss Beale's seat', later to be popularly known as her throne.

View of Stone Carving Studio, 1905.

Detail of some of H.H. Martyn's own carving, St. Philips and St. James Church, Cheltenham.

The 'Builders Journal' of July 5th 1889 has a photograph of the reredos of St. Philip's and St. James' Church, Cheltenham, stating that the sculptor was H.H. Martyn. Middleton Prothero & Philpot designed the reredos and Mr. Martyn probably finished the main figures to perfection, the preliminary work being done by many other craftsmen as it would be too great an undertaking for one man to complete alone. These two examples of his personal skill as a sculptor are particularly fine and show that he was a man of great talent.

Many other statues and busts in the Cheltenham Ladies' College were produced in the studios of H.H. Martyn. Between 1893 and 1896 Martyns also carried out a considerable number of carvings in stone for Cheltenham Gentlemen's College Chapel and H.H. Martyn himself made a gift to the College of the statue of 'Christ the Good Shepherd' which stands over the door looking on to the Bath Road. The gift may indeed have been prompted by the extent to which Martyns was commissioned to produce carvings for the Chapel. However, records are lacking. Boltons was also involved in the work and certainly produced the stone reredos which is very similar to that of Malvern College and Winchester and Truro Cathedrals. The stone carvers were probably the same as Martyns used as the men would go where the work was available. It is on record, however, that the Eleanor Cross by the Bath Road was produced by Martyns at a cost of £387.00. The Eleanor Cross was unveiled on June 26th 1903 by Sir. A. Power Palmer G.C.B. (o.c.) in brilliant summer weather. The eight bronze plaques honour the 54 Old Cheltonians who died in the Boer War.

The stone carvings of the four corner buttresses and the figures at the east and west end of the college chapel and flanking the Good Shepherd over the west door are all Martyns work.

Many churches in villages, towns and cities all over the country were graced with Martyns' beautiful stone carving, like the one for the church of John the Baptist, Kensington, and in 1908 the reredos for Ullet Road Chapel, Sefton Park, Liverpool.

One of the large stone Corinthian capitals for the Geological Museum, South Kensington.
Architect: John H. Markham.

Stone carving department, Sunningend, Lansdown, about 1923.

Stone carvings of St. Michael and St. Gabriel executed for W.H. Bidlake, Architect.

Between 1899 and 1901 the Hon. Percy Allsopp used the services of Martyns for the elaborate restoration of the Lady Chapel in Worcester Cathedral. The screen enclosing the chapel was carved in stone in perpendicular style, surmounted by a rood and fitted with an elaborate retable of fine violets in wood.

Martyns developed a close association with W. Jenkins & Co. of Torquay and obtained exquisite marbles through them. The best marbles came from Italy and the principal of the company himself selected the pieces of marble at the quarries. The company also had its own marble quarries in Devon. Walter Jenkins and A.W. Martyn became lifelong friends.

Martyns' stonecarving art can be seen in the deceptive simplicity of the Cenotaph in Whitehall; Belfast, Lambeth, Woolwich, Bromley and Johannesburg Town Halls; Ulster Parliament Buildings; King's College, Aberdeen; Guy's Hospital — the list is almost endless. Sir Edward Landseer Lutyens, architect of the Cenotaph, entered into an agreement with Martyns on 29th July 1920 licensing the production of scale replicas, though no example has yet come to light.

The following works in stone by Martyns were reported in the 'Architectural Review':

1905 Messrs Speights, Photographic premises, 157 New Bond Street, London, stone carving.

1905 The stone carved gargoyles for the mausoleum of the Campbell family in St. Mary's Cemetery, Kensal Green.

1906 11 Hill St., Berkeley Square, London, in which considerable work was done involving stonework, woodwork, carving and plaster work to dining room, library and boudoirs.

1907 A carved figure of St. John in a niche in the west front of the Church of St. John Evangelist, Dyson Lane, Upper Edmonton, London.

1907 Ditton Place, Balcombe, Sussex, stone carving, also at Hollington House, Newbury.

1908 The offices for the River Wear Commissioners in Sunderland, stone carving.

1909 Stone carving for the New Central Library, Nelson, Lancs. and the Ashton Memorial, Lancaster, by John Belcher R.A., Architect.

1910 Three figures carved for the public library of Dudley, Worcs. depicting 'LITERATURE' 'SCIENCE' 'PHILOSOPHY', together will all the decorative plasterwork.

1911 The Berkshire County Hall, stone carving, plasterwork and wrought iron lift enclosures.

1912 Thames House, Upper Thames St., London. Exterior stone work, very fine work over the corner entrance.

1913 The Civil Engineers Building, St. George St., Westminster, stone carving (some also by W.S. Frith).

1914 The Midland Adelphi Hotel, Liverpool, all the stone carving.

1915 London Joint Stock Bank, Newcastle, all the stone carving and woodwork.

1918 Australia House, stone carving in front of building on the south (Strand) side. W. Jenkins & Co. supervised 1200 tons of marble work for the interior.

From a pre-1935 brochure the following list is reproduced:

STONEWORK & CARVING

Nottingham Exchange; Adelphi Hotel, Liverpool; Martin's Bank, Liverpool; Midland Bank Head Office, Poultry; Ulster Parliament Buildings.

STONE CARVING, ETC.

The Cenotaph; Worcester Cathedral; Belfast Town Hall; Lambeth Town Hall; Woolwich Town Hall; Bromley Town Hall; Johannesburg Town Hall; Ulster Parliament Buildings; Australia House, London; King's College, Aberdeen; Midland Bank Head Office; Eastern Bank, London; College of Agriculture, Cambridge; King's College for Women, Campden Hill; Westminster Opthalmic Hospital; Guy's Hospital; Adelphi Hotel, Liverpool; Birmingham Civic Centre; Swansea Civic Centre; London & Manchester Assurance Co., London; Geological Museum, Kensington; Derby Police Courts; and Lambeth Bridge, London.

From advertisements in the Architectural Review:

1919/23 Thornton Manor, marble organ case, chimney piece etc.

1919/23 Woolwich Town Hall - north facade. Walsall Cenotaph, designed and executed.

1923 Marble statues for Queen Victoria Memorial, Calcutta.

1923/29 Parliament Buildings, Victoria, British Columbia, carved stonework.

1923 King's College for Women, London, — stone carving over east doorway.

1928 Melbourne Grammar School, Australia, Caen stone reredos with glass mosaic figure panels.

1923/29 Malvern College — reredos.

1923/29 Shorditch Maternity and Child Welfare, stone carving over main entrance.

1923/29 Luton Library stone carving.

1923/29 Swan & Edgar's premises, London — vases on the Piccadilly front in Portland stone.

James Howell and Co. premises Cardiff, carved Portland stone panels to design of Ivor Jones and Percy Thomas.

Thornton Manor. Carved marble organ case.

A publication on Cheltenham early in the century stated as follows:

"Certainly it cannot be claimed that Cheltenham is a manufacturing centre in the same sense as Birmingham or Wolverhampton. There is however one unique industry here, and any description of the town would be hardly complete which did not mention the works at Sunningend of Messrs. H.H. Martyn and Co. Ltd. The writer had the privilege of being personally conducted over this remarkable undertaking some little time ago by the original founder, Mr. H.H. Martyn, and a small volume might be written of all that was seen on that occasion. It must be remarked in passing that the carrying on of sculpture carving, architectural modelling, art metal work, etc., would seem to be quite in harmony with the character of the town. At these works — the site and lay out of which are all that could be desired — are to be found studios for modelling and well equipped shops for the execution of high class fibrous plaster work. At the time of writing, such orders were being executed as the stately marble pulpit — in the Gothic style — for Brisbane Cathedral, Australia; an imposing statue for Bloemfontein, South Africa; carved figures of exquisite design in Polyphant stone for St. Ninian's Cathedral; modelling in clay prior to carving in Portland stone — of the magnificent emblematical figures for the London headquarters of the Y.M.C.A.; carving and panelling for Balliol College, Oxford, as also a decorative scheme for one of the new boats for the P. & O. Co. Messrs. Martyn enjoy an unequalled reputation for the excellence of their carving both in wood and stone, and there is probably no living architect unacquainted with their capabilities in this direction, as also for fibrous plaster and hammered metal work."

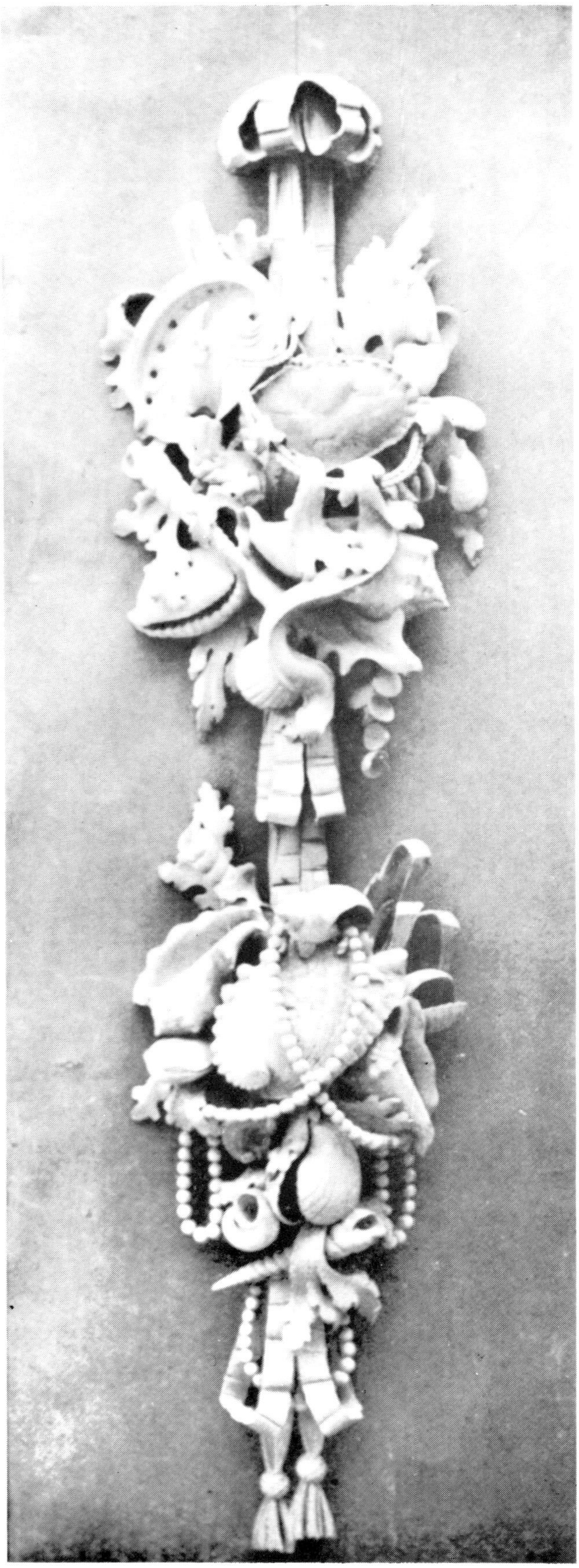

Carved wood drops.

Chapter 3

WOOD CARVING

More than all other activities, woodcarving put Martyns on the road to success. Impressive work is its own best advertisement and it ensured familiarity with the company name nationally and internationally among architects looking to adorn their clients' homes or places of business. Locally, the company soon became known as 'Martyns the Carvers' and many of the older generation remember it still by this name in the 1980s.

The principal reason for this acclaim in the early days of the company was a carver persuaded by H.H. Martyn to join the company in 1899. Henry Arthur Dean (later known as Harry Dean) came from a farming family in Oxford and had carved from his early youth. He already had a name for exquisite work when he moved to Cheltenham and joined Martyns. Harry Dean epitomised H.H. Martyn's goal to produce **'the best'** and for 23 years he did just that. His carving has been rated as good as Grinling Gibbons and it is unjust that his name should not by now be equally well known. Tragically he died in 1922, only 57 years old, a loss to the world of a great artist. Harry Dean was a family man and he and his wife, who came from Devon, had eight children and lived for much of the time at 4 St. Phillip's Terrace (now Gratton Road).

In a small shed at the bottom of his garden Harry Dean carved The Last Supper as a rare private contract for a friend. His children often enjoyed watching him work on that carving. He was very deaf for most of his working life, but he had a good sense of humour and enjoyed sport and

Portion of the Wood Carving Studio, 1905.

politics, which took up a lot of his evenings and spare time. One of his last carvings was for Buenos Aires, probably for the British Embassy. Harry Dean was keen on shooting, as was A.W. Martyn, and it was not unusual for the employer to call while Harry was carving and take him off to Dowdeswell, a few miles east of Cheltenham, for an afternoon's rough shoot. Carvers worked 'flexi-hours', as we would now call them and would come and go as the inspiration took them. If the carving was going well they would work late into the night. They were also permitted a bottle or two of beer by their bench, perhaps to aid inspiration.

There was a blacksmith in London Road, Cheltenham, who was specially skilled in the making of woodcarving tools. He would make them to order to the design and shape the carver would describe, and temper the steel to the optimum for honing to a razor-sharp edge which would last. Martyns' carvers, both stone and wood, used this smith's services from the early days.

In 1905 there were about 20 experienced and gifted master carvers, supported by others of lesser ability and apprentices learning their trade who carried out preparatory work for the top craftsmen to finish.

One such man was W.P. (Bill) Davison. He joined the company as an improver in 1907 at 17 years of age and worked as stonecarver, woodcarver and modeller on half the pay of a time-served carver. He became a journeyman carver after completing his training and it is known that he worked in 1914 at Sledmere Hall, Yorks, working under the eye of the senior plasterer, Mr. Millson, making masters in clay from which the plasterers made the moulds for casting. Bill Davison came from a long line of carvers dating from the 1780s and was fortunate to receive his early instruction from his father. He worked mostly in Martyn's London studios after his apprenticeship and was known to have carved stone decorations for the front of the Midland Bank, Folkstone, in 1924.

Two of this country's finest wood carvers — Harry Breckin (left), Harry Dean (right).

A carver who matched Harry Dean in excellence was H.H. Breckin; in fact they often worked together on the larger pieces. However, Harry Dean worked alone most of the time in the old works in College Road, would not join the Union, was a staunch Conservative and preferred to be apart from the other men, not unusual with artists of his skill.

Herbert Henry Breckin, known to all his friends as Harry, was born in 1860 in Bradford and later moved to Rotherham with his father, who was a carver and cabinet maker for Appleyards, for whom he did work in Rotherham Parish Church and many houses in the Dukeries. Harry Breckin joined Martyns in 1906, taking lodgings with a Mrs. Smith at Angle House, Bath Parade. He married in 1910 Mabel Humphries and had a son and two daughters, one of whom, Mary Martyn, (not a member of the family), kindly gave invaluable help in my searches. Harry Breckin worked on aircraft construction in the Old Winter Gardens during the first war, a far cry from carving. His daughter remembers being lifted up to peer through the window to see the planes.

Times were frequently very hard when craftsmen were without work. Sometimes to keep working they would transfer to Boultons to carve on a project and return to Martyns as other work became available. During one very bad spell when work was short, Mrs. Breckin had to pawn her wedding ring and the family's few possessions of china and silver. Harry had refused a coal heaving job as he was concerned about his hands and its effect on his carving in future, so his assistance money was stopped. Clothes were unpicked and re-modelled so that the children could go to school reasonably dressed. When things improved, Harry Breckin found himself on ship decorative work. His first carvings were in the liner MALOGA, a job he enjoyed so much he wanted his daughter to be christened Maloga. Unfortunately, the ship was sunk in the first world war.

During the 1920s Harry lodged near the Elephant and Castle, London, while working at the Guildhall and on the Queen Alexandra Memorial. Mary Martyn informs me that the top two panels over the door of the College chapel, Cheltenham, illustrating the Tree of Life, were carved by Harry Breckin while the rest and major portion was done by Harry Dean.

From a photograph, a likeness of the late owner of Tunstall Manor was carved in walnut by Harry Breckin and set in the overmantel of the billiards room. The son was delighted with the likeness of his father, a fact to which he testified in a letter to the company. Lichfield Cathedral and Malvern College (The Spandrills) have work by Harry Breckin, and of course hundreds of other venues now lost to memory and record.

Harry Dean, together with Harry Breckin, must go down as key figures in the success of Martyns. Their work is exceptional and its effect was to inspire others in the company to try to equal it. Some of those who watched or received instruction in time came close to matching their brilliance.

Carvers were considered by themselves and some others to be an elite among the workforce, perhaps not quite as high in the scale as a sculptor who both designed and carved. However, life was hard around the turn of the century as although men were well paid when working, they were at once laid off without pay if there were no work. Fortunately layoffs of carvers at Martyns were minimal as the work commissioned continued to increase.

Some of the other carvers in the early years were G.F. Turner, D. Hill and C.F. Yeand, who carved many of the pew ends, which are all different, in St. Phillip's and St. James' Church, Cheltenham.

Other carvers included E. Simpson, T.R. Sheppard, H. Mould, H.W. Foster, A. Turner, R.W. Young, C. Cox, G. Green, W. Chesney, W. Simmonds, H. Moolenaar, J. Hives, R. Quick, C.A. Morgan, J. Spyker, T. Edwards and a certain C. Gisborne who like many of the others was to go on to greater works. He was later awarded the B.E.M. on completing the major part of the carving on the Speaker's Chair for the House of Commons.

J. Hives (brother of Lord Hives of Rolls Royce) was in charge of wood buying — a vital role which took him to Austria for the finest oak for church work, Honduras for mahogany and Mallinson's in London for many of the fine timbers used at the works.

'Archie' Spurr was the manager of this large force of carvers and also of the sculptors; a considerable task. He also travelled to obtain contracts for work.

C.F. Yeand served his woodcarving apprenticeship with Martyn & Emms during their 1874—1888 partnership. He then joined H.H. Martyns as one of its first master carvers, continuing until his retirement at the age of 76. The story told is that he left without a golden handshake, as one of the directors from Maples, who by then had taken over Martyns, said if he has been in regular employment all those years he should not be short of money. Mr. Yeand has left beautiful carvings in wood in churches, houses, cathedrals, palaces and ocean liners, though sadly only some of the pew ends in St. Phillip's and St. James' Church, Cheltenham, carved in 1889, can now be positively identified as his own work. Payment by Middletons, Architects, to H.H. Martyn & Co. for the pews was made on 13th January 1892; a sum of £708.0s.0d. Silent testimony to his skill in wood will outlast the money and gold watch which he would have received on retirement.

David Hill was another carver of exceptional skill who joined Martyns in the early years. In 1906, after serving his apprenticeship with Waring and Gillow in Lancaster, he left to join the prestigious Martyn team of which he was later to become foreman carver, a post which he held for most of his 40 years with the company. David Hill's skilled carving exists in most of the large contracts carried out by the company but his individual works are unfortunately not recorded. One of his later works was for Great Rissington church in the Cotswolds where he worked as foreman carver on the pulpit and screen, and the cherubs which adorn the organ casing.

The lovely carved mirror frames for the boudoir of Haile Selassie's daughter in Ethiopia were David

Tryptych for Jesus Chapel, Worcester Cathedral, 1899. Harry Breckin is known to have carved the six figures in the two groups near the top of the reredos, the central figure of the Virgin and Child and the two accompanying on either side.

Some figures carved by Harry Breckin in 1898. The central figure can be seen top right of the tryptych of Jesus Chapel, Worcester Cathedral.

Hill's very last work for Martyns. Because of advancing age he carved the frames at home to save him the journey into work. They were a fittingly great final work for a man of such skill and one who like many of the early team had been a friend of H.H. Martyn, often visiting his home. For many years too he had received a brace of pheasants for Christmas from his employer and friend. Sadly, after all his years with the company, when he retired in 1947 he received no token of esteem from his later employers.

"Huie" Foster started with Martyns as an apprentice in 1910 in the wood carving studios; he remained with the company for 54 years as a highly skilled carver and modeller, much revered by his own co-workers and the clients for whom he carried out his exquisite carvings. He worked on all the major contracts during his long association with the company, from the Lal Bagh Palace to Caird Hall, Dundee. He also did some interesting fine modelling, such as his head of King George V for use by the Royal Mint to stamp on the penny of the day. Huie's model was sent to a Paris company to be reduced and formed into a die for the Mint, where it was used to make millions of coins. He also made a model for the casting in bronze of a limited edition paperweight of the Oerlikon gun, the real gun castings throughout the war having been cast in the foundry. Foster worked on the Speaker's Chair for the House of Commons. He is among several who worked on the carving; he was also entrusted with carving, in wood, the patterns for the intricate and detailed clasps and scrolls which adorn the Dispatch Boxes, carved first in fine detail in lime wood, to be later cast in the foundry and burnished prior to being affixed to the boxes.

Like many of the early craftsmen, Huie Foster was on good terms with H.H. Martyn and was often at his house for tea in the early days, the two craftsmen no doubt finding much in common.

A notable piece of carving executed in 1899 was the Triptych for the Jesus Chapel of Worchester Cathedral. According to a Martyns brochure of 1905:

> *The work throughout is reminiscent of the finest medieval examples. Every inch of the massive construction is carved; figures in the round, canopies and finials with elaborate Gothic ornament and the wings in bass relief.*

The design was by R.A. Briggs, Architect. The work of Harry Dean and Harry Breckin, as well as other carvers, is exemplified in this Triptych — well worth seeing. On 6th May 1899 the altar and reredos destined for Jesus Chapel, Worcester Cathedral, was put on display in the Winter Gardens in Cheltenham. The Cheltenham Looker-On described it as follows:

There was on private view at the Winter Garden on Monday last, a magnificent specimen of carving in mahogany, executed in the studios of Messrs. H. H. Martyn and Co., of High Street, Cheltenham. It was an altar and reredos about to be erected in the Jesus Chapel of a Cathedral in an adjoining county. The work, which was designed by Mr. R.A. Briggs, F.R.I.B.A., is in the style of the 15th century. In the central panel of the reredos is a figure of the Virgin holding the Infant Saviour on her knee in the act of blessing, and on either side are figures of St. Wolstan and St. Oswald, Patron Saints of the Cathedral. Figures of the Twelve Apostles are on each side of these panels, and on the outer buttresses those of six Bishops. A figure of our Lord is immediately above the central canopy, with Angels bearing the emblems of the passion on either side, and others of St. John the Baptist and Mary Magdalene. An Angel holding a crown forms the apex of the whole. Five sculptured panels depicting five of the miracles are above the table, with an Angel between each panel. The Reredos has two leaves to open and shut, and on these are bas-reliefs of the principal events in the life of Our Lord. The left one shows the Baptism, the Transfiguration, the Temptation, and the sorrowful Journey to Jerusalem; the right, the Triumphal Entry into Jerusalem, the Resurrection, the Appearance to Mary Magdalene, and the Ascension. The Altar, in five panels, has a bas-relief centre, one of the Virgin holding the body of Christ, and others of Angels. The whole work is a superb specimen of modern art, executed with masterly skill.

In 1905 Martyns was entrusted with restorative work to carved panelling attributed to Grinling Gibbons. The screen was moved from Winchester College Chapel and refitted at Hursley Park. The cost of re-assembling from the many broken pieces, replacing and carving, was £1,000 for this masterpiece of restoration.

The screen had been moved from Winchester College Chapel in 1874—5 and had been stored in a heap outside and left exposed to the weather. It passed through several hands in a badly damaged state until thirty years later it was restored by Martyns craftsmen. The screen was then installed at Hursley Park, the home of Sir George Cooper, which he was extending. Additional matching carving and panelling was also executed by Martyns for other parts of the extension.

The stairs at Hursley are another fine piece of work by Martyns, the newel posts having lovely deep-cut carving on three sides, and the supporting posts for the handrail each shaped and carved in delicate design.

Hursley Park was requisitioned by Lord Beaverbrook in 1940 and Vickers Aviation moved in. When their lease expired in 1958 IBM established development laboratories there and in 1960 Capt. Sir John Cooper gave back the panelling to

Grinling Gibbons screen restored by H.H. Martyns for Hursley Park after its removal from Winchester College.

Winchester College, where it was installed in the new hall.

Grinling Gibbons and Martyns 'workmanship', now happily married in the screen, bears out the view that woodcarving at Martyns equalled or even excelled that of Gibbons. Other woodcarving over doorways at Hursley Park also exhibits the Martyn craftsmen's skill in delicate stems, flowers, fruits and even the awns on ears of barley.

Hursley Park, Winchester. Architect: A. Marshall Makenzie and Son. The Grinling Gibbons screen and door restored by H.H. Martyn and Co. with matching balcony wood carving and complementary panelling.

Hursley park. Further carving and panelling.

Hursley Park. Further carving and panelling.

The Tree of Life, memorial to Frederic Myers, Cheltenham College Chapel, carved by Harry Dean.

Detail from Tree of Life.

On All Saints Day in 1907 a fine piece carved by Harry Dean was dedicated in Cheltenham College Chapel. The Myers memorial, as it is known, is placed by and above the south entrance and depicts the symbolic Tree of Life. Carved at Martyns studios in Cheltenham of sycamore wood, it is a masterpiece of the carver's art, yet Harry Dean's name is not mentioned in the chapel as its carver. A wild rose rises from among vegetation in which can be found birds, dragonflies, mice and other small creatures, each creatively carved to lifelike perfection. He borrowed the book "Wee Timorous Beasties" for reference from Ida, A.W. Martyn's daughter.

An interesting coincidence in view of the part Martyns eventually played in the Myers Memorial was the meeting which H.H. Martyn had with Frederick Myers. Myers spent much of his life trying to establish on scientific grounds the doctrine of human immortality. In his researches into the subject he explored many avenues including seances. At such a meeting H.H. Martyn met Myers. In his own words:

> *I was asked to spend an evening with Frederick Myers at the home of a college master, who seemed obsessed with the fourth dimension . . . and well do I remember it. I was introduced into the drawing room, with several ladies and gentlemen seated in the darkened room, with well-curtained windows, waiting while Frederick Myers softly expressed the music of verse with wonderful expression of beauty . . . Alas! the results of that seance were nil. . . .*

Mirror frame carved by Harry Dean for the company boardroom.

Harry Arthur Dean, specialist woodcarver.

The following is quoted from A.S. Owen's 'History of Cheltenham College Chapel' about the carved Tree of Life on the Myers Memorial:

"It is filled with the joy of life; the birdlover will note the different kinds of birds in it, and at its base, the cross-bills, which according to legend, earned their name from trying to pull the nails from the hands of Our Lord on the Cross, the nightingale pouring out its soul in song, the robins, the titmice, the kingfisher, the swallow. There is much symbolism; we can easily see the meaning of the spider's net from which the fly has escaped; but the mole at the base needs a word of explanation; it is there because the first thought of the awfulness of annihilation came to Myers when as a child, he saw a dead mole — but this is a living one."

Harry Arthur Dean brought this concept alive as great artists do — by breathing life into his work, a point beyond fine craftsmanship. Many knowledgeable people have said that Grinling Gibbons himself would not have disdained to own it as his work.

Another great piece which Harry Dean carved was the frame for a mirror which for years graced the board room at Martyns. The illustration can serve better than words to describe its intricate beauty.

An interesting screen in carved wood and wrought iron was produced for the Church of St. Mary, parish church of Monmouth, in the last year of the Martyn-Emms partnership, just prior to the formation of H.H. Martyn & Co. in 1888. It was made in collaboration with William Letheren & Sons, who produced the wrought iron work. Letherens were later to collapse in 1906 and their 'Vulcan Iron Works' at Lansdown were bought by Martyns in 1908 and renamed Sunningend. Letherens had produced very fine wrought iron work such as the gates at Arle Court and St. Gregory's Roman Catholic Church. Thomas Letheren, who was the iron work artist who produced these and many others, joined Martyns after the failure of his father's company to continue his detailed work for them. Cheltenham Ladies' College also boasts some of his finest work in the beautiful ironwork balustrading for the main stairs and the decorative balcony in the library. Middleton, Prothero & Philpot paid Letherens £415 in 1893—4, confirming that their services were used.

Martyns' woodcarvers' art can be seen in the Long Gallery in Buckingham Palace and at Windsor Castle, work for which the company received in 1916 the Royal Warrant 'By Appointment Architectural Carvers and Decorators to His Majesty King George V' and were permitted to display the coat of arms as a mark of the honour. In Westminster Abbey, Harry Breckin worked on the Queen Alexandra Memorial for Edward VII. He was there carving at the time of the general strike in 1926 and was unable to get home for his time off, for the duration of the strike.

St. Paul's Cathedral has a fine pulpit and sounding board carved and built by Martyns at a later date and used for the first time for the funeral of Sir Winston Churchill. The pulpit is so spacious it is said to be like walking on to a stage. The British Empire (O.B.E.) Chapel, St. Paul's, also has wood carving and panelling by Martyns.

Hereford Cathedral, the library panelling; Harewood House, Leeds; Balliol College, Oxford; Belfast, Woolwich and Stockport Town Halls; Ascot Place, Berks; Marsh Court, Stockbridge; Pylewell Park, Lymington; Cowley Manor, Cheltenham; 11 Hill St. Berkeley Square; and many more premises boast of fine work by the artists in wood at Martyns.

In 1908 the New Public Offices at Westminster were graced with particularly fine woodcarving to the principal entrance doors. Other woodwork and carving was also done throughout the building (excluding the boardroom). The plaster enrichments for the ceilings were also produced by Martyns.

In 1916 Mr. Royston, another woodcarver of the Company, received the Civic Arts Association award (£20) for his 'carved wood tablet war memorial'.

Architects from many countries used the extensive facilities and the fine craftsmen of Martyns to execute their designs.

Sir William Richmond R.A. designed a fine frieze with lions among a formal design of trees carved in mahogany at some time prior to 1905. R.A. Briggs, architect, was a frequent client. He was commissioned for much of the re-designing of the interior of Worcester Cathedral at the turn of the century.

G.H. Fellowes Prynne designed many beautiful screens for churches. Screens carved by Martyns to his design can be seen at St. Neot and St. Cleer in Cornwall, as well as an altar screen at St. John's Church, Penzance, beautifully carved and designed to form frames for paintings on a large scale. The paintings were by Edward Fellowes Prynne, brother of the architect, and the dedication took place on 15th October 1902, the complete work costing £450. In the same church there are a fine screen and gates in wrought iron and copper, also designed by G.H. Fellowes Prynne and made by R.E. & C. Marshall of Cheltenham. At this time Martyns had not yet entered into the wrought iron business in an extensive way, this coming about after the move to Lansdown in 1908.

In Cornwall is an oak carved pulpit in St. Columb Major church, Gothic in style, designed by G.H. Fellowes Prynne. The carved screen in the same church is also by Martyns, although the figure of

Woodcarving studio, Sunningend, Lansdown, about 1923. Harry Dean's son second from left.

St. Columb Major Church, Cornwall, Pulpit.

Christ and the adjoining figures were carved by two local lady carvers and incorporated over the screen. In December 1896 Middleton, Prothero & Philpot mention the chancel of St. Michael and All Angels Church, Bishops Cleeve; (to Martyns direct, £60.14s.0d., and in May 1901 Upton Bishop Church, new chancel stalls to H.H. Martyn & Co., £141.0s.0d.).

Other carvings by Martyns were designed by W.H. Bidlake, architect. These include the reredos in St. Pancras Church, Birmingham and the lectern in Emmanual Church, Wylde Green. Geo Hubbard & Son, architects, Stuart House, Cambridge, commissioned panelling for the board room in memory of Mrs. James Stuart. St. John's Church, Wakefield, has a reredos of magnificent proportions with the most intricate carving in pear giving contrast to the heavier surround. Also by Martyns is a screen and calvary at St. Saviour's Church, St. Albans.

The following is a list from the Architectural Review's articles on H.H. Martyn woodwork in their publications.

1906 11 Hill St., Berkeley Square and Belfast Hall, both with wood carving.

1908 Norwich Union Society's offices in Norwich, special woodwork and panelling and enrichments including particularly fine work in the board room.

The Morning Post advertisement hall was panelled in Austrian Oak. In 1909 Glasgow Central Station Hotel had special woodcarving by Martyns in the lounge and dining room. A more simple piece of work in 1909 was the rood beam in silver hardwood with gilded emblems of limewood at Dodford Church, Worcestershire.

1911 Woodcarving for the General Buildings, Workmen's Compensation, Aldwich, London.

1912 Thames House, Upper Thames St., London, woodcarving to interior.

1913 For the Galleries of P & D Colnaghi and Obach at 144—146 New Bond Street, London, particularly fine work for the Georgian Room. Also woodcarving and plasterwork elsewhere in the building.

1915 London Joint Stock Bank, Newcastle, woodcarving.

1916 Stalls designed by Ernest Gimson for Westminster Cathedral and made by Martyns. The stalls are in ebony inlaid with ivory/mother of pearl.

1916 British Dominions General Insurance Co., walnut panelling, also plaster and wrought iron work.

1916 The Ocean Marine Insurance Co., Old Broad Street, London, carvings.

1917 New Government Buildings, Westminster, woodcarving and plaster modelling.

Joinery and woodcarving continued as a mainstay of the Company's work throughout and it was the skill of the workers in wood which made possible entry in 1914 into airframe manufacture. Their speed in adapting to new work and their expertise ensured the success of the early Gloucestershire Aircraft Company. The company's first aircraft, the Bamel Mars I, was designed, built and flown in four weeks, a record unlikely to be beaten.

The skills of 80 years of carving and woodworking were passed from man to man in the apprentice scheme which ran its continuous thread from 1888 to 1969. After Martyns closed, some of the custodians of these skills formed their own companies. One of the ex-employees, Ted Clifford, calls his company Sunningend Joinery and Cabinet Makers at Bourton-on-the-Water with some pride and produces high quality furniture in the style of Martyns — **'the best'.**

Ted Clifford, as with all the work force, was grieved at the news of the close-down in 1971 and decided to set up a joinery business in partnership with three others from Martyns, R.J. Duester, D. Stevens and W.D. Rowe. They also employ several other skilled men from the old company.

11 Hill Street, London W. Architect J. Leonard Williams. Doorway to library showing woodcarved embellishments.

Their work, like Martyns before them, is still sought after by the discerning far and wide. Ted Clifford also has an apprentice scheme, though he says it is difficult to run one now, as the youth ends up being paid more per hour than a skilled man owing to the shorter hours worked with a day off at technical college, an anomaly brought about by union terms and unpopular with the skilled men.

Ted remembers that in 1936, when he started at Martyns on a five year apprenticeship, his pay was 6/- (30p) per week for the first year, 8/- (40p) second year, 10/- (50p) third year, 15/- (75p) fourth year and £1 fifth year. After he had served his time he was later made manager of the joinery and cabinet making department and then company surveyor. Much of his time was spent estimating for various jobs, ship interiors being the most taxing as the work plan was often on a small scale for so large an undertaking.

He remembers the extensive work in wood, plaster, bronze and stone for the Cardiff Civic Centre. The order for the work was through Sir Percy Thomas who placed many other orders as the City clients were so delighted with the work.

Graham Grinnell was one of the very last woodcarving apprentice of Martyns. A particularly gifted and skilful craftsman, he now carves in his own studio in Cheltenham.

The last cabinet apprentice at Martyns was Keith Bawden. His talents are sought after for restoration work as far afield as the West Indies. His pride in his association with Martyns, as with many who worked there, is fierce, positive, even protective, toward its name and achievements. His enthusiasm helped considerably to spur me on with the extensive research required for this book.

Mr. Lashford-Spinks, now a member of the Guild of Woodcarvers, also carries on carving in his small workshop at Winchcombe, fine work, much of which goes to the United States. It is a pleasure to watch him at work. Incidentally, both Mr. Lashford-Spinks and Graham Grinnell use old wood carving tools with initials on the handles which show they were the tools used by the first carvers at Martyns, such as Harry Dean, Harry Breckin, C.F. Yeand, Charlie Gisborne and many others. The men are scattered but the skills persist. With no apprentice scheme now, for how long will woodcarving of such high quality survive? An example of this impending problem already showed itself in 1951. Sir Richard Coppock said of carving work which had to be done in the House of Commons to restore war damaged areas: "There was certain woodwork in the House of Commons which could not be done by modern woodworkers and we had to send to Cheltenham (Martyns) for special men, the youngest of whom was over 70."

As well as the House of Commons, Martyns carvers in 1953 were entrusted to work on the Gothic style woodwork of the beautiful Guildhall, London, much of which was destroyed in the Blitz. Sir Giles Gilbert Scott said the Martyns craftsmen had "done a magnificent job". He was

St. Lawrence's Church, Reading. Architect, S. Slingsby Stallwood, Rood screen and rood carved in oak.

particularly pleased with the oak panel surmounted with crown and supporting lions. The work he said, was well up to the standard of other work carried out by the Company in London for him in the past.

A list of some of the wood carving and joinery contracts before 1934 is as follows:

JOINERY & WOOD CARVING
Hereford Cathedral
Westminster Cathedral
St. Nicholas, Cole Abbey
St. Paul's, Wilton Place
Central Hall, Westminster
Buckingham Palace
Windsor Castle
Harewood House, Leeds
Balliol College, Oxford
Belfast Town Hall
Woolwich Town Hall
Stockport Town Hall
Nottingham Exchange
Hursley Park, Winchester
Ascot Place, Berks

Messrs Novellos' premises. F.L. Pearson, architect. Marble fireplace and carved overmantel.

Marsh Court, Stockbridge
Pylewell Park, Lymington
Cowley Manor, Cheltenham
Midland Bank Head Office
Standard Bank of S. Africa, London
Australian Mutual Provident Soc., London
General Assurance Offices, London
Central Station Hotel, Glasgow

More recently, in 1950, the seats for the new chapel at Sandhurst Military College were carved by Les Timms and Sam Bourne. Each pew end had a different regimental coat of arms and each colonel of the particular regiment inspected his own carved crest to ensure it was perfect in every way, even to counting tiny details such as pearls. Les Timms' first regimental crest was his own father's, The Royal Horse Artillery.

Messrs Novello's premises. Detail of door pillars and pilasters.

Right, Maurice Norman and left, Fred Arkell carving royal coats of arms from a drawing.

Les Timms was a wood and stone carver trained in the Gothic tradition at R.L. Boultons with Fred Arkell in the early 1930s. He then went on to A.R. Mobary of Oxford, another company well known for its church carving. He moved to Martyns in 1939 to work on the building of aircraft, mostly Horsa gliders and Albermarles; after the war he was involved in carving candelabras and wall brackets for Maples to sell in their London store. He also worked a great deal on shaping furniture legs. He was involved in particularly demanding and interesting work in connection with the plaster department at a later date.

Maurice Norman, who became principal wood carver in his time, carved a magnificent Hereford bull for the Hereford Herd Society. When the carving was complete several stock judges of the society visited the works to see if the bull's conformation was representative of the best of the breed. Apparently they were satisfied and gave him Supreme Champion status. It certainly stands lifelike and proud and carved to perfection.

The Speaker's Chair in the House of Commons took six months to complete and was made in Australian black bean wood. It is 14 feet high and carved to the design of Sir Giles Gilbert Scott O.M.R.A. similar to the one destroyed in the 1940 Blitz. One of the first carvers who joined the company at the turn of the century, Charlie Gisborne, was awarded the M.B.E. following his work on the Speaker's Chair.

The fine Dispatch Boxes for the House of Commons, in wood with bronze fastenings, were made at this time by Martyns. In Somerville College, Oxford, carving for the organ case was produced in Gibbons's style. Carvings were also produced for King Carol of Rumania's palace at Bucharest.

From advertisements in the Architectural Review:

1919	Eton College, African War Memorial, carved in wood.
1919/23	Hyde Park Terrace — library chimney piece — including limewood carving.
1919/23	Offices of Australian Mutual Provident Society, London. Carving in limewood.
1919/23	Midland Adelphi Hotel, Liverpool, carving and oak panelling. Sefton dining room.
1919/23	Anchor Line Buildings, Liverpool, carving.
1919/23	Woolwich Town Hall — Mayor's chair.
1919/23	Middlesex Guildhall, carving, panelling etc.
1919/23	Hursley Park, Winchester, carving and panelling.
1923/29	St. Lawrence's Church, Reading, rood screen and rood in oak.
1923/29	Greenways, North Ferriby, Yorks, wood carving and panelling.
1923/29	Paisley Grammar School, oak memorial and bronze tablets.
1923/29	Bournville Church, oak litany desk.
1929/39	Imperial Chemical Industries offices, Millbank, London, wood carving to door of chairman's room and other portions of the interior.
1929/39	Lancashire County Offices, Preston.
1929/39	St. Stephen's Church, Birmingham, carved triptych. Architect W.H. Bidlake.

Thornton Manor, executed for Mr. Lever. Architect: Paul Waterhouse. Woodcarving, pilasters and panelling.

Cardwainers Hall. Architects: Best and Lloyd. Panelling and carving.

Cardwainers Hall, panelling and carving.

Pews, screen and pulpit carved for the chapel at Sudeley Castle, Winchcombe.

The following list of clients and venues is taken from a 1905 brochure and shows an extensive clientele and range of work:

WORKS EXECUTED FOR

Her Late Majesty Queen Victoria
J.S. Alder, Esq.
McVicar Anderson, Esq.
J. Arnold, Esq.
Messrs. Boehmer & Gibbs
Messrs. Buckland & Farmer
Sir Arthur W. Blomfield & Sons
R.A. Briggs, Esq.
Messrs. W. & C.A. Bassett-Smith
Swindon Barter, Esq.
Messrs. Banister, Fletcher & Sons
Messrs. Baines & Son
W.H. Bidlake, Esq.
J. Banks, Esq.
Messrs. Carpenter & Ingelow
Messrs. Cossins, Peacock & Bewlay
G. Cuthbert, Esq.
Messrs. Cox & Silk
Somers Clarke, Esq.
A. Conder, Esq.
E. Dunn, Esq.
Messrs. Douglas & Minchul
Messrs. Essex, Nichol & Goodman
R. Fowler, Esq.
E. Goldie, Esq.
Messrs. Gordon & Gunton
G.H. Gadd, Esq.
H.S. Gamble, Esq.
H.B. Guest, Esq.
Messrs. Higgs & Rudkin
Messrs. Henman & Cooper
Messrs. W. Hale & Sons
Messrs. T.H. & F. Healey
Ralph Heaton, Esq.
J.J. Holding, Esq.
J. Hopkins, Esq.
Messrs. Ingoll & Son
Messrs. Isaacs & Florence
E. Kirby, Esq.
F. Kempson, Esq.
W.T. Lowdell, Esq.
Messrs. Martin & Martin
Messrs. Newland & Higgs
Messrs. Nevison & Newton
T. Norton, Esq.
E. Nicholls, Esq.
Lloyd Oswell, Esq.
A. Beresford Pite, Esq.
G.H. Fellowes Prynne, Esq.
Messrs. Protheroe & Phillott
Messrs. Potts, Son & Pickup
C.E. Ponting, Esq.
J.A. Pippett, Esq.
Messrs. Pugin & Pugin
Sir William B. Richmond, R.A.
E.R. Robson, Esq.
P. Robson, Esq.
Greenwood Stephenson, Esq.
G.H. Shepherd, Esq.
Messrs. Sinnott, Sinnott & Powell
J.J. Talbot, Esq.
Messrs. Treadwell & Martin
Bruce Vaughan, Esq.
Messrs. Waller & Son
Aston Webb, Esq., A.R.A.
T.B. Whinney, Esq.
Messrs. Worthington & Son

A carved figure by Harry Breckin.

WORKS EXECUTED AT

Canterbury Cathedral
Worcester Cathedral
Gloucester Cathedral
Tewkesbury Abbey
Malvern Abbey
All Souls College, Oxford
Cheltenham College Chapel
Cheltenham College
Ladies' College, Cheltenham
Malvern College
St. Agatha's Church, Birmingham
Harborne Church, Birmingham
Stirchley Church, Birmingham
St. Edward's Church, Birmingham
St. Simon's Church, Birmingham
St. Oswald's Church, Birmingham
St. Paul's Convent, Birmingham
St. Patrick's Church, Walsall
Parish Church, Stone, Kidderminster
Parish Church, Bewdeley
St. Simon's, Paddington, London
St. Lawrence's Church, Old Jewry
St. Saviour's Church, Ealing
Holy Trinity Church, Roehampton
St. Peter's Church, South Tottenham
St. James' Church, Muswell Hill
Parish Church, Leamington
Hawkesyard Priory, Rugeley
St. Saviour's Home, Hendon
Parish Church, Shenley, Bucks.
St. John's Church, Sidcup, Kent
Trinity Church, Henley-on-Thames.
St. Mark's Church, Brighton
St. Andrew's Church, Starbeck
Lowe House, St. Helen's
St. Nicholas Cathedral, Liverpool
St. Thomas's Church, Waterloo, Liverpool
St. Wilfrid's Church, Preston
Parish Church, Chorley
Roman Catholic Church, Chorley
St. Werburgh's Church, Chester

St. Barnabas Church, Sutton, Surrey
St. Peter's Church, Stalybridge
St. Thomas's Church, Bedford Leigh
Manafon Church
Parish Church, Upton Bishop, Ross
St. Mary's Church, Monmouth
Parish Church, Ilfracombe
St. James' Church, Devonport
St. Neot's Church, Cornwall
Sheviock Church, Cornwall
St. John's Church, Penzance
The Parish Church, Cheltenham
Christ Church
All Saints' Church
St. Stephen's Church
St. John's Church
Church of the Holy Apostles
St. Mark's Church
Leckhampton Parish Church
Cleeve Parish Church
Prestbury Parish Church
Ashorne Hill House
Cowley Manor
Thornton Manor
Brockhampton Park

Tunstall Manor
Gifford House, Roehampton
Addersley Park
Severn End, Worcester
Battenhall Mount
Sudeley Castle
Madresfield Court
Blakesware
Berkeley Castle
Pyports, Cobham
Blackpool Town Hall
Assize Courts, Birmingham
New Library, Birmingham
Kyrle Hall, Birmingham
Christchurch Buildings, Birmingham
London C & M Bank, Birmingham
London C & M Bank, Chepstow
London C & M Bank, Salisbury
Manchester College, Oxford
Metropolitan Fire Offices, Moorgate Street, London
Lloyd's Advertising Offices, London
Buildings, Oxford Street, London
The Exchange (extension) London
Queen Anne Schools, Caversham
Lloyds Bank, Cheltenham

Woodcarvings in the style of Grinling Gibbons.

Sledmere House, Yorkshire. Decorative plaster work. Architect: W.H. Brierley.

Chapter 4

DECORATIVE FIBROUS PLASTER WORK AND CARTON PIERRE

The fibrous plaster department at Martyns was an early addition to the original wood and stone carving. It is one of the most beautiful of decorative art forms. However, it is the least glamorous of all the arts in which to work, being a messy business involving a wet slurry on the one hand and fine dust when the plaster dries on the other. The workers were known as rag and stick men!

In the late 1890s H.H. Martyn heard of a talented artist producing fine plaster ceilings in London and he determined to get him to come to Cheltenham, promising him all the work he could do and more. Thomas Claridge moved to Cheltenham with his two sons Thomas and Edward, his brother-in-law Charles Bryan and others in about 1900 and set up in business at the back of the Hewlett Arms pub. Later they moved to Manson Avenue.

Thomas Claridge's father had also been in the fibrous plaster business in London and had invented a way of making ornaments to apply to walls and ceilings in carton pierre. This was made from scotch glue thinned down with hot water in which paper was dissolved and further mixed with whitening. It was kneaded to a putty and pressed into a mould cut in reverse. A few of these exquisite moulds were saved from several thousand when the company records and artifacts were burnt.

At first a lot of work was passed by H.H. Martyn to the Claridge family and all went well but in about 1906, after a long quiet period, Thomas Claridge was persuaded to move to Sunningend in the High Street and act as manager of the plaster department of H.H. Martyns. Martyns thus acquired an experienced team of craftsmen of the highest skills and artistic talent. The department now expanded quickly as the work increased and more skilled plasterers were brought from London, Manchester and Birmingham. These included Arthur Copp (London), and Tommy Piers, Joe Anderson and Joe MacCarthy (Manchester). They all stayed on for the whole of their working lives. Local plasterers were also trained to run cornices and mouldings in situ and to bed up enrichments cast mostly from wax moulds.

Wax for moulding was resin softened with beeswax to make it pliable when immersed in warm water. It would then be poured on to the carved model. The making of highly decorative plaster cornices or whole ceilings was a complex and skilful operation. Some idea of the work and skill involved is conveyed in the following description of the making of a fibrous plaster cornice written for me by Albert (Jack) Claridge, grandson of the Thomas Claridge who developed carton pierre.

"The profile of the cornice is cut to shape from sheet zinc, fastened on to a wood background and held in position on a wood frame called a template. This is run along a screed on a bench while the plaster shape is gradually built up; the enrichments are then bedded into position to the length required giving the model from which the mould is made. The model is coated with shellac to seal the surface, then greased all over and covered with clay about ½″ thick. A plaster cast known as a case is made off the back of the clay, the case and the clay removed and the case treated with shellac after large holes for pouring and small holes to let the air out are cut. The model and case are oiled and the case is put over the model and fastened down. Pouring funnels (usually drainpipes) are stood vertically over the large holes and held firm with plaster.

Melted gelatine is poured into the funnels until the gap between the model and case is filled. When the gelatine is set the case and the gelatine are removed with the gelatine lying in the case. The face of the gelatine is hardened with alum or given two coats of paint to prevent the damp from the plaster cast penetrating into the gelatine.

The mould is now ready for casting. Before each cast is made the mould must be given a hessian scrim about ½″ mesh with the ends and sides hanging over. This is brushed in with plaster, and the strengthening wood strips, usually 1″ x ¼″ after brushing with plaster, are placed in position.

Plaster department about 1923, "Rag and Stick Men". Right hand side, Edward Claridge, manager.

Plaster moulds, about 1923.

The scrim is turned over, covering the wood strips, and the whole brushed in with plaster; the cross brackets are placed in position and covered with hessian scrim and plaster. The back of the cast is splashed with plaster to the required thickness. When the cast is set it is taken out of the mould and the process repeated."

Jack Claridge also told me of some of the contracts on which he had worked. When I remarked that a particularly intricate pattern set in a complex corner must have been difficult to achieve he made the following spontaneous reply: 'There is nothing diffcult in this world but that knowing how makes it simple.'

Jack worked at Harewood House, Leeds, on Princess Mary's private apartments, part of which involved cutting away a ceiling and dome and replacing the plaster to match the original. Whilst there he lodged with one of the workers on the estate. The worker paid one shilling (5p) per week rent but received 52/- (£2.50) Christmas gift from his employer, in effect having a house rent-free. Jack was quite a young boy when working at Harewood House and was accompanied by the outside manager, Mr. Joe Anderson. At 14 Jack was working solely in the works in Cheltenham and remembers producing the fine plaster work for Sledmere House, Yorkshire, as well as the Lal Bagh Palace, India, for which each piece was numbered with a key plan ready for easy assembly in India by local labour. The final finishing was carried out by Martyns craftsmen. All went smoothly despite the ornate work and the long period of three years to completion.

Later Jack Claridge travelled away to work on the Nottingham Exchange and the New India Building, Liverpool.

While working on a bank in Derby, he and Joe Anderson called in to see the team who were working on the Elite Theatre, Nottingham, a very decorative piece of work. Much good work went into cinemas during the inter-war years.

Another important work supervised by Jack Claridge was the restoration of St. Andrew's Church, Holborn, London, which was gutted during the Blitz in 1940. Working from charred fragments brought down to Cheltenham and faithfully copied and also from drawings of the original Wren designs, the whole interior was painstakingly recreated from the plaster ceilings to the wood panelling. Sealey and Padget were the architects in charge.

Important in the team who produced the ornate mouldings were the men who carved and modelled

St. Andrews Church, Holborn, London. Designed by Wren. Decorative plaster and wood work faithfully restored.

in clay or wood the delicate and intricate designs, often in reverse. Martyns had a great many artists capable of this beautiful and skilled work. One of these was Carl Roberts, a sculptor and woodcarver particularly skilled in designing and making the moulds in reverse for the plaster. He was an early apprentice, going straight from school to Martyns. Fred Shepheard was another skilled in this art. His son Ron Shepheard followed in this work and his twin brother Fred Shepheard became a skilled joiner.

An unusual contract for plaster decorative work was part of the 1937 Coronation decoration for the front of Selfridge's in Oxford Street. The theme was 'The Empire's Homage to the Throne' and consisted mainly of 20′ high plaster panels in bas-relief surrounded by colourful standards, shields and flags forming a pelmet. The corner groups which were 35′ high, depicting Canada and India, were modelled in clay and moulded in plaster in the fibrous plaster department of Martyns. The entire decoration was later transported to India and erected at the palace of a Maharajah.

Bill Tovey, who started with Martyns in 1919 as a tea boy and then worked as foreman of the plaster department until its closedown, cast the large corner groups for Selfridge's at the works from clay originals which had been modelled by the sculptors H.J. Youngman (Canada) and H. Cawthra (India).

Bill Tovey worked on many marvellous decorative contracts in his 40 or so years with the company. Several were in Belfast, at Queens University and Stormont, on which Martyns had the contracts for some of the largest rooms. The work to be done was so extensive that many other companies were involved in other parts of the building.

Bill also worked on the Co-operative Hall and the general offices of the Flax Spinners in York St. Belfast. He particularly remembers remodelling the old plaster for the Great Hall of the City Hall, Belfast. The Hall was 120′ long by 20′ wide and had been totally destroyed by enemy action on 4th and 5th of May 1941. Reconstruction was from fragments of the old plaster copied in the works in Cheltenham. Bill Tovey had seventeen men working with him to fit the work on site. There were seven pieces to each beam and it took seven men to lift each one into position. Seventeen railway containers of finished work were sent from Cheltenham. Some of those working in Belfast were Ted Hampton, Jack Gay and Vic Childs.

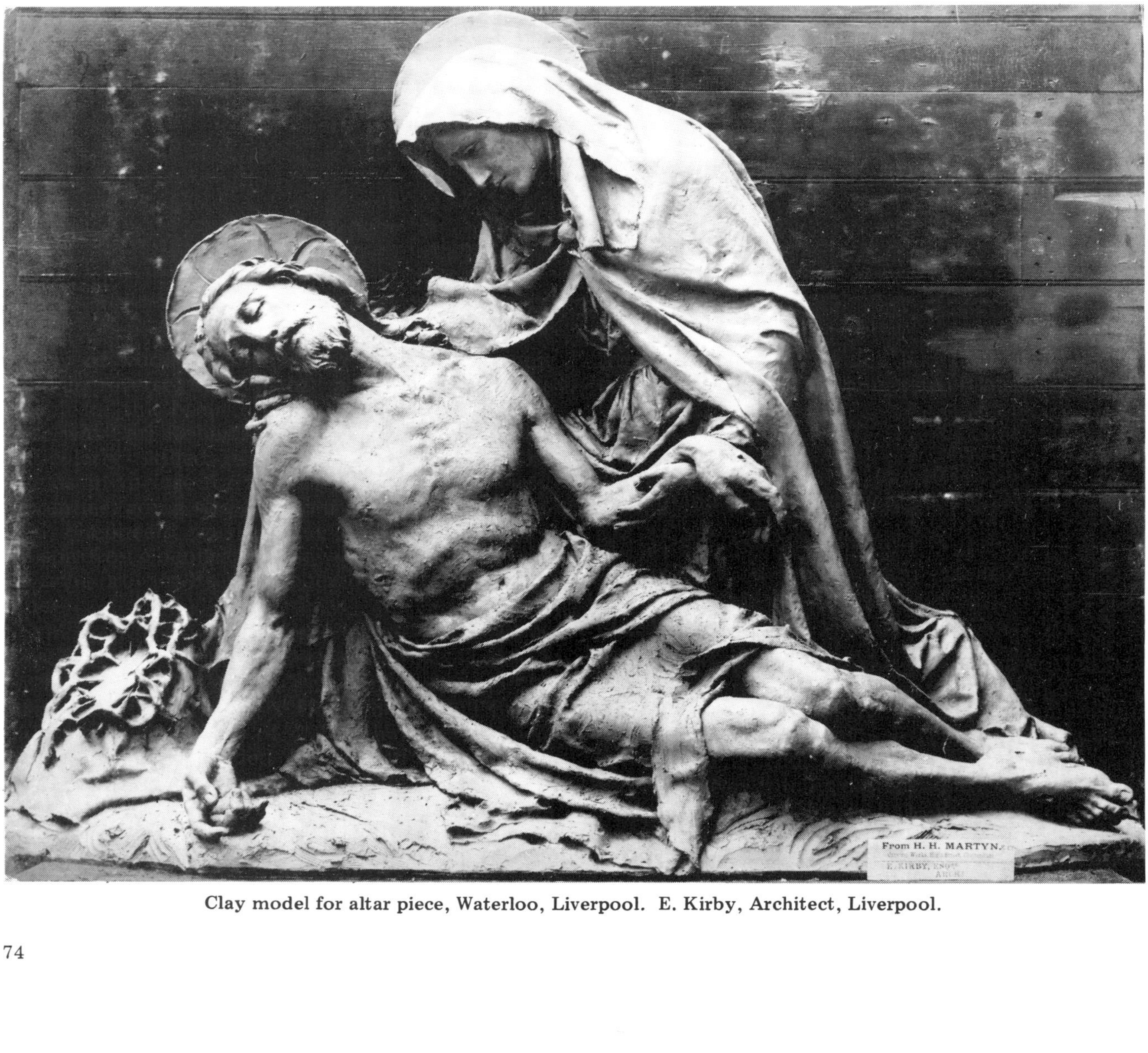

Clay model for altar piece, Waterloo, Liverpool. E. Kirby, Architect, Liverpool.

Bill Tovey is full of admiration for Jack Claridge, whose skill in making the castings in the works was exceptional, as was his ability to draw, plan and execute to the fine limits required to ensure a perfect fit on site.

Bill's brother Frank was another talented member of the family; he was foreman of the joinery department from 1925 and also worked for the company for about 40 years.

Martyns enrichments were incorporated in many luxurious liners and appropriately, in the Ocean Terminal building, Southampton.

Other locations include: Guernsey Courts; City Hall, Belfast; Stormont Castle; Stormont Parliamentary Buildings; Royal Palace, Baghdad; Houses of Parliament, Baghdad; Notre Dame; Leicester Place, London; India Buildings, Liverpool.

For most of the time that decorative plasterwork was carried on at Martyns, i.e. from the 1890's to about 1966 when the department closed down from lack of work, the Claridge family was at the forefront. Thomas Claridge managed the department first from 1906 to 1920 when he retired due to chronic arthritis. Edward Claridge then became manager but later left to start his own business — Claridge (Putney) Ltd. Tragically, Thomas Claridge the third was killed at Passchendale, one of the many men whose talents were buried in the mud of Flanders.

Selfridges, Oxford Street frontage, decorated for the 1937 Coronation celebrations, showing the plaster panels of historic events.

India, one of the 35 feet high plaster panels made for the front of Selfridges. By Hermon Cawthra, R.B.S.

Canada. By Harold J. Youngman, A.R.B.S.

For a time after Edward Claridge left, Archie Spurr became manager of the plaster department as well as wood and stone carving and decorating, but later Albert (Jack) Claridge became manager and remained as such until 1962 when he left, having worked for the company since 1918 — 44 years. George Hawling, the joinery manager at the time of Jack's retirement, took over for the last few years.

Almost the last job for the plaster department was for Newstead Abbey, Nottingham (Lord Byron's home at one time). Jerry Barnes, foreman of the plaster department secured the contract. He heard on the BBC morning news bulletin a report of the fire at the Abbey followed by a statment that the decorative plasterwork had been destroyed and could never be replaced. On his own initiative he telephoned the BBC and informed them that they were incorrect and that the plasterwork could be renewed if Martyns was given the opportunity. He said that the department had restored decorative plasterwork in a number of fine buildings following fire and bomb damage.

After various consultations Martyns was awarded the contract and Huie Foster and Les Timms modelled from the pieces of charred plaster so that the new plasterwork resembled the old to the last leaf and curl.

The work of all these men exists today for everyone to see and admire throughout the world. Few, if any, who see the beautiful work, know who the men were who carved, set out the cases, set the scrim and the supports, poured the gelatine, splashed and brushed and poured gallons of wet plaster slurry to set into beautiful forms for future generations to enjoy.

Detail of H.W. Foster's clay model for Lal Bagh Palace, India.

Model in clay for frieze.

Clay modelling shop. H.W. Foster working left. (Note previous picture.)

New Court, Lansdown Place, Cheltenham. Architect: Healing and Overberry. Plaster enrichments to ceilings and walls.

The following decorative contracts in plaster are mentioned in the Architectural Review:

1906	11 Hill St., Berkeley Square, London, plasterwork for dining room, library and boudoirs.
1908	New Public Offices, Westminster, plaster enrichments for the ceilings.
1910	93 Mortimer St., London W., decorative plasterwork.
1910	Plasterwork for the Public Libary, Dudley, Worcestershire.
1911	Modelled plasterwork for Third Church of Christ Scientist, Curzon Street, London.
1913	For the Galleries of P & D Colnaghi & Obach at 144-146 New Bond Street, plasterwork.
1916	British Dominion General Insurance Co., plasterwork. Stuc decorations. throughout Cardiff Empire including the great frieze in the auditorium.
1917	New Government Buildings, Westminster, plaster modelling.

Public offices, Westminster, S.W. Architect: Sir Henry Tanner. Modelled plasterwork.

Nottingham Exchange. Architect: Cecil Howith. Reception room, decorative plaster ceilings, columns and bronze light fittings. Woodwork, marblework, fibrous plaster, wood carving, painting, wrought bronze and cast bronze, wrought iron and cast iron, was carried out in the committee room, anteroom, Lady Mayoress's room, dining hall, lobby, Mayor's private room, small private rooms and council chamber, also exterior stone carving.

The following list is from a pre-1934 brochure:

FIBROUS PLASTER

Third Church of Christ Scientist
Central Hall, Westminster
Nottingham Exchange
Caird Hall, Dundee
Municipal Concert Hall, Newcastle-on-Tyne
Municipal Baths, Westminster
Adelphi Hotel, Liverpool
Park Lane Hotel, London
Strand Palace Hotel, London
Harewood House, Leeds
Keddleston Hall, Derby
Sledmere, Yorks
Shugborough Hall, Stafford
Lal Bagh Palace, Indore
Pylewell Park, Lymington
Standard Bank of South Africa
Phoenix Assurance Offices, London
Martin's Bank, Liverpool
Ulster Parliament Buildings
New India Building, Liverpool
Eaves Hall, Clitheroe
Cardiff Empire
Elite Picture Theatre, Notts.
Majestic Theatre, Leeds
Regent Cinema, Bristol
Savoy Cinema, Brighton
Paramount Theatre, Manchester
Whitehall Theatre, Charing Cross
Savoy Cinema, Burnley
Swansea Civic Centre

Also plasterwork for Buckingham Palace
Derby Police Courts
Wiltshire County Offices
Saville Theatre, auditorium, stalls and bar etc.
Edinburgh Savings Bank
Newport Civic Centre, S. Wales
Angel Hotel, Cardiff
Brotherton Library, Leeds University
Cardiff Civic Centre

Martins Bank, Liverpool. Decorative plaster ceiling.

Leeds University. Decorative plaster work.

CINEMAS

Granada, Manchester
Fibrous Plasterwork and Decorations.
Benslyn & Morrison, F./A.R.I.B.A.

Granada, Woolwich
Fibrous Plasterwork and Decorations.
Cecil Masey, Esq., F.R.I.B.A.

Granada, Bedford
Fibrous Plasterwork and Decorations.
Benslyn & Morrison, F./A.R.I.B.A.

Regal Cinema, Brighton
Fibrous Plasterwork and Decorations.
W.R. Glen, Esq., F.R.I.A.S.

Regal, Birmingham
Fibrous Plasterwork and Decorations.
W.R. Glen, Esq., F.R.I.A.S.

Regal Cinema, Liverpool
Fibrous Plasterwork and Decorations.
W.R. Glen, Esq., F.R.I.A.S.

Regal Cinema, Marble Arch
Decorations and Seating.
Clifford Aish, Esq., F.R.I.B.A.

Regal Cinema, Cheltenham
Fibrous Plasterwork and Decorations.
Leslie C. Norton, Esq., L.R.I.B.A.

A list of ship work involving plaster will be found in the chapter on ships.

From advertisments in the Architectural Review:

1915/19 Aldford House, Park Lane London, plaster and metal work.

1915/19 Novello's premises, London, plasterwork.

1915/19 9 Hill Street, Mayfair, London, plasterwork.

1919/22 Anchor Line Buildings, Liverpool, plasterwork.

1919/23 Australian Mutual Provident Society, London, plasterwork.

1919/23 Cardiff Empire, plasterwork.

1919/23 Tudor Grange, Birmingham, plasterwork.

1919/23 City of Nottingham Exchange, plasterwork.

1923/29 Lexden Grange, Colchester, plasterwork.

1923/29 Daily Mirror Offices, London, plasterwork.

1923/29 Lal Bagh Palace, Indore, India, plasterwork faithfully copied from a Jagatsarwanji Temple at Amber.

1929/39 Hill Grove, Kidderminster, plasterwork.

1929/39 Martins Bank, Liverpool, plasterwork etc. etc.

Ascot Place, Berkshire. Architect: A. Mitchell. Decorative plaster work.

Ascot Place, Berkshire.

Ascot Place, Berkshire.

Ascot Place, Berkshire. Decorative ceiling and columns.

Drawing Room, Hill Grove Kidderminster. Architects Messrs Pritchard and Godwin. Decorations.

Imperial Hotel, Torquay. Architects: Messrs Watson and Watson. Entrance Hall decorative plaster work.

Aston Lodge. Detail of plaster enrichments.

Novellos' premises, London. Architects: F.L. Pearson.
Plaster Shield.

Aston Lodge, Birmingham. Architect: Chevion Richardson. Decorative plaster ceilings, walls and pillars.

11 Hill Street. Decorative plaster ceiling and fire place and drops carved in wood.

11 Hill Street, London W.1. Decorative plaster work, panelling and wood carving to the boudoir.

S.S. Otranto, Lounge. Architect: A.N. Prentice.

S.S. Otranto, Dining Saloon.

Turnbury Hotel. Architect: J. Miller. Decorative plasterwork and wood panelling.

Turnbury Hotel. Further plaster enrichments.

India Buildings, Liverpool. Decorative plaster ceilings and bronze entrance doors.

Swansea Civic Centre. Architect: Sir Percy Thomas. Decorative plaster and bronze light fittings.

Walcott Hall, Shropshire. Decorative plaster ceiling.

Cardwainers Hall. Decorative plaster ceiling.

The Commando Memorial Group receiving finishing touches at the hand of A. Merrett.

Chapter 5
BRONZE CASTING

— Little drops of water little grains of sand make the art of moulding the greatest in the land.
— foundry workers' saying

Bronze is a metal with traditions in art going back to the Roman Empire, and beyond to the Egyptians and the Chinese. Since man discovered the nature of this alloy he has used it to cast some of his finest works of art. Part of A.W. Martyn's expansion plan was to open a large foundry for bronze casting and to offer architects an even more comprehensive service. In about 1907 A.W. Martyn looked over Letherens' old works at Lansdown and determined to take over the premises while still keeping on the works in High Street and College Road, at least for a few years. Some small casting work was carried out at the College Road works. Advertisements dating from May 1908 onwards to the end of the year state: 'Gun metal, Bronze, Marble and Brass Memorial Tablets, Sunningend corner of College Road'. The facilities already existed at Letherens for wrought metal work, as well as the space to expand to large bronze casting and to extend the already growing wood, stone and plaster works which were outgrowing the High Street premises. At the end of July 1908 H.H. Martyn & Co. opened at Lansdown, renaming it Sunningend. The manager was Mr. Camden, who was in charge of all wrought and cast work. The High Street, Sunningend branch continued to advertise up to 1916 — 'Monuments executed and forwarded to all parts of the world.' It then closed and all the men and equipment moved to Lansdown.

Martyns' entry into large scale bronze casting depended on obtaining an impressive initial order to warrant the expenditure on a much larger plant.

A.W. Martyn travelled a great deal to London to meet architects and clerks of works, from whom he obtained contracts to keep the expanding company busy. He travelled in the early days in top hat and frock coat by train, first class, from St. James Station, Cheltenham. On one such visit to London in 1908 he obtained the vital order from Sir H. Tanner, architect, which was to ensure that the bronze casting department and the ironwork department would be enlarged and that Martyns would enter with style into the big league. The order was for a great screen with massive central gates, flanked by carriage and pedestrian gates, which were to stand at the northern end of East Carriage Drive as the Cumberland Screen at Marble Arch, London.

It took almost 80 men over three months to make these ceremonial gates. They were adorned with the Royal Arms, surrounded by the chain of the Order of the Garter, surmounted by a crown from which hung a festoon of laurel. The side gates were ornamented with the Royal Cypher

Marble Arch Gates.

surrounded by laurel wreaths, over 10,000 individually made laurel and palm leaves forming part of the design. The main gates weighed more than 40 tons and cost £3,000. They were transported by the Great Western Railway on a special low loader owing to their great height.

Unfortunately, Martyns' triumphant entry into large significant bronze and wrought iron work was removed from its prominent position in the Capital's heart to make way for the ever increasing number of cars. Traffic flow took precedence and the gates, pillars and lanterns were removed in 1959 after standing splendidly for 50 years. One set of gates then deteriorated and was later sold for scrap, a Salford factory having agreed to buy and then later declining them. The other set, with pillars and lanterns, was later shipped to Canada for erection at a park entrance in Saskatchewan. The University of Saskatchewan also ordered gates later from Martyns.

As the foundry grew and the work increased, A.W. Martyn sought someone of outstanding talent and experience for the increasingly complex and demanding castings which were required. It was fortunate that the noted sculptor and architect Walter Gilbert, who had used the services of H.H. Martyn for many years, still had associations with the Bromsgrove Guild, of which he was founder, where fine casting in bronze had been a long-standing tradition.

Walter Gilbert was friendly with Arnold Edwards of the Bromsgrove Guild. Understanding that this talented man needed a larger foundry to expand his work and realise his potential, he and A.W. Martyn persuaded Mr. Edwards to leave the Bromsgrove Guild and join Martyns as foundry manager, a move which was beneficial to all parties.

Arnold Edwards joined Martyns as foundry manager in 1919 and for the next 30 years stamped his remarkable personality on the enterprise. Edwards was a perfectionist and a man of great skill in the handling and blending of metal, a medium for which he had a 'feel'. He loved his work and trained a team of men who had a great respect for him. Many were afraid of him, since he could be a hard taskmaster and demanded the highest standards of work and effort. Edwards formed and nurtured the foundry, which acquired the reputation of the finest source of cast art metal work in 20th century Britain.

In his youth Mr. Edwards was reputed to be a rough diamond. The story told is that as a young apprentice in Halifax, when paid his 5s. (25p) wage he would slap it down on the table and offer to fight anyone for the same stake. His aggressive style was certainly channelled to good effect if his success at Martyns is anything to go by.

At its height from 1920 to around 1938 Martyns foundry cast 75% of all art metal work required in the country. Its main competitors were the Bromsgrove Guild, Birmingham Guild and Singers of Frome. However, there was a degree of co-operation between the rival firms; for instance, on 9th June, 1937 an agreement with the Birmingham Guild was signed, committing Martyns to manufacture for them architectural castings of a heavy nature (excluding iron) and which exceeded a superficial area of ten square feet, at 10% discount. Castings were produced in most metals, including silver, bronze, silver bronze, nickel, gun metal, phosphor bronze, silver iron, copper and lead. Often casting in eight different metals took place in one day, requiring great care and cleanliness to prevent contamination.

The managers' and foremen's job was to preside over the complicated task of blending. They prepared the complex mixture of metals which determined the colour of the finished bronze, dark or light, silver or golden and whether it changed colour with maturity or remained constant. Great personal skill and knowledge were required.

One such colour requirement was that of the Stag monument at Victoria, London. Mr. Reed, the manager who succeeded Mr. Edwards, had to guarantee that it would weather to the same colour as Eros in Piccadilly. He carried out tests on various combinations to ensure that the aluminium would in time resemble old bronze — quite an undertaking.

For Arnold Edwards, casting was only the beginning. He applied the same high standards of craftsmanship to assembly, chasing and erection on site. He made the foundry a great asset to the company by his total dedication and brilliant skills. His only relaxation, apart from his home life, was his love of cricket. The annual cricket festival at the Cheltenham College ground was his delight, especially when Yorkshire was playing, and this was the only event likely to draw him away from his foundry.

So many castings have been produced over the 53 years of the life of the foundry that the great majority are impossible to trace, being scattered far and wide throughout the world, but those mentioned and photographed will serve as witness to the greatness of the foundry.

Another important man in the team involved in the work with metal was F.G. Taylor. Fred Taylor joined Martyns in 1917 at 13 years old as a trainee metal worker and tea boy. He was to prove quickly that he also had a 'feel' for metal. A pond at Bull Hill holds no doubt to this day the evidence of a 13 year old's fear of retribution. Fred Taylor, working on a capstan lathe, was drilling and tapping a knob of the Bristol Fighter control column when he snapped the tap off. At 13 he was so afraid he popped the evidence in his pocket and at the first opportunity threw it into the pond.

Arnold Edwards, manager of the foundry from 1919 to 1949.

Fred Taylor became outside foreman at 23 years old in 1927, his pay being 1s. 5d. (7p) per hour plus 3d. (1¼p) for being in charge, plus one guinea lodging allowance per week, one weekend home in six weeks and one week's holiday a year with no pay. His pay rose to 2s. (10p) per hour by the second world war. It sounds incredibly little but adds that life was simpler, with none of today's luxuries. Above all he loved his work and has a passionate pride in what he produced and in having been associated with so great a company as Martyns.

In Fred Taylor, Arnold Edwards had a man who could deal with any eventuality, being able to talk on equal terms with architects, manage his men effectively and overcome the on-site problems which can always arise. A case in point was the installation of the largest set of doors of their kind in steel and aluminium for the new government offices in Whitehall Gardens in 1951. The doors, operated by Dowty hydraulics, were 16′ wide, 22′9″ high and 11″ thick, each weighing 5 tons. Fred Taylor designed and built on site special floor boxes to hold these massive doors and finely adjust them to the fixing position, overcoming what appeared to be an insuperable problem. It was often said that nothing was too big or too small — Fred Taylor could be relied upon to deal with it.

As Martyns expanded the foundry business two types of casting were undertaken. The one using sand as the moulding material was run by Mr. Edwards, and the other using the lost wax process was run by the Mancini family.

Bill Wykes and Fred Taylor (on steps) working on the bronze statue of Queen Victoria for Birmingham city centre.

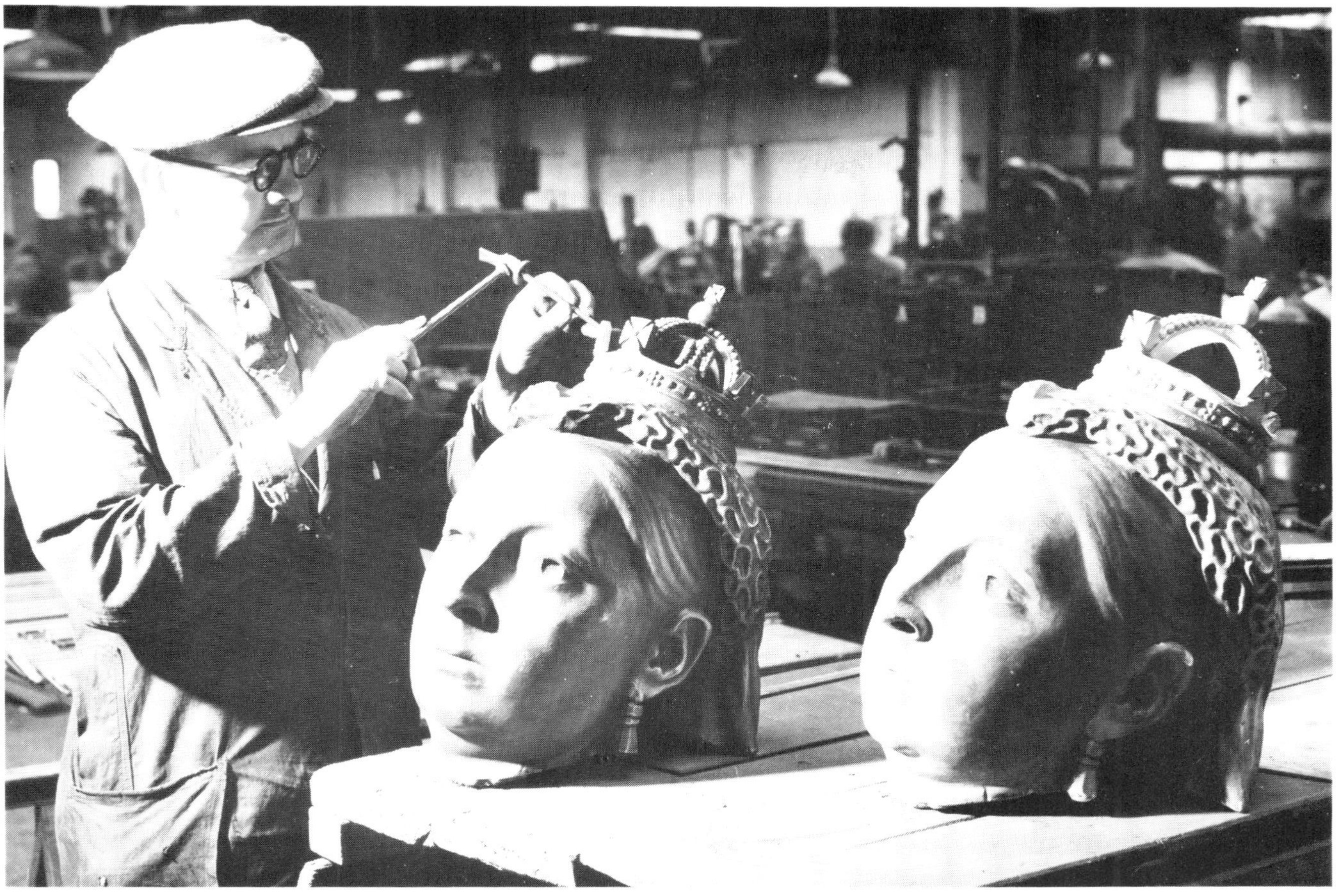

F.G. Taylor chasing bronze head after the re-casting of the Queen Victoria Memorial for Birmingham.

Bronze finishing department, Sunningend, Lansdown. The Mancini family at work.

Liverpool Exchange Memorial awaiting despatch in the works.

In sand casting, plaster or wood models were used as patterns for pressing the sand moulds, especially when making lettered tablets, the letters being of lead set in the plaster. Sculptured work was first modelled in clay, waste moulded and a plaster cast made, usually in several pieces. To obtain intricate detail in a casting the sand would be sieved — the finer the sieve the finer the detail.

To make a waste mould, sections of the clay model are covered with coloured plaster about 3/16″ thick then backed up with ordinary white plaster to a sufficient thickness to give strenth. The sections are then removed from the model, cleaned and washed over liberally with soft soap to stop suction. A plaster cast is made and the mould chipped off with a hammer and chisel, the coloured coating showing when close to the cast.

In the lost wax process a plaster model is made as in the sand process, then a plaster mould made in small pieces to avoid any undercuts. The plaster mould is put together covered in wax to the thickness required in bronze, the inside is filled with a core of poor plaster and the whole heated in an oven to a very high temperature. This melts out the wax, leaving a cavity between the mould and the core into which bronze is poured. Bronze shrinks 3/16″ to a foot, the weak plaster in the core allowing this to take place.

Another member of the foundry team was Mr. A.H. Nottingham who kindly wrote the following for me:

"I started work at H.H. Martyn, Sunningend Works, in January 1917 as a tea boy in the wrought metal department under Mr. Hancock and Mr. Millward. There were five blacksmiths, two welders and about 150 other men and women. We worked a fortnight nights and a fortnight days, 6.30 a.m. to 6.00 p.m. — 6.30 p.m. to 6.00 a.m. When the war ended in November 1918 the work force was greatly reduced, and eventually in 1919 I was taken on as the first apprentice in the new foundry under the manager Mr. Edwards and Charles Dennis the foreman, just the three of us.

"After two or three months two more apprentices and about ten men were taken on, and the foundry began to develop, mainly casting in bronze the many war memorial tablets and also casting lead garden figures. As the foundry progressed the castings became larger and more intricate, demanding a steady hand and great concentration. Charles Dennis, Fred Palmer and I were responsible for moulding in sand, casting in bronze the work of many famous sculptors including Lindsey Clark, Gilbert Scott and Reid Dick. I recall the Broken Limber, Commando Group at Spean Bridge and two castings of Queen Victoria 14′ from base to top of head and 4′ in width, one of which went to Troon in Scotland.

"We were the first foundry to cast doors in one piece, including the revolving doors at the Bank of England. We made a fourposter bed in nickel silver for a Rajah in India and screens for Cambridge University in aluminium bronze. There was a lot of ship work, tables in cast iron and bathroom and swimming bath fittings in stainless steel.

Bronze memorial tablet cast in the sand process by Alf Nottingham when an apprentice of only seventeen.

"Another big job was the Liverpool Cathedral gates in bronze, and interior work including several small figures for the altar rail. For the War Memorial tablets for Australia we had to make special equipment as there were four panels each about 14′ by 6′ with hundreds and hundreds of names. The pattern was in plaster with lead letters stuck on for the names. We moulded the tablets in sand and cast in bronze.

"We used two types of moulding. Using green sand, you made your mould from whatever pattern you were using and cast the same day. Using the other method, you made the mould in the same way but stored it until it was thoroughly dry. That was called dry sand casting. All tablets and false core work, anything of importance, was always dried.

"We had six furnaces with normal draft in which we could melt up to 900 lb. of metal. For anything requiring above that amount we used the cupola which was normally used for melting cast iron. We used two kinds of sand, synthetic, known as sea sand, and silica sand which readily binds together.

Cambridge University Library. Main entrance in bronze.

The sea sand was mixed with a glycol substance, then stored. After a cast it became rock hard and could not be used again. The silica sand was used over and over again.

"The crucibles for melting were made of graphite and if used carefully would last for a long time (40 melts). It used to take about 1½ hours to melt 100 lbs. bronze at 900°C. 50 lbs. stainless steel would take about two hours at a temperature of 1600°C. Temperature for lead was 300°C., aluminium required 600°C. and brass and copper, 900°C. We often mixed our own bronze, 60 copper 30 zinc 10 tin or 70 copper 25 zinc 5 tin. Brass was 50 copper 40 zinc 10 tin or 60 copper 35 zinc 5 tin. Nickel silver 65 copper 20 nickel 15 zinc or 60 copper 20 nickel 15 zinc 5 tin. The mixes were sometimes varied with additions of small amounts of lead or aluminium. We often used eight different kinds of metal in one day.

"There were only five of us who could do the false core work and during the slump in the 1930s we had 75% of the architectural work of the whole country; men used to queue at the works gate for a job. There was a period when the foundry kept the firm going because of the lack of work in the other departments. There were very highly skilled craftsmen in many of the departments, like Mr. Sheppard and Mr. Foster in the modelling shop, Mr. Claridge and his son Jack in the plaster department and Mr. Hill and others in the wood carving shop. Mr. Spurr was the manager over these departments. Mr. G. Hawling, was under manager, in charge of woodwork and the foreman was Mr. Brown.

"We did a lot of work in cast iron and bronze for Selfridges, Derry and Toms, The Bank of England, Cambridge University and Alfred Herbert, and we made a bust of Winston Churchill. We made the toll booths in cast iron and the ventilator shafts in copper for the Mersey Tunnel.

"Part of the foundry was given over to a family of Italians by the name of Mancini, who had been brought in because of their special skills in the lost wax process; making the mould in plaster with a thickness of wax between the mould and the core. It took several days to dry plaster and melt wax before casting. They did not stay long. Sometime later, maybe about the start of the Second World War, Mr. Meigh was given some of our men and they commenced making castings in aluminium bronze for the Admiralty using the Durville method of casting."

A.H. Nottingham was a key member of the foundry team for about 29 years. His ability was evident, and after he had completed his apprenticeship of five years and spent one year as a qualified foundry man, Mr. Dennis the first foreman of the foundry, died, and Mr. Nottingham was immediately made foreman. At only 22 years of age he had a force of 66 men to manage. He proved his skill in this task and the handling of the metals. He had to ensure that no mix-up occurred or contamination was caused by carelessness, no easy task where casting in many different metals took place in a single day. The high international standing of the foundry is testimony to his and the whole team's professionalism and skill.

Bronze figures in the altar rail at Liverpool Cathedral. Craftsmen and Designers: Walter Gilbert and L. Weingartner.

The foundry mixed all its own metals and Mr. Nottingham described the process for me:

"To mix bronze: the copper would be put in the crucible first, since it has the highest melting point, followed by the tin and then the zinc. A graphite plunger would be used to introduce a small quantity of boron to drive off the oxygen.

"To make nickel silver, nickel went in first, (looking like ball bearings), then copper in sheets 10′ x 6′ x ¼″ thick, then the zinc. The copper would have come from Broken Hill, South Africa, as it was very pure. Later in the 30s, ingots of ready mixed bronze and gun metal were purchased from the South Wales smelting works of Cohen's but all other metals were still home produced. The metals for mixing or straight use came from various sources, lead mainly from Australia; tin and zinc from the various importers; tin in bootlace like strips about 18″ long about 1 lb. in weight; zinc in slabs of 20 lb. weight."

Lead was used to cast garden figures, gutters and downpipes, for which antimony would be added to stiffen the lead. Sheet lead for roofing was poured on an open bed of sand levelled on a table about 3′ high with sides, also carefully levelled. The lead was melted on an open fire in a ladle and transferred to a hinged container which was the width of the table to give a full even pour. With skill, the exact quantity at the right speed on a level table could give an even sheet of lead 1/8 or ¼″ thick as the quantity dictated, the molten lead solidifying after it had spread out evenly."

Sequence for casting bronze tablet for Commercial Bank of Sydney, Australia. Plaster model laid in sand face up on foundry floor, all contours to pattern covered with false cores, moulding box on the right.

Model in position as shown in photograph. On right is the bottom part of finished mould to the face of the tablet. The large open frame standing centre is the surround to support the false cores, which forms the deep moulding of the tablet.

The mould closed and ready.

Foundry team pouring the molten bronze. Skilfully united team work.

The pattern maker was another skilled member of the castings department. A.D. Ingram, who was a nephew of Arnold Edwards the foundry manager, was one of the team of pattern makers and he described for me the work and the traditions. He started straight from school in 1935 as an apprentice. He said: 'A clean white apron was worn until you were 18 when a smock was the order. A collar and tie was customary'. In his own words he continues:

"Apprenticeship at Martyns was unhurried. The first year was often spent in little more than making tea and sawing wood for the men but during this time the apprentice absorbed the atmosphere of the workshop and learnt to appreciate the craftsmanship of the older men and to develop a proper respect for them and their work. Teaching was by observation and practical instruction. In general the pattern makers were helpful and approachable but the element of respect was essential in developing a relationship conducive to learning. The atmosphere in the workshop was disciplined. Shavings were swept from the floor twice daily.

"As the apprenticeship progressed other tasks were allocated to the apprentice, who by this time would have collected a number of tools at his own expense. One of his first tasks would be to select carefully suitable timber with which to construct a tool box.

"A number of patternmakers lived in Gloucester and travelled by train using a workman's ticket. Trains were frequent and two main line stations were conveniently near the works.

"Local patternmakers usually cycled to and from work, or walked from nearby St. Mark's estate.

"Architectural patternmaking is a unique and intricate craft. It took a considerable time to understand and for the craft to take shape in the mind. It couldn't be learned from theory from a textbook. The older men were a mine of information and gradually the details of core prints and core boxes and the technique of making the castings hollow would be absorbed before advancing to more complicated work.

"Patterns were made from Honduras mahogany and sugar pine. They were supported on a bed or cradle made of deal before being rammed with sand in the foundry. This bed or cradle of deal would be held together with screws usually size 1½" long and no. 10 diameter. Screws as small as ¼" long and no. 0 diameter were used for some of the smaller pieces of work in mahogany. Larger screws were first dipped in Russian tallow to ease their insertion. Even the core prints were fixed with screws and not simply held in place with glue and panel pins. Sometimes a job had to be handed over from left to right and so it was essential that core prints could be taken off without damage.

"Sometimes patterns in this field of ornamental bronze work required carved embellishments. Carvings were made in lime and the wood-carver worked in a quiet, well-lit position. The carver would not need to concern himself with the core prints and core boxes required for the pattern but he would need to ensure that the article had the required amount of taper for it to lift out of the sand cleanly without dislodging it.

Rangoon Court Entrance Gates, Rangoon, Burma.

"The patternshop had a distinctive and pleasant smell. It was compounded of fresh sugar pine, glue and wax, only marred occasionally when the glue over-boiled or the wax pot got too hot. Glue had to be used very carefully; any excess would become sticky in the damp sand of the foundry and cause difficulty in removing patterns from the sand.

"All patterns and core boxes were varnished with shellac before leaving the patternshop. Each coat was carefully rubbed down with fine sandpaper between applications. This needed care because some of the patterns had features which

Carved wood models for part of casting for Rangoon Court gates. Note position in gate.

could easily be ruined by careless use of sand-paper. Beeswax was heated and spread into any blemishes with a small flat stick sharpened at one end to help spread wax into the screw slots and so obtain a perfectly smooth surface. Any scratches, such as those made with a marking awl, had to be avoided because if lines became transferred to the casting during moulding they would be very difficult to remove at the fettling and fitting shop stage of the work.

"It was helpful to the apprentice patternmaker to spend a little time in the fitting shop, and this was usually arranged. It was interesting to watch the chasers tapping away with small tools to sharpen the image of the castings and clear away any gritty formation which might fill up and mar a feature of the work. The apprentice also benefitted from a little time spent in the core shop corner of the foundry. The cores were baked after they had been rammed up in the core boxes. Cores were extended to balance in the core print shape in the mould as left by the pattern and its respective core print. This was in turn an extension of the pattern but with the required reduction in size from the pattern determined by the thickness of the metal. Metal thickness of the bronze castings was usually accepted as 5/32″ and all work had to be uniformly consistent.

"A turned pattern was made in two halves, one for one half of the moulding box and one for the other half. This was done by screwing the two pieces of wood together with a screw at each end. Brass peg and cup dowels were usually used, but for large work, iron plate dowels were used. The two wooden parts had a piece of newspaper inserted between them and lightly glued. This prevented shake during turning and also facilitated the separation of the pieces. A chisel was inserted and the pieces separated quite easily as the paper gave up its hold.

"Cores were not always needed. They were not used for work such as radiator grilles or ornamental shapes to fit within the framework of an interior door or balustrade. Such pieces were said to "leave its own". On exterior doors, the panels, usually with some carving embellishment, could be cast flat, in with the door panels. It was most unfortunate if any holes appeared in the finished casting because they had to be drilled out, tapped, and a threaded piece of bronze stick inserted. This was screwed up tightly, filed smooth on the surface and carefully rubbed with emery cloth, but this practice was never completely satisfactory and its use was discouraged. The mixture of metal in the insert might vary slightly from the original, or its flow give a different grain since it was inserted "end on". After weathering, these differences could show up in the casting giving an effect like raindrops.

"Colouring of finished bronze castings was done in the colouring shop and the normally acceptable finish was described as "penny bronze". This was a very special job usually entrusted to one man in particular. Sometimes the work would include enamelling and nothing looked more pleasing to the eye than a coat of arms in all the splendour of fine colours. Gold leaf was applied in appropriate circumstances.

"Some specialised attention in addition to actual patternmaking was also carried out in the patternshop; for example, the insertion of glazing in a viewing pedestal. The glazing was cushioned with piping and the container used to display a scroll containing a roll of honour. A bronze knob was supplied so that the scroll could be revolved and read.

"The carved features which ornamented decorative work of this kind were sometimes uniform and repeats in the wax moulding were allowable if the design formed a continuous surround, but more often the design was individual and the whole thing had to be carved separately.

"Martyns was responsible for many memorial tablets throughout the country. Here great care was necessary to ensure uniformity of spacing so that the finished work was aesthetically pleasing. Oblique lines such as those required for L/Cpl would often occur continuously for a time and it was necessary to keep the angle of the slope consistent.

"Tablet backgrounds were first set in their framework and letters made of lead were stuck on with shellac. The letters varied considerably in size, but no matter how small, they were first cut in wood stuck on to a block with a central strip to take the main flow and with smaller runners to each letter before being sent to the foundry for casting in lead. The patternmaker would then clean the letters with special small German files taking care to preserve the slight degree of taper.

"After use these letters could be eased off their background with a chisel and used again for other tablets. Letters made to special order, for example the Hebrew alphabet, would probably be left on the pattern for convenience of storage and taken to the pattern store, which contained a wealth of patterns from past work and was an ideal place in which the apprentice could browse and gain an insight into the nature of the work.

"The shellac used for fixing the lettering was kept separately from the shellac varnish. Shellac varnish is spirit based and it was first allowed to evaporate until it reached the required consistency. Too thick a varnish would leave a seam which would show in the finished casting and be impossible to remove without damaging the lettering; too thin a varnish would cause letters to come loose in the sand and give the moulder endless trouble. On rare occasions the imprint might become torn by a pattern when it was removed from the sand. This necessitated the "laying in" of a little make-up piece to help the moulder, but usually the moulder, adept with his many shaped tools, would overcome the difficulty.

"The patternmaker's knowledge of the foundry would cause him to adhere to the principle that the joint line would determine which was to be the pattern half of the moulding box and which would be the core half. The pattern half would

Plaster model ready for casting for the British General Insurance Company.

contain the main features and the core half would contain the underside. For a two-half pattern — the half with the cup dowels would be placed on the moulding platform and one half of the moulding box rammed up on top of it. The box would then be turned over and the mating half of the moulding box, with its own pegs, would be placed on top of it.

"The pattern half containing the peg part of the dowel would be located into the rammed-up part of the pattern. Parting sand would then be shaken over the existing sand and 'plumbago' over the pattern to facilitate its easy removal. The second half would then be rammed-up with sand, and smoothed off flush. It then only remained to separate the two moulding halves and remove the pattern halves one at a time.

"Gates, vents and risers, terms used in moulding practice, were the responsibility of the foundry. For large work, 'rapping plates' would be inserted, strategically placed on the joint faces to enable the moulder to insert a spike and tap it to loosen the pattern from its hold in the sand. Without rapping plates it would be obvious that the pattern could be split, and this deterioration was not acceptable, especially if more than one casting was required from the pattern.

"Mention must be made of the draughtsmen at Martyns, whose immaculate work provided the foundation for the patternmakers' effort. Drawings were to full size scale. Printing and dimensions were clear and of artistic style to interpret the architect's requirements. The appearance of these drawings and the impression they created left no doubt about the standard of work expected.

"Some work had to be set out on a large board and this usually took some time to inscribe before the actual woodwork could commence. For handrail curves the patternmaker constructed a mock-up former which the fitting shop could use to set up the finished work and make it true to the fall of the staircase. Handrail sectional design and brackets were individual. The final fixing was done with screws, usually of the raised head slotted variety. On front faces, screws were usually covered with a decorative 'patera'. If screws couldn't be covered, each slot had to be turned to the same angle to avoid distracting the eye from the best possible visual effect. Nothing was done haphazardly, and nothing was slipshod or casual. Everything had its form and contributed to the firm's prestigious reputation.

"At the end of each day, time was allowed to clear away tools and leave the bench tidy. This usually took about a quarter of an hour. All work had to be protected from sunlight especially when left for long periods, for example over the weekend, to prevent dimensional alterations of the woodwork.

"Allowance had to be made for metal shrinkage. A special ruler known as a contraction rule was used. The contraction was calculated according to the mix of metal used in the foundry. For smaller items a commercially produced contraction rule could be used, but no specified contraction in metal generally accepted elsewhere applied to the special bronze mixture of metal used at Martyns' foundry. This discrepancy was slight when applied to work involving small dimensions and the small metal contraction rule was easier to use than the large one specially made at Martyns, which was long and unwieldy.

"When the patternmaker required his saws sharpened or chisels wet-sandstone ground he filled in a simple requisition form and this work was carried out by another department. Patternmakers who took pride in their work — and this included all patternmakers at Martyns — lined their toolboxes with green baize. All tools were located in their own special place and always carefully kept in that place. Tools were never strewn carelessly over the bench. Those in use were placed fanwise towards the user with the cutting face uppermost, not down on the grit of the bench, in case this damaged the fine edge.

"Planes were rested on a strip of wood to keep the cutting edge of the blade up and away from any foreign matter they might otherwise be liable to encounter. Should a spot of rust appear on a tool it reflected discredit on the owner and was speedily removed with a little emery dust and a spot of oil (if one was lucky and the rust not too deep).

"Patternmakers who worked at Martyns could regard themselves as lucky indeed to be in the patternshop. It was a quiet, well-disciplined room with pleasant odours exuding from the pine shavings, the wax and the varnish. Of all the scents to permeate one's clothing these must surely be amongst the most acceptable. One could certainly have gone further and fared worse. To be a patternmaker at Martyns was to be in a gem of a position.

"Not everyone accepted the self-discipline involved in perfectionism, but for those who did, the work became an inseparable part of each individual's personality. Work and home life became welded into an integrated whole which gave satisfaction, but it had far-reaching effects on one's attitude to the world outside Martyns, where such standards were not always obtainable. This could give rise to great personal frustration, but that was a small price to pay for enjoying experienced craftsmanship **at its best**."

The next foreman of the foundry was F.J. Hopkins who described some of his experiences.

"I signed my indentures with H.H. Martyn on 12th December 1931 and served 18 months as tea boy and lamp dryer, which means skin drying moulds on the floor of the foundry prior to casting. As the next apprentice was taken on I began working with the men until I was thought good enough to work on my own. For this I was paid 8/- (40p) a week for one year, 10/- (50p) a week for the second year, the third year 13/- (65p) fourth year 16/- (80p) and fifth year 18/- (90p). After that I served another year as an improver at £1.1.0 (105p) per week. As time went on I worked my way up to charge hand, then to under-foreman. Mr Nottingham the foreman retired for health reasons and I took over the senior foreman's position which I held for 23 years, in that time working on all types of architectural castings.

29th July 1955.
AE/LH.

MR. HOPKINS.

There is an apprentice (Colin Palmer) commencing in the foundry on Tuesday -(7.30 a.m) on architectural work. Please take care of him.

Re Dowtys' castings.

There is a letter in asking for immediate delivery of these - they are wanted very urgently.

St. Avold.

Please do not lose any time in starting on the doors for the above, as we have received a letter demanding delivery. You will require one of the men from the iron side to assist C. Wintle.

Re Tablets for Tower Hill.

Just a reminder - 3 lbs. of tin to 100 lb. architectural ingots.

A Edwards

P.S. I think previously I gave you 2 lbs. per 100 lb. but actually the maximum quantity should be 3 lb.

I hope you have had a good holiday - one of the best ever.

Memo from A. Edwards to Fred Hopkins.

These included statues, fountain groups, and bronze doors. A few of the most memorable were; Sir Walter Scott, Sir Winston Churchill (Guildhall), Three Commandos (Fort William), Queen Victoria (Birmingham), The Stag (London), Despatch Boxes and Speaker's Chair (House of Commons), Gates to Royal Canadian Air Force (Trenton, Ontario), Mersey tunnel and last of all, Robert the Bruce, one at Sterling and one at Calgary, Alberta, Canada.

I would like to say these were very happy years and the men I worked with were some of the best craftsmen in the country. It was a tragedy when we were all declared redundant and pushed on the scrap heap".

The final statement made by Fred Hopkins is expressed in similar terms by almost all the men who like him found that the company was to be wound up. The name of Maples was very unpopular.

Fred Hopkins was less than pleased when asked to cast Maples' founder in bronze; it was an arduous task for him as Maples was so disliked.

The statue of Sir Walter Scott was cast in 1939 and stood in the yard for the duration of the war. It was badly damaged by shrapnel and bullets. Fred Hopkins repaired it after the war and it was delivered to Lady Kennet Scott, for whom it had been cast.

Fred also cast a recumbant figure which now lies in the church of All Souls, Tower Bridge, London.

The internal memo reproduced here is an interesting surviving document from Fred's files.

Some of the early work executed in the foundry was the production of memorials in the wake of the first world war. Communities wanting to honour the men of their area who had lost their lives desired suitably fitting, often elaborate work. Some of those cast were: a bronze memorial for Jesmond Dene, Newcastle on Tyne designed by W. Gilbert with figures cast in the round and finely lettered tablets. A Roman lettered tablet for the 107 employees of the Raleigh Cycle Company who gave their lives. In Greek style, the Moss Steamship Memorial to their staff who died. Conservative Club, Glasgow in bas relief. A 10′ high 26 cwt. figure of Britannia designed by W. Gilbert for the Crewe War Memorial. The Masonic Shrine in Great Queen Street, London, W.I., a magnificent example of bronze casting and a supreme test of the skill of the bronze caster; an elaborate and beautiful design again by W. Gilbert. A set of cast and wrought iron gates for Nottingham War Memorial by T. Wallis-Gordon; and further afield, the Victoria Memorial in Calcutta designed by Vincent J. Esck, architect, where the 16ft victory figure with trumpet stands high on its dome overlooking Calcutta.

Beautiful work was done for His Highness the Maharaja Tukoji Ras Holkar of Indore. Martyns had obtained the contract through the architect Mr. Bernard Triggs for the entire palace, even to the furnishings. The porte cochere in bronze, and a nickel silver bed and elaborate washbasin for the Holkar are just a few examples of the work in the palace.

Standard lamps for Mersey Tunnel awaiting despatch from Cheltenham.

The Masonic Shrine, Great Queen Street, London, cast in bronze with gilded figures. The Roll of Honour is guarded by kneeling figures representing the fighting services.

Mould for Grand Temple door, Great Queen Street, standing in the foundry, Cheltenham.

Great bronze doors to the Grand Temple, Great Queen Street, London. Inner face.

Outer face of the Grand Temple doors. Each door cast in one piece 12′ x 4′ weighing 1¼ tons.

Later work was the extensive Cambridge University entrance gates to the quadrangle, the library entrance portico in bronze and the reading room gates in aluminium bronze, all cast about 1934. Still later, in 1952, was the impressive casting of Oscar Nemon's sculpture of Churchill seated, weighing half a ton, now in the Guildhall, London. Incidentally a local Police Sergeant from St. Marks sat for Nemon to help him sculpture Churchill's large frame. Also dating from 1952 is the larger-than-life Commando Memorial now standing in dominant splendour on a 600 ft. hill at Spean Bridge in Scotland, the site where 35,000 officers and men of the Commandos were trained during World War Two.

Probably one of the most taxing tasks undertaken was the casting of the Australian Memorial Tablets with all the thousands of names of the Australian service men who died during the war. The tablets were 16′ x 8′. Each name, each letter had to be cast perfectly. After the sand mould had been impressed with the lead letters set in plaster, it had to be checked for sharpness, particularly as letters such as 'o', 'a' and 'p' tend to lose their centres by suction when the impress is lifted. Any such faults or breakdown of sharp edges had to be made good by hand; a long, tedious and skilled job done on the knees. Mr. Nottingham said he spent hours on hands and knees perfecting the letters in the Australian Memorial. Many hundreds and thousands of letters had to be checked and perfected with tool and finger.

The Naval Memorial at Plymouth, designed by W. Macmillian, R.A., is another major work of the company. It consists of two bronze groups depicting Aphrodite and Neptune and has tablets with 15,600 names of officers and men whose only known grave is the sea. The Memorial was made in 1954 and it took the company six months to complete, each group weighing a ton. It was unveiled by Princess Margaret on Plymouth Hoe.

Robert the Bruce, seated on his powerful horse in splendid array, was another fine and complex casting. The statue was designed by Charles d'O. Pilkington Jackson and paid for by Eric Harvie of Calgary, Canada and by public subscription. The four-ton bronze took four and a half days to travel from Cheltenham to its destination at Bannockburn and was unveiled by the Queen there in 1964 to mark the 650th anniversary of Robert Bruce's triumph over the English. The cost of the statue was reputed to be £27,000 and the donor was so delighted with the first casting that he asked for a second to be made and sent to Calgary, Canada, to symbolise Calgary's Scottish links.

Cambridge University Library. Aluminium bronze screens to reading room.

The following photographs illustrate the process involved in casting the equestrian statue of Robert the Bruce. Sculptured by C.d'O. Pilkington Jackson, A.R.S.A., F.R.B.S., F.R.S.A. Photographed by S.F. Scorey.

The sculptor C.d'O. Pilkington Jackson dwarfed by the plaster cast taken from his model.

Mr. Reid (manager) and F. Hopkins (foreman) setting out runners and risers for casting head of horse.

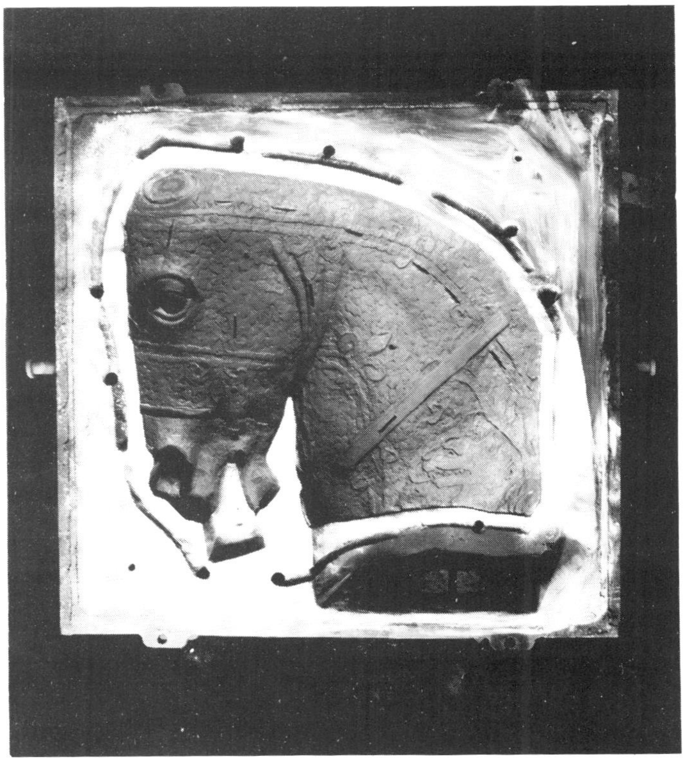

Head of horse with runners and risers (sand mould top half).

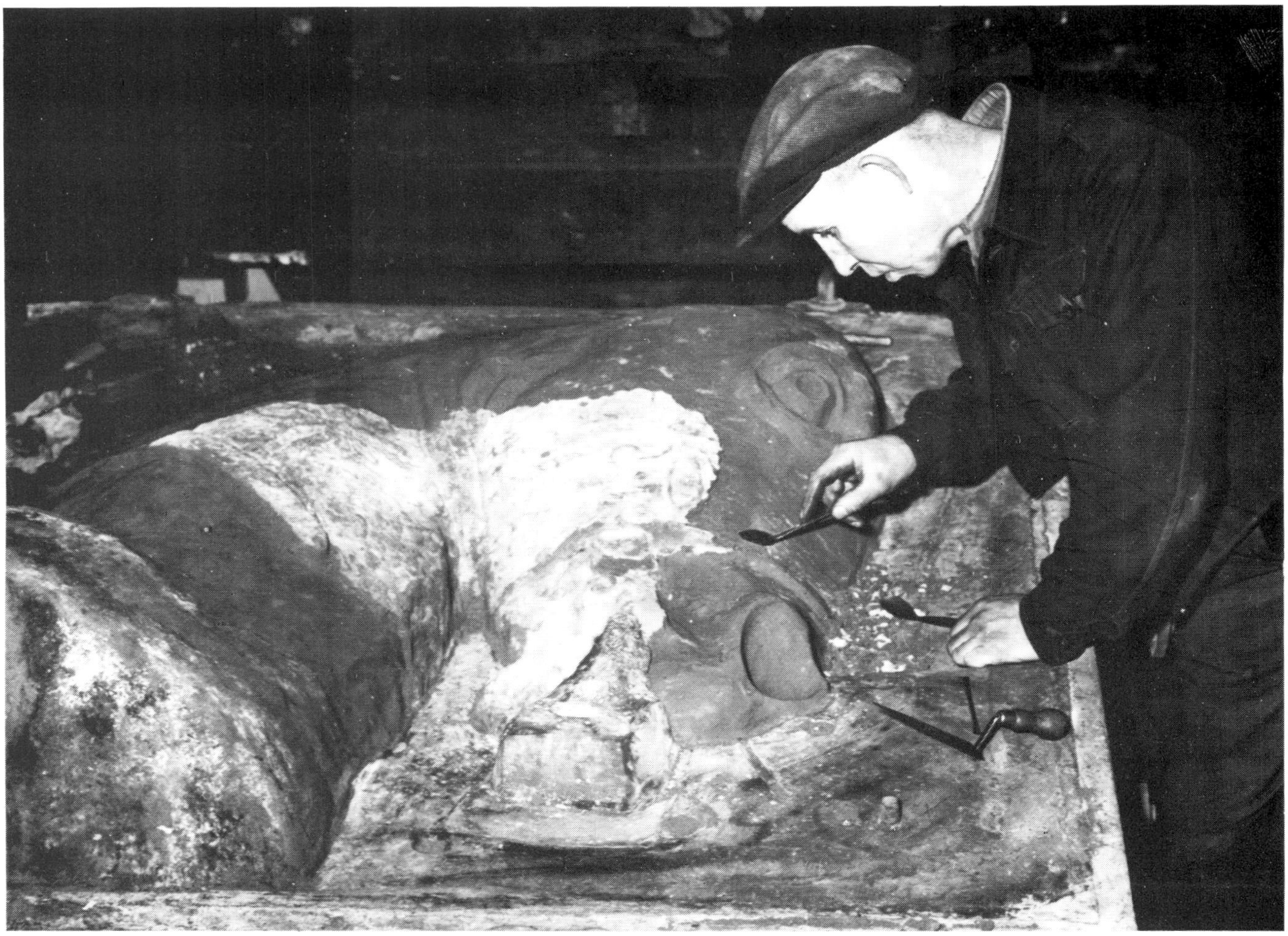

J. Gunyo cutting thickness on inner core.

F. Hopkins making false cores on undercuts of drapes.

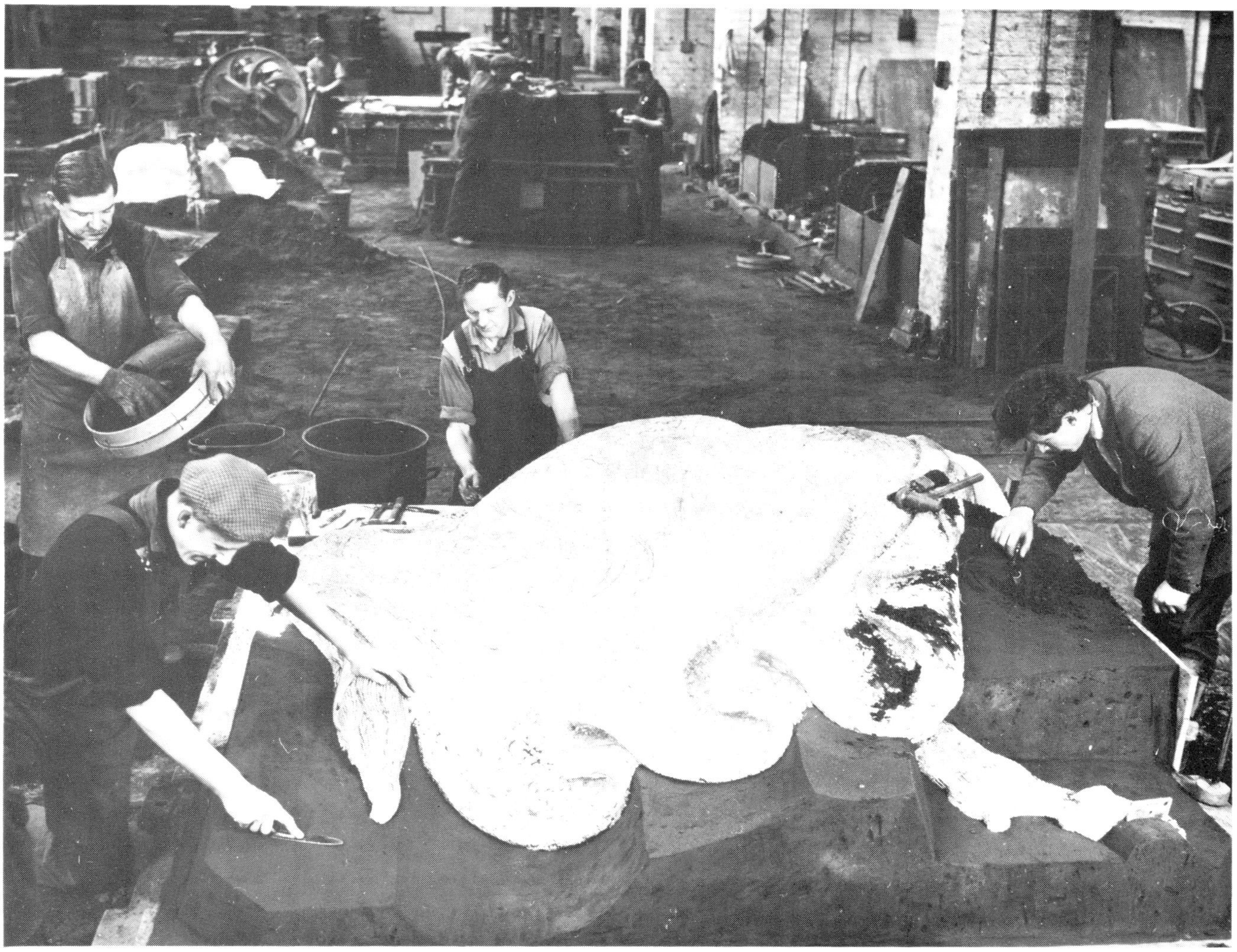

F. Hopkins, centre, W. Mitchell left hand side and apprentice right hand side, setting out drapes on 'odd side' ready for moulding.

W. Mitchell working on false cores prior to making top half of mould.

False core being lowered. J. Price and W. Mitchell guide it into position to ensure even space for the molten metal to run all around.

C. Wintle and apprentice working on the front section of the horse (plaster).

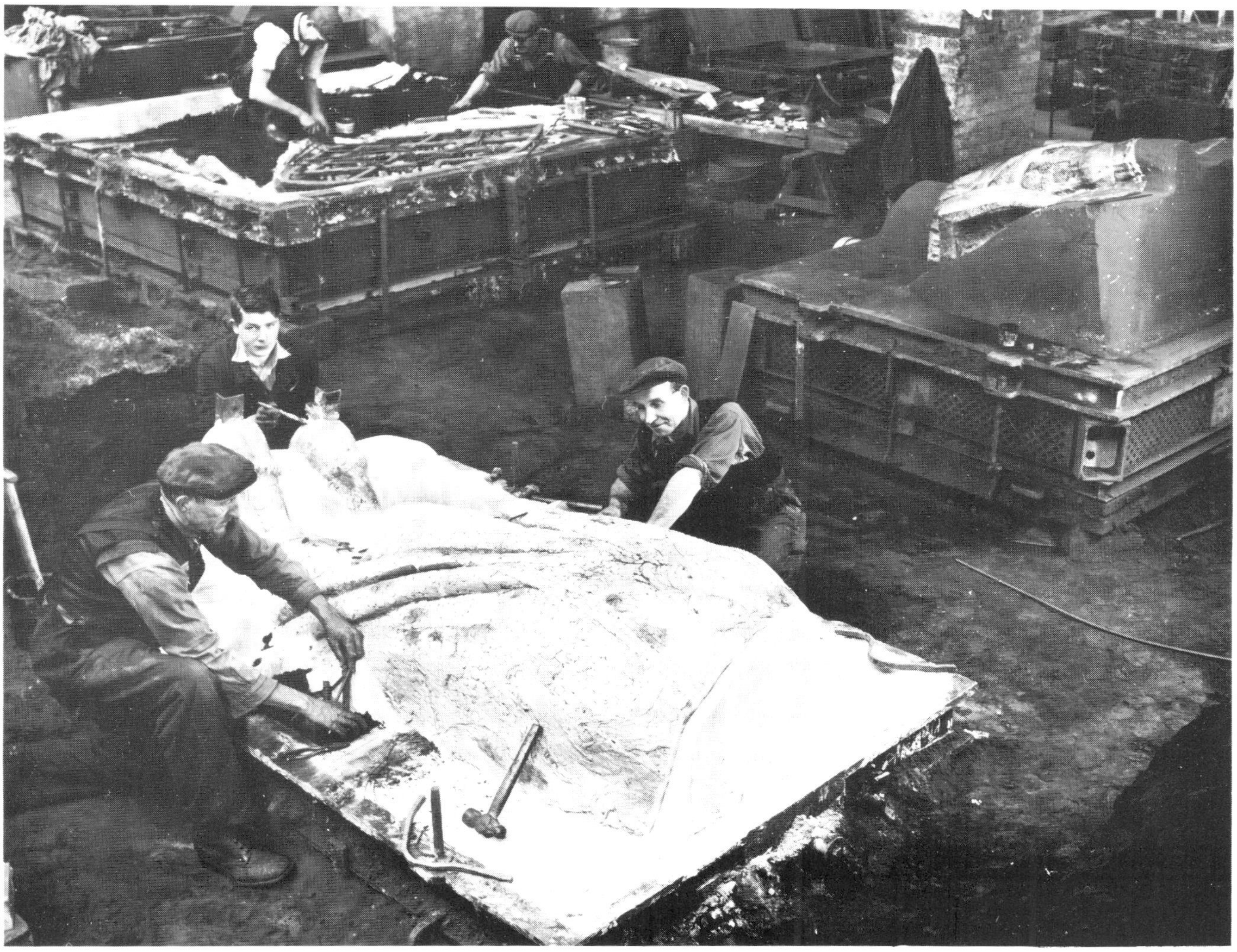

The team working on the drapes (top of picture) and on the front section of the horse.

Casting one section, with G. Cook and J. Gunyo holding plugs and waiting for foreman's call to lift them and allow metal to flow through the mould.

W. East working on the head.

C. Twinning, fitting shop foreman, adjusting arm prior to welding.

W. East chasing.

C. Twinning (top) who did the colouring of the bronze in acids and powders. W. East chasing, and A. Merrett who welded all the sections of the massive statue together.

Finished bronze of Robert the Bruce awaiting transport from the Cheltenham foundry to the site of his triumph at Bannockburn.

Cast bronze figure of Sir Winston Churchill by Oscar Nemon. The final touches by Tom Weeks at the works prior to despatch to The Guild Hall, London.

C. d'O. Pilkington Jackson took ten years from first idea, with four years' serious sculptural work to complete the statue. To get the actual likeness of Robert the Bruce the sculptor consulted dentists and surgeons who were able to examine the exhumed skull of the subject and formulate professional opinions as to his likely living appearance. The head and face certainly have a splendid, noble and commanding force in keeping with his historic reputation. The casting, finally, was so well done that the sculptor's care for detail and accuracy are clearly recorded in bronze.

Smaller, though no less remarkable, is the Castle Bromwich, Birmingham, R.A.F. Memorial crest cast in bronze, the R.A.F. emblem of the albatross set in the ten foot high memorial to almost half its height.

Two life size racehorses were cast in the foundry, Hyperion in 1962 and Chamossaire in 1966. Both were sculptured by Prof. John Skeaping. The 1933 Derby winner Hyperion took two to three months to cast, weighing 1,020 lb., and was shown at the 1962 Scottish Royal Academy Summer Exhibition. Prof. Skeaping had modelled the horse by carefully following the measurements of the bones of the skeleton while having a live horse in the studio for animation.

There was an episode concerning the plaster model of Hyperion from which the bronze casting had been made, which cost the company a great deal of money. Following the casting of a sculptor's work the model is usually required to be broken up. In the case of Hyperion all was broken up, but by mistake, chance or design the head survived. Some several months later the plaster model of the head appeared, treated and sprayed to look like bronze, in a café in Winchcombe, Glos. Prof. John Skeaping got to hear of it and rightly held Martyns responsible. They had to buy it back for a reputedly large sum of money and carry out the job with the hammers which it had escaped before. No doubt greater care was exercised from then on. Hyperion stands at Lord Derby's Stanley Stud, and Chamossaire at the Snailwell Stud, Newmarket.

Other famous sculptors who entrusted their work for casting at Martyns were Henry Moore, Huxley Jones, Lynn Chadwick, who would not on any account have the cast wire-brushed, preferring the untouched surface, Dennis Cheyne Dunlop and many more. G.W. Reid was the manager who ably controlled the casting and metal department in the latter years and F.J. Hopkins was foreman.

The statue of Queen Victoria was re-cast in 1951 from the old marble statue which had suffered from acid erosion for nearly 50 years in Birmingham's centre. Impressions were taken from the marble sculpture and the 1½ ton 12 ft. high statue re-created in bronze. Mr. William Bloye F.R.B.S. re-touched the marble prior to the taking of impressions. Bill East, Alf Merrett, Henry Wykes and Fred Taylor put the final touches to the bronze before it left the works for its pedestal in Birmingham again.

A rather controversial casting was that of the doors for the New Whitehall Building, or Temple of Bureaucracy, as it was dubbed at the time in 1951. The cost of £13,000 incensed some people as a waste of money, although they provided work for a lot of men. Cast in aluminium, 22'9" high, 16' wide, they weighed 10 tons together, made up of 8 tons of steel and 2 tons of aluminium.

Robert the Bruce, William III, Sir Winston Churchill and Queen Victoria were all notable bronzes, but Miss Christine Edwards told me that her father Arnold was proudest of his creation in the foundry of the three Commando figures, each nine foot tall and in full battle dress with rifles slung across their shoulders. This memorial took twelve months to complete in the foundry. It was designed by Scott Sutherland of the Dundee School of Art, who succeeeded in portraying great strength in the figures by their size and by the deliberate carelessness of their clothes, baggy battle dress, enormous boots and the battered untidiness of their balaclava hats. Their faces are those of tired but purposeful men, rough-hewn and determined. The monument was unveiled on September 27th 1952 by the Queen Mother.

By contrast an aluminium spire and cross for a cathedral in Ethiopia was made in 1962, spire and cross being some 54' in height.

Closely associated with the casting department were the sculptors, carvers and modellers who produced the originals from which the casting was taken. Paramount at Martyns were the sculptors, artists who worked from their own ideas and created the whole work of art. One of these was Robert Lindsey Clark R.S.B.S., one of this country's finest sculptors, who was referred to in an earlier chapter. He started with the company in its very early days prior to the move from the High Street.

Robert Lindsey Clark was apprenticed to Martyns in the early 1900s and soon showed evidence of his skill as a sculptor, which led in 1911 to his being made a member of the Royal Society of British Sculptors, an elite of only 200. His talents were soon recognised at Martyns and in 1905 he was appointed Chief Sculptor and was already exhibiting at the Royal Academy and the Liverpool Walker Art Gallery. Liverpool Corporation awarded Lindsey Clark first prize of £100 for his design for the Queen Victoria Memorial. His connections with Martyns were severed for a time after his marriage when he left to study at the Lambeth School. Later he returned as head sculptor and art director, a position which he held until his death in 1925. Among his many works, some of them very large indeed, the one for which Robert Lindsey Clark was most acclaimed was his bronze sculpture called 'The Broken Limber'. Generally regarded as his most successful work, it received universal admiration at the 1924 Royal Academy Exhibition. The piece depicted an eighteen pounder gunlimber of the Royal Horse Artillery of the 1914–1918 war. The two horses, lunging to drag the limber from the mud, are perfectly sculptured to show the strength of each muscle. The experienced soldier riding the near side horse is controlling the pair in spite of the broken limber pole which has given under the strain. Jimmy Babbage, who lived in Market Street and who did short hauls for Martyns with

Robert Lindsey Clark's model for "The Broken Limber".

his horse and cart, sitting up front in flat cap and fine moustache, stood with his horse for the sculptor to work from for many hours. Three copies were cast at the foundry by Mr. Edwards and his team. One is in the Cheltenham Museum and Art Gallery, another was purchased by John Player of the tobacco company and the third by A.W. Martyn. He was greatly impressed by the work and it graced his home, The Hearne at Charlton Kings, to be admired by many who visited there.

Alf Nottingham was still an apprentice when he was entrusted with the job of forming the moulds for Lindsey Clark's 'Broken Limber', a complicated and skilled operation which he described to me.

"The pattern would be placed in position and fine sand dusted all over it through a sieve to a depth of about one inch and pressed down hard. Then two inches of coarser sand would be rammed down also and then pricked all over as close as possible with a fine needle, an arm-aching task which if skimped would result in the gasses being unable to escape, causing blowholes in the surface of the casting. Next, three to four inches of courser sand were firmed down and vented with 3/16th wire all over.

"The whole box is then turned over so the pattern can be pulled out with guides to ensure it can be replaced later with absolute accuracy, after the imprint has been dusted all over with loam and coal dust. Now the pattern is replaced, turned over and rammed firm again and a two inch covering of coke breeze applied, then pierced with tubes about eight inches to a foot apart again to let the gasses out when casting. The box is reversed again and the pattern withdrawn. Another pattern is made now to form a back so that the metal is about 3/16th inch in the finished casting. The whole is then stored until perfectly dry, the two parts put together facing each other and prepared with runners and risers through which the molten metal is poured."

One of the great disappointments to the staff and men working at Martyns at this time was that the 'Broken Limber' was not chosen as Cheltenham's War Memorial. It would have cost the town £200 more than the present stone obelisk made by Boltons, but the committee of the time turned it down. But what a wonderful attraction and spectacle it would have been now in the Promenade, cast life size as was intended!

The Lindsey Clark family carry on the tradition as sculptors. Philip Lindsey Clark was a pupil in his father's studio at Martyns but in 1910 moved to London. He had a notable career as a sculptor. Robert's grandson Michael Clark (he dropped the Lindsey) is the third generation to be made a member of the Royal Society of British Sculptors, unique in the Society. How fortunate Martyns was to have the talent and art direction of Robert Lindsey Clark almost from the start of the company until he died in 1925. There is no doubt that a company is only as good as the men who make up its number. Martyns were rich in fine craftsmen and the company's success was largely due to such men.

The following metal work contracts of H.H. Martyn & Co. were described in the Architectural Review:

1911 Lift enclosures in wrought iron for Berkshire County Hall.

1913 Hong Kong and Shanghai Bank, Gracechurch Street, London, E.C. Art metal work, bronze doors.

1916 British Dominion General Insurance Co., wrought iron work.

1916 Cardiff Empire, two bronze cartouches for the facade.

The headquarters of the Alliance Building Society were totally fitted out by Martyns, who also cast the coats of arms in bronze for each branch.

A very late major casting done by the Martyns foundry was 'Heleos the Sun God' and the fountain group which now stands in the Television Centre at Shepherds Bush, London. It is fitting that such a piece in 'gold' should stand, in its way, a token of the golden years of the foundry.

These are some of the more important metal work contracts executed before 1934, taken from a company brochure:

BRONZE WORK
Middlesex Guildhall
Courts of Justice, Rangoon
Queen Victoria Memorial, Calcutta
India House, London
Hong Kong & Shanghai Banking Corp, London
Australian Mutual Provident Society, London
Liverpool Victoria Friendly Soc., London
Ulster Parliament Buildings
Strand Palace Hotel
Midland Hotel, Bradford
Drovers, Singleton
Middlesex Guildhall
New India Building, Liverpool
Marble Arch Gates
National Bank of India

Other works researched from various sources:

Halifax Building Society, Coventry
Bronze work.

Halifax Building Society, Hull
Bronze work.

Cable House, London
Bronze entrance doors, balconies etc.

Rolls Royce Ltd., Crewe
Main staircase in bronze.

University Library, Cambridge
Bronze entrance, aluminium bronze screens.

Nottingham Exchange
Bronze work.

Birmingham Civic Centre
Bronze work.

Newport Civic Centre
Bronze work.

Swansea Civic Centre
Bronze work.

Hornsey Municipal Buildings
Exterior bronze work.

Martins Bank, H.Q. Liverpool
Bronze work.

Martins Bank, Lombard Street, London
Bronze counter grilles.

Midland Bank, H.Q. Poultry, London
Bronze doors, bronze staircases.

Lloyds Bank, H.Q. London
Bronze windows.

Hong Kong & Shanghai Bank, Hong Kong
Bronze entrance and lift doors.

Edinburgh Savings Bank
Bronze counter screens and lanterns.

Bush House, London
All the bronze work, entrance screens, doors and staircases etc.

India Buildings, Liverpool
Bronze work.

Victoria House, London
Bronze and lead work.

Lambeth Bridge, London
Four bronze pineapples.

Cumberland Hotel, London
Cast metal doors.

Philharmonic, Liverpool
Lead cresting.

Leeds Synagogue
Bronze work.

Bank of England, London
Internal bronze doors, bronze figure of Ariel on dome.

Bank of England, Southampton
Bronze entrance doors.

Geological Museum, Kensington
Lead facing.

Bronze victory figure for Victoria Memorial, Calcutta, India. Architect: Vincent J. Esch.

Detail of bronze gates, Victoria Memorial, Calcutta, India.

Cast bronze heads for Derby Bridge.

Chichester County Offices
Bronze doors and screens.

Wandsworth Administrative Buildings
Bronze fountain.

Manchester Town Hall Extension
Bronze work to bridges, balustrades, show-cases etc.

Selfridges, London
Main entrance doors and cast iron windows.

61 St. James Street, London
Bronze shop front.

Derby Bridge
Relief heads in bronze.

Palace at Buccharest for King Carol
Bronze work.

Lal Bagh Palace, India
Bronze work.

Falkirk, Scotland
Bronze shop fronts.

Cathedral in Ethiopia
54′ high spire, aluminium.

The following is a list of men working at Martyns in 1935 supplied for me by Mr. A.D. Ingram:

FOUNDRY DEPARTMENT

Manager
Arnold Edwards

Department Secretary
Reg Hall

Foundry
Alf Nottingham — Foreman
? Nichols (Snowball) — Furniceman
? Jones — Coremaker
Frank Whittle — Moulder
Dennis Randal — Moulder
Tommy Crook — Moulder
Len Hatch — Moulder
Joe Guest — Charge Hand
F.J. Hopkins — Apprentice
— and others

Foundry Fitting Shop
Harry Lewis — Foreman (later under-manager)
Harry Lewis Senior — Locksmith
Arthur Lidiard — Storekeeper
Ernie Butler — Metal Polisher
Alf Merrett — Welder
Fred Wallace — Chaser
Fred Green — Chaser
Ted Gillard — Fitter
George Skinner — Fitter
Harold Dickenson — Fitter
Bill East — Fitter
Les Humphries — Metal Turner
Wally Gapper — Fitter
— and others

Art Metal Department
Albert Millward — Foreman
Ron Wilkes — Guillotine Cutter
— and others

Away Fixing
Fred Taylor

Setter Out
Tom Ellis

Colouring Shop
Fred Green

Foundry Pattern Shop
Frank Abbey — Foreman
George Ainge — Charge Hand
Charlie Lee — Labourer
H. Foster — Woodcarver
Bert Young — Apprentice
Larry Gibbons — Apprentice
Jack Webb — Apprentice
Fred Ingram (self) — Apprentice
Bill Shaw — Patternmaker
Bill Robinson — Patternmaker
Tommy Salter — Patternmaker
Chris Brennan — Patternmaker
Robert Hendry — Patternmaker
— and others

OTHER DEPARTMENTS

Cheltenham Main Office
David Longden — Managing Director
Charles Denley — Works Secretary
R.J. Maxfield

Drawing Office
Jimmy Lloyd
Sam Wilcox
Hardy Evans
— and others

Miscellaneous
Bill Austin — Wages
? White — Medical
? Wimblett — Canteen Manager
George Martin — Wood Yard
Nevil Payne — Woodmill Foreman
Bill Dent — Works Van Driver
? Friedloss — ‘C’ Block (Maples) Arthur Beach — Works Painter
? Stanford — Works Painter
(colour used ‘Leaf Green’ by Walpamur)
Andy ? — Plaster Shop
Teddy Black — Works Storekeeper
? Hauling — Joinery ?
Archie Spur — ?
Reg Cooper — Joiner Apprentice
Jack Brush — Joiner Apprentice
— and others

A list of castings on which Mr. A.D. Ingram worked:

Mersey Tunnel

Kingston Guild Hall
Balustrade.

Sandford Park Lido, Cheltenham
Opening tablet.

Ocean Terminal, Southampton
Opening tablet.

Regal Cinema, Cheltenham
Canopy, lamp pendants, handrail.

Cambridge Guild Hall
Doors, handrail, caskets, pillar crests.

Cambridge American Cemetery
Doors, flagpole and base.

Tewkesbury, Gloucester
War Memorial tablets.

Churchdown, Gloucester
War Memorial tablets.

Gloucester City
War Memorial tablets.

Lancaster
War Memorial tablet (horizontal with urns).

Royal Air Force Base
Doors etc. (probably Cranwell).

Chatham War Memorial
48 tablets (not standard type).

Nelson
War Memorial tablet.

Port Talbot
War Memorial tablet.

Seabank Hotel, Porthcawl
Entrance handrail.

Royal Palace, Bucharest
Radiator grills etc.

Otranto, Rangitata, Rangitoto, Orontes, Caronia
Ship work, doors, panels, radiator grills, etc.

Stratford-on-Avon Town Hall
Radiator grills.

Strathspey
War Memorial tablets.

Gloucester Technical College
Doors, window boxes.

Cardiff
Football park gates.

Epsom Parish Church
War Memorial.

House of Commons
Dispatch box, loudspeaker grills.

Liverpool Merchant Navy
Parchment roll of honour console.

Cheltenham Cemetery Chapel
Memorial tablet, civilian dead.

Pitlochry Hydro Electric
Tunnel replica tablets, tablets for flooded land.

Jewish Synagogue
All Hebrew lettering tablet.

Bank of England, Southampton
Doors.

Bank of Hong Kong
Doors.

St. John's Conduit, Bristol
Tablet.

St. Mary Redcliffe, Bristol
Two tablets.

W.D. & H.O. Wills, Bristol
War Memorial tablet.

Selfridges, London
Shop front.

Ventnor, Isle of White
Direction indicator.

Bournemouth (a restaurant)
Two urns with sea lions.

Institution for the Blind
Tablet.

Northern Ireland Government Offices, Regent St., London
Sir William Cooper's room, balustrade, flagpole.

From advertisements in the Architectural Review:

1923/29 Empire House, St. Martins-Le-Grand, bronze entrance doors.

1923/29 Commercial Bank of Sydney, Australia, 11′ x 7′ bronze lettered tablet cast in one piece.

1928 Cross and candlesticks for All Saints Church, Springwood, Liverpool.

1928 I.C.I. Millbank, doors.

1929/39 Selfridges, Oxford Street, London, central figure cast in iron from model by Reid Dick, Esq., Sculptor. Also the whole window and entrance to Selfridges.

1929/39 United Newspapers Ltd., London, bronze doors and oak office front.

Bronze Tablet. All Saint's Church, Highgate.

Garden ornament, one of a large range produced by the company, offered in 1950 at £47 bronze, £26 lead, £17 cement.

Bronze fountain figure for Crawley.

A plaster model by Robert Lindsey Clark A.R.B.S.

One of a variety of cast iron grilles for Derry and Toms' premises, London.

Sculpture by Henry Moore cast at the works.

U.S.A. Cemetery, Cambridge. Base of flag pole being worked on by Harold Dickenson.

Alliance Building Society. Aluminium bronze bass relief group (shop fitting also by H.H. Martyn).

Romano's, Strand, London. Cast figures and wrought iron garlands.

Martins Bank, Liverpool. Cast bronze entrance doors.

Wrought iron gates for the war memorial, Nottingham. Erected on the Victoria Embankment. Architect: T. Wallis-Gordon.

Chapter 6

WROUGHT IRON

Sweat, noise, heat, hammering toil: amid such conditions artists produce from hard unyielding metal the lace-like beauty of wrought iron. Leaves, hearts and honey-suckle, twists, tendrils, scrolls combine in intricate patterns. By 1905 art metal work was being advertised by Martyns as one of the many skills it offered to architects. The contracts for wrought iron continued to increase and after the move to Sunningend, Lansdown, where the cast metal department began to enlarge its scope, the two progressed together. Frequently wrought metal work would be combined with cast work.

Wrought iron work grew from the blacksmith's trade. Almost every village had its blacksmith, and towns would have several in the nineteenth century. Many smiths graduated to the greater skill of artistic iron work. The work in the past was very different from the welded iron of today. Now the pieces in a design are stuck together with weld, and however expertly done a shoulder or ridge is evident. In the past, the joins between stem and leaf, scroll and upright would first be made malleable in the forge and then beaten, tapped and coaxed until the separate pieces became one, uniting the iron so the scroll or leaf appeared to emerge from a continuous piece without a join.

Martyns drew its decorative iron workers from men already skilled and with traditions of excellence going back generations. William Letheren, who had the Vulcan Iron Works at Lansdown before it was taken over by Martyns, was a master of the art. He had awards and medals for his work dating from 1865 to 1885 for 'elegance of design and excellent workmanship'. His son Thomas inherited his father's skill with metal and after Letherens ceased trading in 1906 he joined Martyns to carry on his artistic work for them.

Charles William Hancock joined Martyns in 1908. Prior to that, he had been carrying out at his own works much of the art metal work for Martyns and it was agreed that if A.W. Martyn could secure the order for the Marble Arch Royal Gates, Mr. Hancock would be asked to join and manage the department. He was probably trained by Letheren and coming from an ironworking family he too brought exceptional talent to the works when he became manager in 1908.

Both these men helped train the future generations of ironworking craftsmen for the company, passing on the skills of generations past. It is no wonder that the staff of the wrought iron department held a position of excellence equal to the best of the other departments, and that their work was appreciated and requested by architects and clients alike, world wide.

Charles Hancock managed the wrought iron department from 1908 until he set up his own business again in 1925 following the combining of both departments under the management of Arnold Edwards. However, his son, Harold Hancock, continued for many years as a draughtsman for Martyns.

Another important member of the metal work department was H.J. Lloyd, who worked for the company from 1917 as their chief metal work designer and draughtsman, a post which he held for 45 years, except during the second world war when he worked as a jig and tool draughtsman. During his long working life with Martyns H.J. Lloyd worked on most of the prestigious contracts and is known to have worked closely with Herbert Rouse, architect for the Mersey Tunnel. H.J. Lloyd also worked on designs for all the great ships including

Detail of wrought iron and bronze entrance gate, Castle Park, Colchester. Architect: Duncan Clarke.

the Queen Mary; other contracts were the Philharmonic Hall, Liverpool, the Bank of England, and Wembley Civic Centre. He worked in the design department with Harold Hancox, Arley Evans, Sam Wilcox, Percy Edmonds and H. Johnson. He was also an accomplished water colour artist who learnt his skills at the Birmingham School of Art and later passed on his knowledge to the next generation at Cheltenham School of Art, where he was a part-time teacher.

Lou Back, who was to join Martyns later in his career, served his apprenticeship in art metalwork with Charles Hancock at his works in Bennington Street, Cheltenham. His first job he remembers was the fine canopy for the Ellenborough Hotel in the town. Charles Hancock's business closed down after his death in 1937 and Lou Back joined Martyns, bringing the skills in which he had been trained from a master of the art. He continued for Martyns for many years, producing exquisite work. Some of his commissions that he mentioned to me were the fire grates for the House of Commons, various iron work for the liner Queen Elizabeth and the handrails for the staircases in the Canberra and Q.E.II.; The Collegiate, London; a massive staircase for Alliance Insurance, Hove; and Robert the Bruce. During the war he worked on aircraft and toolmaking. Since setting up his own business he has been in great demand as the 'last of the few' capable of the old methods. He renovated the gates, overthrow and lamps of Wrexham Parish Church, now classed as a National Monument.

Other men trained by Charles Hancock were his son Walter (Hatt) Hancock (blacksmith), and Harry Meredith. Others in the same art metal department were Alf Merrett, welder, a master of the art, of whom it was said: 'he could weld paper if you asked him', Charlie Grinham and his son Jack, Arthur Smith (blacksmith), Tom Letheren (blacksmith) youngest son of William, Johnny Thomas (blacksmith), ? Thompson, Fred and George Dymock, Percy Goulter who was an artist at beating out leaves for flower designs and Fred Jones, who was foreman.

In the 1920s the men of the art metal department worked out their designs to chalked lines on the floor. After the metal was heated they were able with great skill to twist and shape bronze or iron handrails to the complex curves of flowing staircases for ships, palaces and stately homes. H.H. Martyn and William Letheren had certainly met by 1887 when their firms collaborated in producing a wood and iron work screen for the Parish Church of St. Mary, Monmouth. Since this was just prior to the formation of Martyns it must have been in conjunction with the Martyn & Emms partnership that the carved wood part of the screen was made.

Albert Millward joined Martyns as foreman of the wrought metal department and later became manager. In 1929 he formed a company, H. Millward & Co. Ltd., Engineers, which his son ran for him. They often machined and drilled castings from the Martyns foundry. One such contract in 1943 was finishing cast control boxes for submarines.

Some wrought metal work contracts from early brochures:

Derby Police Courts
Metal work.

Barnsley Municipal Buildings
Metal work.

Hackney Town Hall
Metal work.

London University
Wrought iron railings.

Clare College, Cambridge
Wrought iron work.

St. John's College, Cambridge
Wrought iron entrance gates and railings.

Bank of England, Southampton
Wrought iron work.

Martins Bank, H.Q. Liverpool
Wrought iron work.

Midland Bank, H.Q. Poultry, London
Wrought iron work.

London and Manchester Assurance Co., London
Wrought iron grilles.

National Library of Wales, Aberystwyth
Wrought iron balconies, lamp standards.

National Central Library
Wrought iron work.

Philharmonic, Liverpool
Metal work.

Ulster Parliament Buildings
Wrought iron.

Blacksmith/Wrought Iron Shop.
Left to Right — Tom Letheren, Mr. Millward (Manager), Tom Weeks, Arthur Smith, Charlie Livsley, Johny Thomas, Greville Dyer, Percy Goulter (white smock).

Wrought iron gates for Hampstead University College School.

Part of the Wrought Iron Shop about 1922. Mr. Albert Millward, manager, standing centre. The pair of dog irons being worked on centre foreground were made as a wedding gift for A.W. Martyn's daughter Ida (Whitaker).
Left to Right foreground — Percy Goulter, Birt Denchfield, A. Millward, Tom Ford, Fred Ford, Charlie Lewis.

Wrought iron gates, Royal Canadian Air Force Memorial, Trenton, Canada.

Metal Machine Shop, about 1922.

Wrought iron doors, Aldford House, London. Architect: G.A. Crawley.

Inverforth Gate, typical of many made by the company.

From advertisements in the 'Architectural Review':

1915/19	Hampstead University College School, wrought iron gates and lamps.
1915/19	Plas Wern Fawr, Harlech, Wales, wrought iron gates.
1919/23	Castle Park, Colchester, wrought iron and bronze entrance gates.
1919/23	Middlesex Guildhall, wrought and hammered bronze electrolier lights.
1919/23	Alford House, London, wrought iron doors.
1919/23	Hexham Abbey, entrance gates.
1923/29	Grovelands Park, Southgate, London, wrought iron "Inverforth Gate".

An Architectural Metal Work Association existed and at a meeting of the association on 15th December 1936 held at 11 Ironmongers Lane. The following were present:

Mr. H.G. Howitt	— Chairman
Mr. E.A. Jackson	— Birmingham Guild Ltd.
Mr. G.H. Whewell	— Bromsgrove Guild Ltd.
Mr. H.C. Bevan	— H.H. Martyn & Co. Ltd.
Mr. W. Morris	—) Morris Singer Ltd.
Mr. R. Hudson	—

also Mr. D.E. Bachelor of Peat, Marwick Mitchell & Co. It appears that the association had recently been formed, Peat, Marwick & Mitchell being recently paid £100 for its formation. The meeting also agreed to assist others in the association asked to quote for 'additional work' on a contract on which a member was already engaged and the parties to protect each other on quotations.

Formation flight by Gloster Gladiator, Gloster-Meteor N.F.14 (centre) and Gloster Javelin F(AW) MK 4 (top). Gladiator full throttle, the others with the brakes on!

Chapter 7

H.H. MARTYN GLOUCESTERSHIRE AIRCRAFT GLOSTER AIRCRAFT

The 1914–1918 war was a difficult period for Martyns as it was for the entire country but it proved to be a stimulating challenge to A.W. Martyn, who was determined not to let the company collapse and with it the jobs of the one thousand men it employed.

A.W. and his father H.H. Martyn had often discussed the possibility of aircraft manufacture, H.H. Martyn being amazingly keen on the new technology of flight considering his age when the first planes took to the air. So when Hugh Burroughes (who was later to become a director) asked A.W. Martyn, Percy Mott and S.J. Waring of Waring & Gillow, all principals of high class woodworking companies, to meet him at the RAeC Club in London, early in 1915, to discuss subcontract work on airframes, the prospect of aircraft production was already in A.W.'s mind.

Following the joint meeting in London, Hugh Burroughes and Guy Peck visited Sunningend and were immediately impressed by the range of equipment and the skill and expertise of the men employed. Shortly after returning to Hendon, Hugh Burroughes arranged the first contract for Martyns, a trial order from the Aircraft Manufacturing Co. for Maurice Farman Longhorn and Shorthorn spares and components. They were produced speedily and efficiently and stood up to searching inspections, with the result that many other contracts followed, including fuselages and wings for Maurice Farman Longhorn and Shorthorn types, D.H.2s, D.H.4s, D.H.6s and B.E.2c, Bristol and Nieuport fighters.

On 14th July 1914 William James Davidson, of Liverpool joined Martyns as works manager and surveyor on a five year contract for a monthly salary of £41.13s.4d. plus travelling expenses and one month's holiday a year. It was he, as general manager, who welded the creative skill of Martyns craftsmen into a highly efficient production unit capable of building aircraft at a great rate. He quickly steered the workforce through the difficult change from decorative art work to aircraft production with the minimum of disruption.

The ever-increasing quantities of airframes required for the war effort meant that additional space was required and Martyns looked locally for more factory space. The Winter Gardens in Cheltenham was an early site, an unusual venue for building aircraft if ever there was one. Rather like a miniature Crystal Palace or giant domed greenhouse situated in Imperial Gardens, it housed teams of workers making and assembling D.H.6 and Bristol Fighter fuselages.

Work was carried out in the Winter Gardens from about 1916 until the end of the war. On Armistice Day crowds packed the Promenade and workers marched from Sunningend through the town. A D.H.6 fuselage minus wings but with tailplane was paraded triumphantly by the Martyns, and the now Gloucestershire Aircraft Co. workers, down Cheltenham Promenade, amid the cheering crowds.

A letter from T.D. Nicol, Ministry of Munitions of War, Aircraft Production, Kingsway, W.C.2. 26th November, 1922 reads:— "Gentlemen. I am directed by the Minister of Munitions, Winston Churchill, to express his great appreciation of the assistance rendered by you and your employees in the supply of munitions during the war."

The Gloucestershire (Gloster) Aircraft Co. employed quite large numbers of women engaged in the production of aircraft parts. Some of the work at that time was particularly suitable to the special skills in which most of the women were already practised. The handling, cutting, stitching and fitting of the canvas which was used to cover the wooden frames of the aircraft were all carried

Armistice procession from Sunningend to Promenade, Cheltenham. 11th November 1918. Aircraft, Bristol Fighter.

Plane Shop. Some of the men who made the successful change to aircraft manufacture, 1915.

out by women. Jack Claridge (manager of the fibrous plaster dept.) introduced the writer to his wife, who described the work she carried out on the aircraft. She had joined the workforce soon after the first world war began and was set to work attaching canvas to the wing sections.

"We had twelve inch long needles. A girl would stand on each side of the wing, which was standing on end between us. The needle was passed through next to a rib and passed back by the other girl opposite, who ensured that the needle entered on the other edge of the rib. The first girl would then make a knot and repeat the process all along the rib, back and forward.

"When the canvas was stitched securely to the wood ribs and spars of wings, tails or fuselage it would go to the Dope Shop where it would be treated so that the fabric would stretch tight. When the dope dried it made a very strong combination."

Mrs. Claridge also worked on balloons, which were used for observation. As with the previous work, this was carefully inspected to see it was perfect. "We had to sew by machine four rows of stitches at each seam or joint to ensure it was gas proof; each seam was passed over a light box to show up the stitches to see they had held the material evenly and with no misses anywhere. It

Bristol Fighters being assembled in the Winter Gardens by H.H. Martyns' craftsmen about 1916.

Woodwork Department, early in first world war. Tail unit for aircraft, left foreground.

would all have to be unpicked if a fault was found." The Dope Shop, worked entirely by women, was not popular and Mrs. Claridge was glad not to be asked to work in it.

Mr. Dilly was foreman of the Dope Shop, which he had to ensure was maintained at a constant temperature. He also had to see that the women working there had their pint of milk at each shift to protect them from the harmful effects of dope fumes. Mrs. Eales, the daughter of Charlie Allen, worked in the Dope Shop and received for working days: £2.9s.0d. (£2.45) per week, or nights: £2.12s.0d. (£2.60) working from 6.30 a.m./p.m. to 6.30 p.m./a.m. For working in the Dope Shop an extra ¼d per hour (equal to 1p for 10 hours) was paid. Overalls were supplied and no food could be taken into the factory. All those working with dope were examined every two weeks by Dr. Hebblethwaite to ensure they were not being affected by the fumes.

The idea of forming The Gloucestershire Aircraft Company came to A.W. Martyn when he took a discriminating look forward and questioned how to keep the staff of H.H. Martyn supplied not just with sub-contract work but with a lasting involvement in aircraft manufacture. He was sure that there was a future for aircraft for defence and for civil transport.

Just eighteen months from the time of the first contract from the Aircraft Manufacturing Company, A.W. Martyn had formulated his plan to get into aircraft development and manufacture himself. In the spring of 1917 he arranged a meeting with Hugh Burroughes of the Aircraft Manufacturing Company in order to present his imaginative plan. Simply it was that a new company should be formed, with A.W. Martyn and his board having 50% of the holding, the Aircraft Manufacturing Company holding the other 50%. He proposed that the new company should take over the Aircraft Manufacturing Company's sub-contract work, rent the Sunningend factory of Martyns and utilise its expert workforce. It was a bold and ingenious scheme from which both companies could benefit. Both boards were enthusiastic and adopted the idea.

A.W. Martyn now entered aircraft production and development with his usual enthusiasm and Cheltenham became a home of this new industry with all its many benefits.

With a capital of £10,000 the Gloucestershire Aircraft Company Limited was registered on June 5th 1917. A.W. Martyn was chairman and managing director, the other directors being George Holt Thomas, who acted as chairman for a few months but then retired owing to ill health, Hugh Burroughes, David Longden and Guy Peck.

The Gloucestershire Aircraft Company grew rapidly. By January 1918 there were 650 employees, by June of the same year 780. The orders were good, covering 150 D.H.6 and D.H.9 fuselages, 461 complete Bristol F2B and 165 FE2Bs plus Nieuport Nighthawk fighters. One and a half million pounds worth of Government orders had been produced up to Armistice Day for the Allied air offensive, so much work in fact that several local companies were needed in their turn as sub-contractors. By the spring of 1918 Gloucestershire Aircraft at Sunningend was capable of producing 45 aircraft a week, a considerable asset to the war effort.

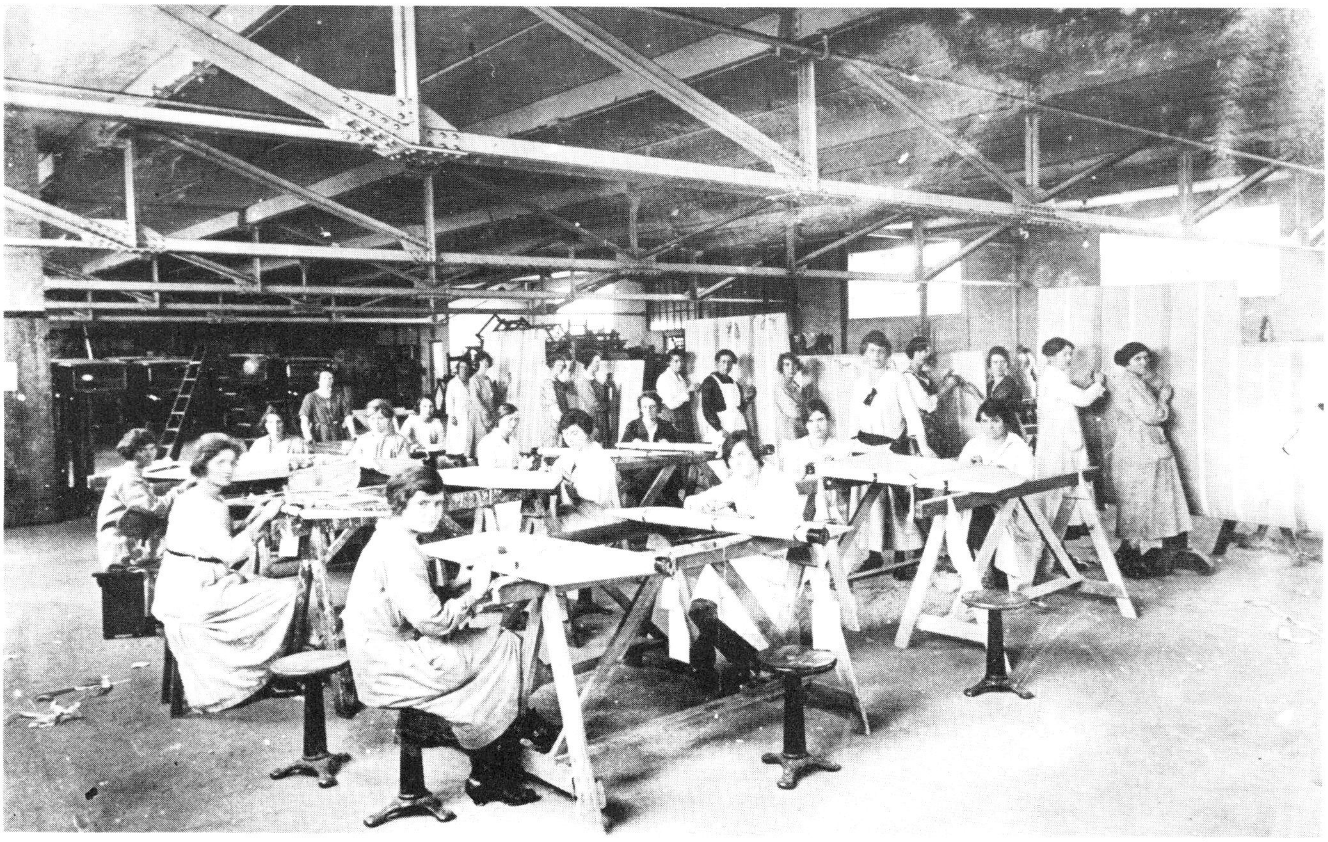

Women seated sewing canvas on to tail units and women standing sewing canvas to wings.

Women in the unpopular dope treatment shop.

Dope treatment shop; note large extractor fan at floor level in background.

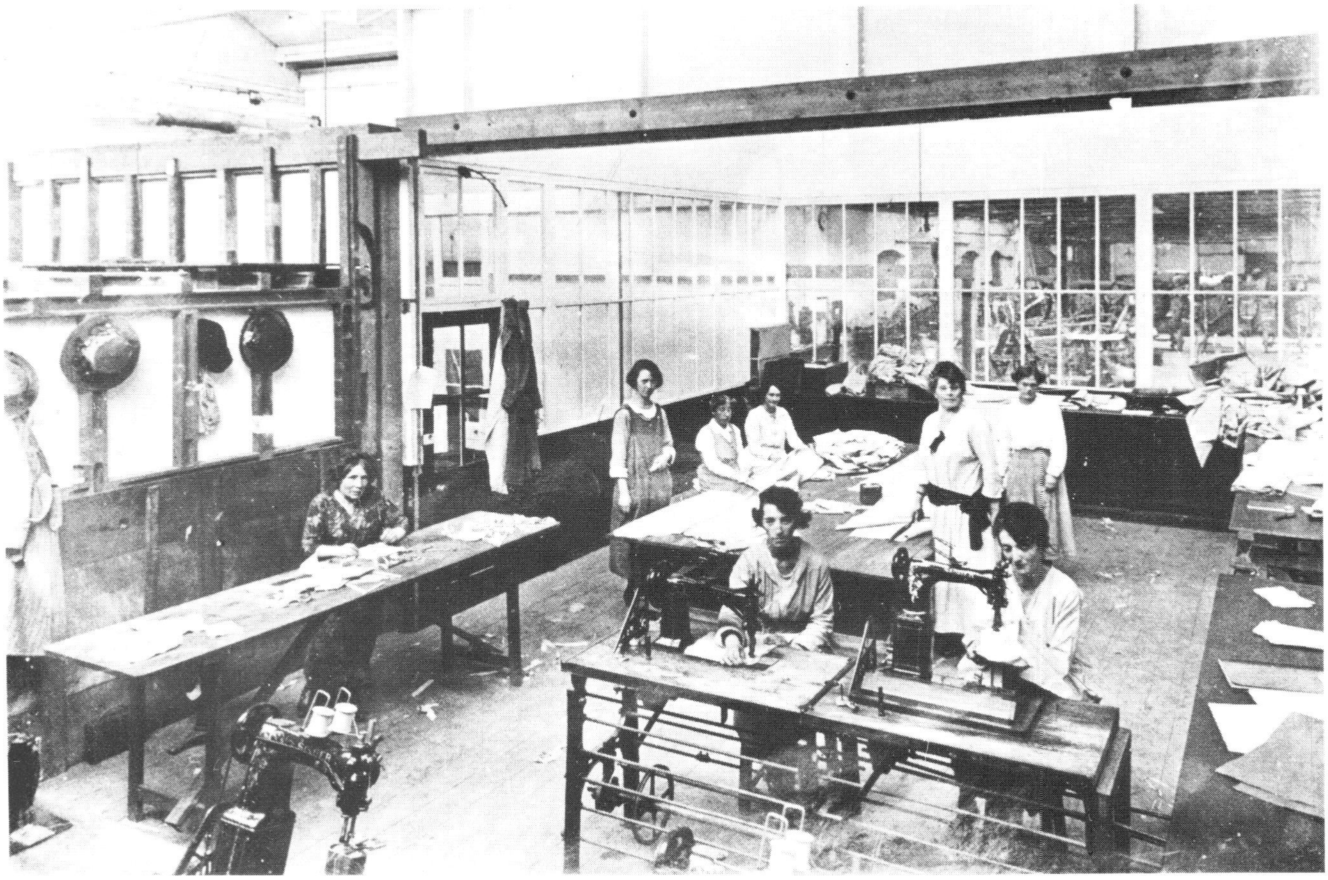

Women at work in the stitching shop.

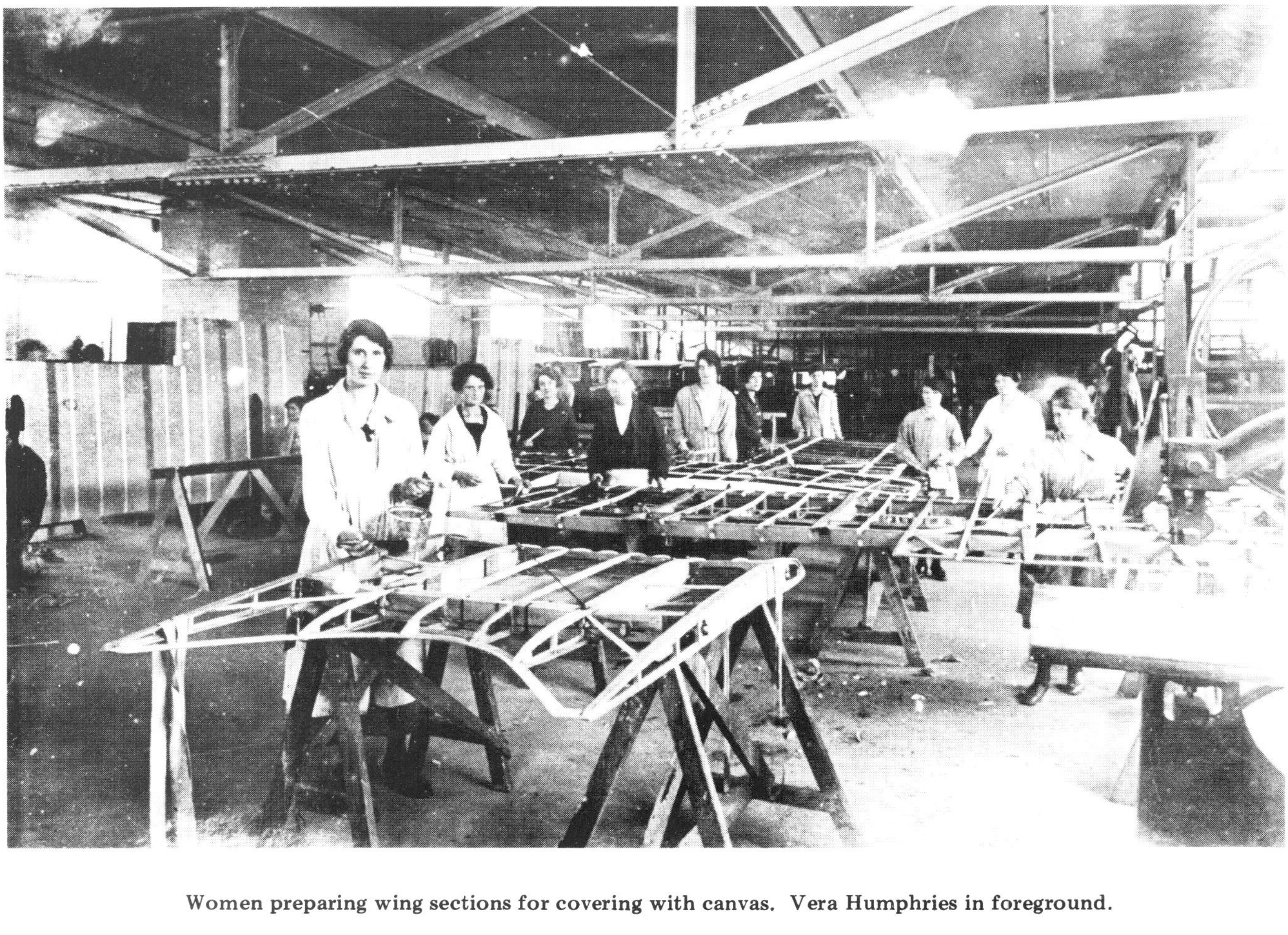

Women preparing wing sections for covering with canvas. Vera Humphries in foreground.

Wing Assembly Shop. Jack Worteley, foreman.

Woodwork Shop 1923.

Formers for base of fuselage. Bert Brown, foreman, in suit.

Aerofoil Shaping Department, with jigs in foreground.

Rudder Assembly Department. Hand mitring machine right-hand side foreground.

Longer view of same workshop, tail plane assembly. Suction pipes and ducting remove shavings. W. Beveridge, Manager (foreground in suit).

Another part of the wing assembly shop. Bristol Fighter fuselages complete in background.

Tail Assembly Department; note architectural work adjacent centre right-hand side, and spars, hollowed out for lightness, in foreground.

Fuselage assembly of Mars VI Nighthawks.

Fitting Nighthawks with radial engines, probably 325 HP. Bristol Jupiter III. Bill Carr, Foreman, left-hand side wearing trilby hat.

Test flying of aircraft had to be done at Hucclecote, Gloucester, where there was a long clear space to take off and land, a facility lacking at Cheltenham. In the early days the aircraft minus its wings was hoisted so that its tail rested in the back of a Ford lorry and was then towed on its own landing wheels along the then winding road to Hucclecote. Hubert Martyn (nephew of A.W.), who worked in the aircraft design office, told me with some amusement that the first aircraft towed in this way suffered from very overheated stub axles, which were of course only designed for quite brief use in taxiing, take-off and landing. However, the overheating was overcome in the innovative way of early pioneers; the men urinated in turn on the overheated wheels and proceeded in short stages to Hucclecote! Later they took cans of purer liquid to cool the axles, though the journey was still broken at the Oddfellows Inn on the Bath Road for refreshment.

The end of the war meant greatly reduced aircraft orders so by the end of 1919 many men were back to decorative work in Martyns, the close link between the two companies proving beneficial both to management and to workers as it caused the minimum of disturbance in the changeover. However, the directors intended to remain in aircraft manufacture and David Longden and A.W. Martyn succeeded in buying a considerable quantity of Nighthawk components from the Government as part of a contract settlement. This proved to be a profitable and farsighted move which helped the company over the next few years as it developed its own products.

From 1918 through 1920 a progressive return to the traditional work of H.H. Martyns took place, mainly with ship interiors and architectural decoration. It was still a period when new ideas and products were needed to maintain the large labour force. Work was obtained from Rover and Siddeley Deasey for motor components. Wolseley car radiators and wings were produced and cars assembled at Sunningend.

Many requests for unusual jobs were received as Fred Willis, manager of the 40 man strong tinsmiths and coppersmiths found. Two of the more unusual jobs they performed were the moulding of the cowlings for the Schneider Trophy seaplane entries, and the radiators for Sir Henry Seagrave's Golden Arrow land speed record car of 1919. The two large side panels for the car which acted as radiators were produced by Mr. Willis and his team. The side panels were designed to be packed with ice for cooling. At the end of the record breaking run of 231 mph the ice had turned to boiling water!

A motor scooter was developed and produced at Sunningend but it was too far ahead of its time. The Vespa of later years was very similar in design but by then young men and women proved to be ready and eager customers.

Erecting Shop 1922. Mars VI Nighthawks capable of 150 m.p.h., for Nos. 1 and 8 Squadron R.A.F.

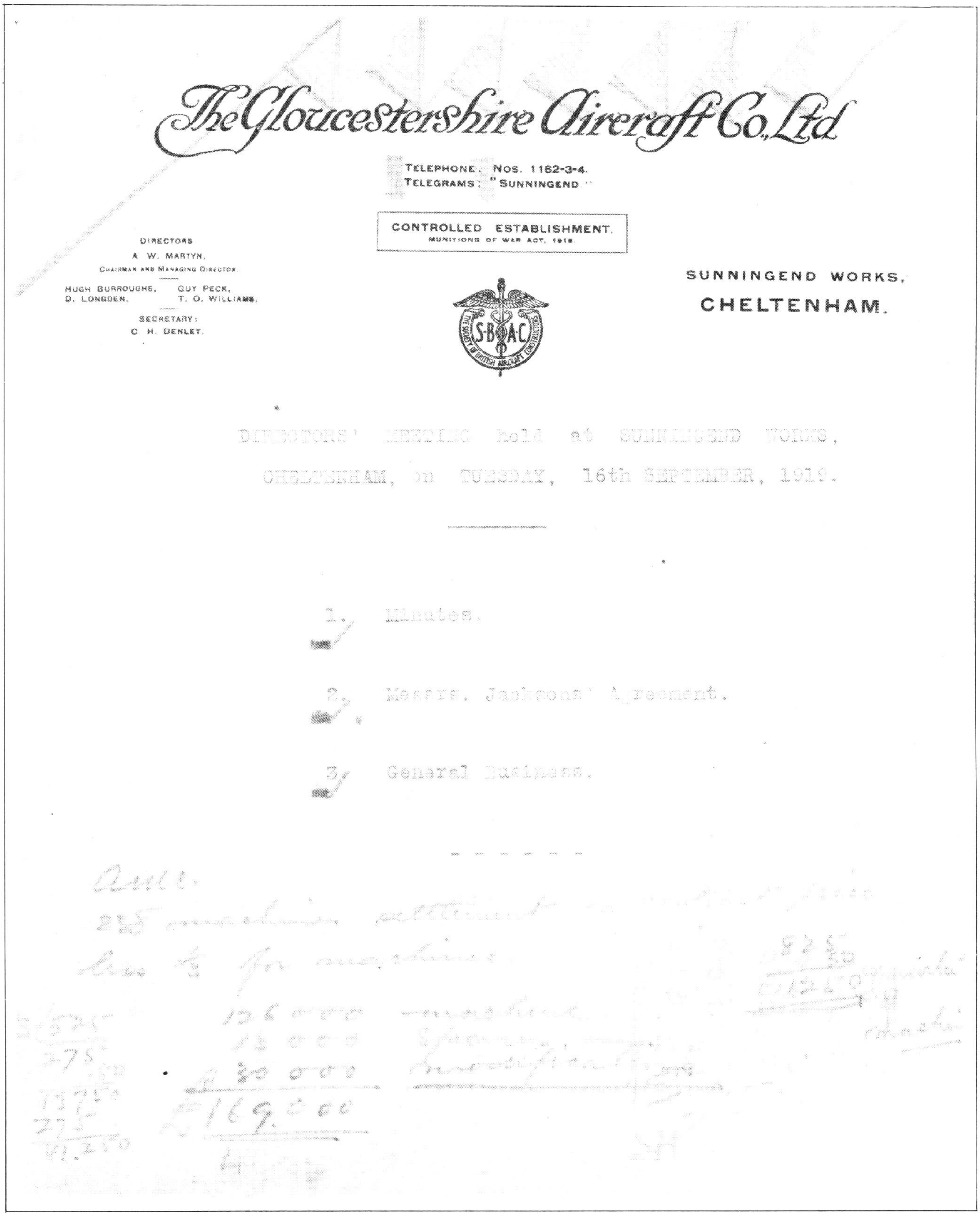

The Gloucestershire Aircraft Co. Ltd

TELEPHONE. NOS. 1162-3-4.
TELEGRAMS: "SUNNINGEND"

CONTROLLED ESTABLISHMENT.
MUNITIONS OF WAR ACT, 1915.

DIRECTORS
A. W. MARTYN,
CHAIRMAN AND MANAGING DIRECTOR.
HUGH BURROUGHS, GUY PECK,
D. LONGDEN, T. O. WILLIAMS.
SECRETARY:
C. H. DENLEY.

S.B.A.C.
THE SOCIETY OF BRITISH AIRCRAFT CONSTRUCTORS

SUNNINGEND WORKS,
CHELTENHAM.

DIRECTORS' MEETING held at SUNNINGEND WORKS,
CHELTENHAM, on TUESDAY, 16th SEPTEMBER, 1919.

1. Minutes.

2. Messrs. Jacksons' Agreement.

3. General Business.

AMC.
825 machine settlement
less 1/3 for machines

126 000 machines
13 000 spares
30 000 modification
£169 000

825
275
1375
275
41.250

Early letterhead and agenda complete with jottings.

Tinsmith Department, 1922. Albert Mills centre in white apron, Bob Wyatt left foreground and Jack Crankshaw right foreground.

Wolseley car assembly 1922/3.

Unfortunately, this youthful market did not exist in 1920. The minibus, as it was named, with its bucket seat, shaft drive, aluminium disc wheels, sprung front forks and rear wheel and a number of other advanced features failed to find a market and the project was abandoned.

As contract work for aircraft declined it was evident to the directors that if they were to remain in aircraft production an experienced designer was needed. In January 1921 H.P. Folland was persuaded to act as consultant engineer designer to develop the Nighthawk for production at Sunningend. At this time Folland was still working for part of his time for the Nieuport Company, which was being wound up. In 1920 the board of directors of the Gloucestershire Aircraft Company consisted of A.W. Martyn, chairman and managing director, G. Turner, T.O. Williams, and now rejoining the board, David Longden and Hugh Burroughes. The directors decided to ensure that the company was recognised by the Ministry of Aircraft Production, a source of valuable orders, by winning a reputation for high speed aircraft.

H.P. Folland was certainly the right choice, as he had a conception for streamlining to reduce drag which was well ahead of his contemporaries. His reputation for designing fast aircraft was international. He was known as the king of racing aircraft designers and 'the man who made a too fast machine' following his design in 1914 of the SE4 which the authorities thought too fast at 135 mph. He also developed the famous SE5 and designed the SE5a, the Nieuport Nighthawk and the Goshawk, which on its first flight broke the British Speed Record at 166.5 mph.

On 1st August 1921 Folland joined the Gloucestershire Aircraft Co. as chief engineer and designer bringing with him most of his design team including H.E. Preston, a specialist on stresses. The new team immediately set out to design the first of the company's racing bi-planes, the Mars I/Bamel which was based on the Nighthawk design. The Mars I/Bamel was a great success and holds a number of records, not least that it was conceived, built and flown in less than four weeks. The Mars I/Bamel GEAXZ was entered in the Aerial Derby of 17th July 1921 and won at 163.3 mph, piloted by Gloster's first test pilot, J.H. James. On 12th December the Bamel, again piloted by J.H. James, set a British air speed record of 196.4 mph.

On 7th August 1922 the Bamel and J.H. James won the Aerial Derby at 177.85 mph and on 6th August 1923 the Bamel won the aerial Derby for the third year running, this time at 192.4 mph and with a new pilot, L.L. Carter.

These early successes were a great boost for the company, owing much to the skill of H.P. Folland and his team in re-designing to reduce drag, and of course to the skill of John James and Larry Carter in getting the best performance from the aircraft. These successes firmly established

David Longden receiving the Aerial Derby trophy, won by the Gloster Mars I Bamel three times in the early 1920s.

Bamel being lifted from Ford towing vehicle after its journey from Cheltenham to Gloucester.

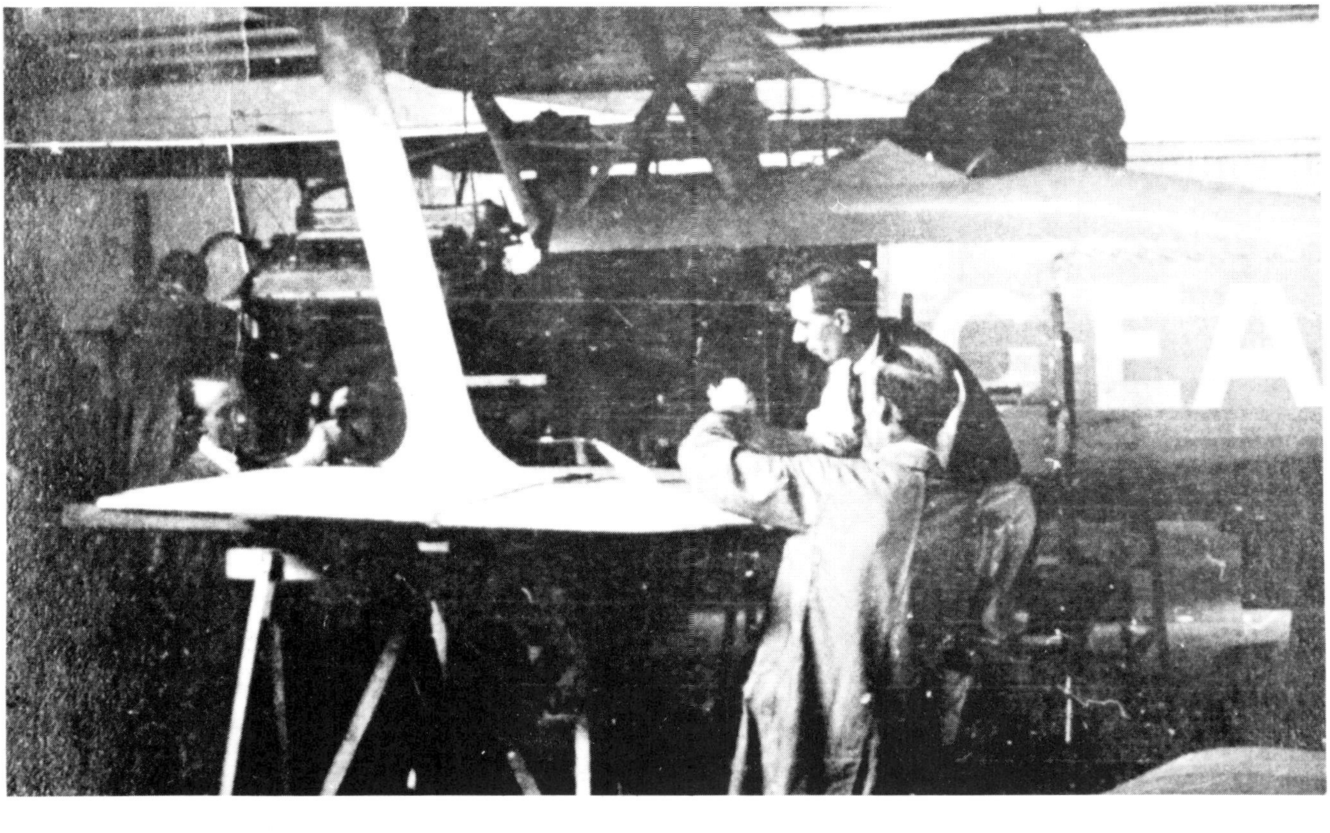

Mars I Bamel: Erecting Shop, Sunningend, 1923, left to right — T. Jones, T. Stinchcombe, Bert Brice working on the Bamel.

the Gloucestershire Aircraft Company as a leading pioneer in high speed flight in the United Kingdom and focussed the attention of the Air Board on the Company, with the result that they received the official stamp of ministry approval: the appointment of an A.I.D. approved works inspector.

The unusual nickname Bamel attached to the Mars I came from Hugh Burroughes remarking to Harry Folland that the fuselage in its half canvased state in which he saw it was 'half bear' and with the hump of the fuel tank up front — 'half camel', so this hybrid animal the 'Bamel' was adopted as the unofficial motif for the racing team and appeared on the cockpit side, John James riding it with scarf flying in the wind.

Of course the main aim in designing to win races and break records was the eventual production of military aircraft in quantity for the Air Ministry. The spectacular performance of the Gamecock in 1925 brought orders both from the Ministry and overseas. Thirty Gamecocks were ordered by the Ministry, at a cost of £79,500, and in 1926 No. 23 Squadron, Henlow, took its first aircraft. A further 58 Gamecocks were ordered at a cost of £145,600. Aircraft were delivered to Nos. 3 and 17 Squadrons at Upavon, Nos. 32 and 23 Squadrons at Kenley and No. 43 at Tangmere.

The Gamecock was popular at air displays both with pilots and the public, and the R.A.F. gave notable displays with it at Hendon from 1926 to 1931. In 1927 the Gamecock demonstrated its racing pedigree by taking the first three places in the race for the Sassoon Cup, the winner averaging 156 mph. In 1931 a fine display was given of integrated aerobatics by Flt. Lieut. M.M. Day and Pilot Officer D.R.S. Bader in two Gamecocks. An order from Finland for two Gamecock aircraft resulted later in the aircraft being produced in quantity in Finland under contract. The Imperial Japanese Air Force were eager customers: 30 Mars II, 10 Mars III and 10 Mars IV aircraft were ordered. Later they produced the Gambet under contract. New Zealand ordered three Grebes.

The early days in Cheltenham ensured that the factory space of Martyns at Sunningend and the work force were both utilised to the full, since men and space could be easily transferred either to aircraft or to architectural work. Photographs show each type of work going on side by side in some parts of the factory. However, it became necessary as the aircraft work increased that more factory space and closer runway facilities were needed, so over a period of about five years beginning in 1925 and culminating at the end of 1929 Gloster's one thousand employees were finally established in the Hucclecote factory, Gloucester. Glosters was now, in the words of the Gloucester Journal, 'one of the biggest and most important air industries in the British Isles.' Unfortunately, the founder, A.W. Martyn, retired,

Gloster Mars I Bamel at Croydon 1923 after winning the Aerial Derby. H. Folland holding wing tip right-hand side, pilot Larry Carter.

somewhat unwillingly it is believed, from both Glosters and H.H. Martyn & Co. in September 1927 and did not take any further part in either company though as already described he did re-enter the aircraft world with George Dowty in 1936 when he became chairman of Aircraft Components Ltd. later Dowty Equipment Ltd.

The Gloucestershire Aircraft Co. changed its name to Gloster Aircraft Co. in 1926, for the benefit of its overseas customers who found 'Gloucestershire' confusing to pronounce and spell.

The 1920s were particularly exciting years for all who worked at Martyns and Glosters, as in those days a man engaged in work on an aircraft was more likely to see the finished article and have a personal sense of achievement in its flight.

The Schneider Trophy racing sea planes were all built in Cheltenham, even after Glosters had completely moved to Hucclecote. The usual pair of aircraft for the race were hand built by Martyns in Cheltenham, a fact not generally known but confirmed to me by men who worked personally on the aircraft.

Many experimental aircraft were built over the years as 'private venture' projects unconnected with ministry contracts though prompted in some cases by ministry specifications, as a result of which most of these one-off aircraft have a familiar look to them. Gloster T.S.R.38 appeared much like the Fairey Swordfish, the plane which eventually won the ministry contract. The Gloster F 9/37, George Carter's first design for Glosters tends to look more like the Blenheim than the Bolton Paul Defiant which met the aimed at Ministry specification.. Others included the Gannet, built in 1923, the smallest at only 16' x 18'; Guan, 1925, two built; Goral, 1926, one built; Goring, 1926, one built; Goldfinch, 1927, the first to incorporate a metal structure, one built; Gambet, 1927, one built, (150 built by Japanese on contract); AS31, 1929, two built and used for photographic survey by the Aircraft Operating Co. Ltd., for ordnance survey work; TC 33, 1931, bomber/transport, one built; TSR 38, 1931, one built; F 5/34, 1936, two built; F 9/37, 1938, two built; E 28/39, first Allied jet to fly, 1941, two built; E 1/44 jet, six prototypes built. Many other designs only reached the drawing board stage but each advanced in greater or lesser degree vital knowledge which enabled the achievement of more successful flight at each subsequent step.

The Schneider Trophy particularly helped with valuable technical development and was of world-wide interest, bringing national prestige to the winning country and distinction to the company which built the plane. It was an event of great importance and held in high esteem in the aircraft world. Glosters unfortunately never won the event though it did come second at Baltimore in 1925. The airframe was only part of the story, a reliable engine being equally important, and Glosters failed to win not on design of airframe, which was excellent, but on repeated engine failure. The high standard of airframe design was shown in the speed record taken by Glosters and still held to this day of 277.1 mph by a float bi-plane at the 1927 Venice Schneider Trophy Contest.

The Gloster IV had to retire soon after breaking the record with a split propeller shaft. Flt. Lt. Kinkead was fortunate in that he detected the fault in time and landed safely. The other two Gloster IVs were unable to fly due again to persistent engine troubles. For what proved to be the final Schneider Trophy contest, H.P. Folland designed probably his finest aircraft, the Gloster VI. Named the Golden Arrow, it looked every inch a winner and was Folland's first venture into mono-plane design. One newspaper reported: "It seems more the conception of an artist who can make and create his own lines by the stroke of a brush, than the work of a designer who is bound by the principles of engineering and the comparative inelasticity of metal and timber. The Gloster Aircraft Company has never produced a finer example of aircraft construction and it is an outstanding testimony to the high standard of

The aircraft supplied to the Royal Air Force Fleet Air Arm were:

	MARS VI	MARS X	GREBE II	GAME COCK II	GAUNTLET I	GAUNTLET II
R.A.F.	4		129	82	24	204
Fleet Air Arm		22				

	GLADIATOR I	GLADIATOR II	SEA GLADIATOR INTERIM	SEA GLADIATOR II
R.A.F.	231	252		
Fleet Air Arm			38	60

	METEOR F & NF	METEOR FR	METEOR PR	METEOR T	JAVELIN FAG	JAVELIN T
R.A.F.	2,354	126	58	602	407	23
Fleet Air Arm	3			38		

Totals: R.A.F. 4,496
Fleet Air Arm 161

Gloster VI Golden Arrow at Calshot 1929. Two built at Sunningend. Held world speed record of 336 m.p.h. N.249 painted-fuselage Cambridge blue, wings and tail unit bronze, floats and struts white.

Gloster Napier IV for Schneider Trophy Contest, Venice, built at Sunningend Works, Cheltenham 1926.

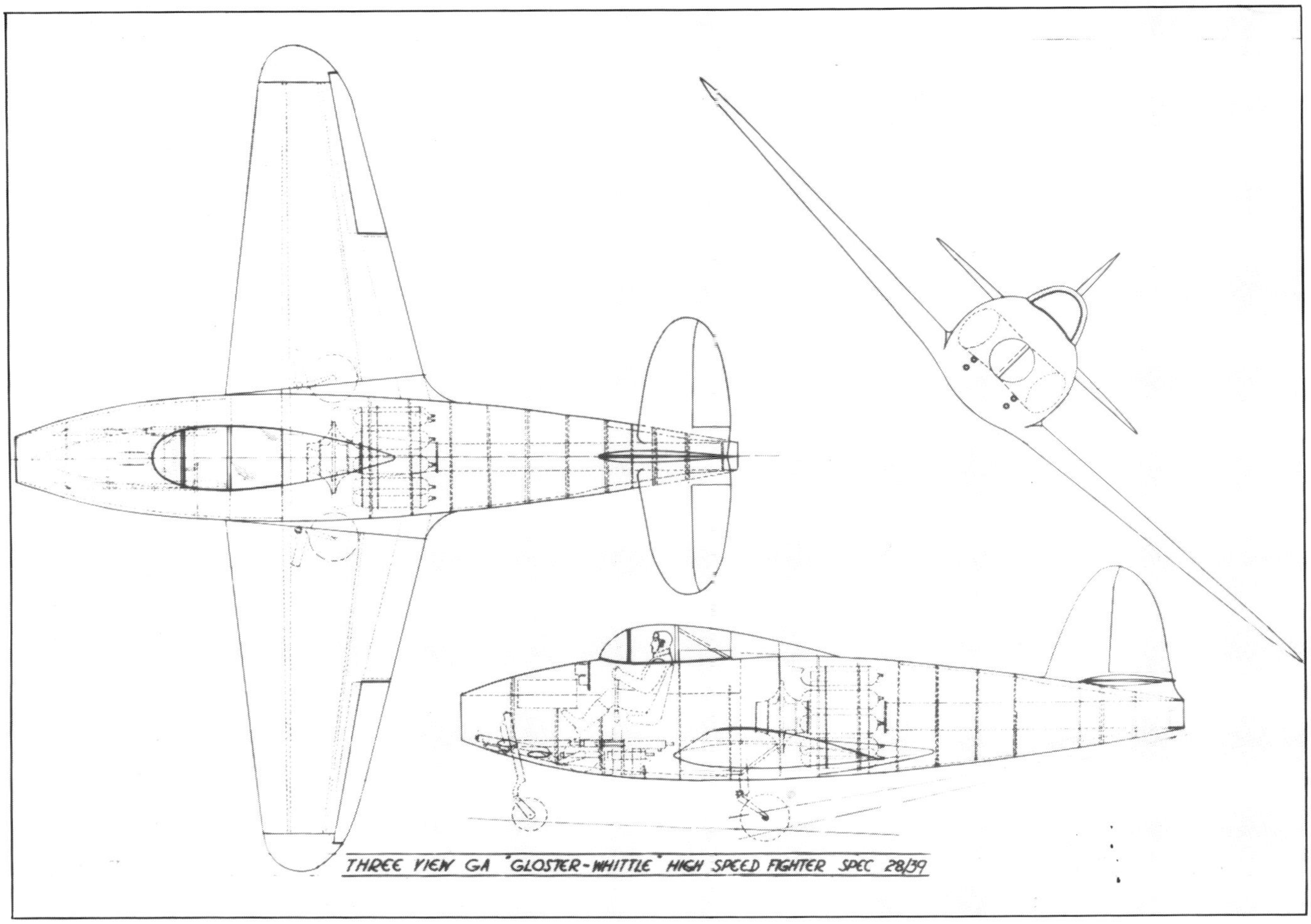

Drawings for Gloster-Whittle.

Gloster-Whittle E28/39 the world's first jet-propelled aircraft to be successfully developed. First flight 15th May, 1941.

their workshop practice just as the design itself is a triumph for Mr. H.P. Folland and Mr. H.E. Preston." This potentially fast aircraft was also plagued with engine failure and the Napier Lion engine cut out whenever the plane turned steeply, a manoeuvre constantly required on the circuit.

The Gloster VI flown by Fl. Lt. G.H. Stainforth attained an average speed of 336.3 mph, notified as an Absolute Speed Record, but this was later broken by the Supermarine flown by Sqdn. Ldr. A.H. Orlebar, which won the 1929 race outright in spite of being withdrawn from the race at Cowes in 1929. The Gloster VI took part in the Lord Mayor's Show in the procession through London on 9th November, a fitting accolade to the company and the men who had contributed so much to aircraft design, production and development and who were to contribute even more in the forthcoming years of the war of 1939 to 1945.

Henry Folland designed 30 types of aircraft during his time with Glosters, manufacturing some 1300 planes from 1921 when he joined to 1937 when he left the Company. One of his many successful designs was the Gloster Grebe, ordered in quantity for the R.A.F., prior to which it was used for experimental work with the Hele-Shaw Beecham two blade variable pitch propeller. Another experiment was the memorable launching of two Gloster Grebes from the airship R.33 on October 21st 1926. At 2500 ft. over Norfolk the first Grebe was released piloted by Flying Officer R.L. Ragg, the second at a greater height flown by Flying Officer C. Mackenzie-Richards. Both engines were started by a Bristol Gas Starter prior to release and dived for about 100 feet before levelling off to land at Pulham.

Glosters built under contract for other companies. Documents state that on September 22nd 1927 Armstrong Whitworth Aircraft signed an agreement for the production of Siskin III aircraft, on July 7th 1928 Westland Aircraft Works ordered steel wings for the Wapiti and on March 18th 1930 Societa Aeroplani Ugo Antoni agreed patent rights for the 'Widgeon' aircraft.

A number of patents were taken out on behalf of employees and were often adopted by Glosters. Gordon Weston Charley invented in January 1930 'Improved riveted and bolted joints', Pat No. 326235 purchased by the Gloster Aircraft Company for £25.0s.0d. H.P. Folland and H.E. Preston, the company's aircraft designers, appear in documents from 1922 to 1929 to have been credited with eight inventions covering aircraft controls, shock absorbers, highlift wings and radiators. Steel wing patents brought the company £575 in 1930 for an amazing list of inventions, 73 in all. In 1931, 59 patents realised £633.0s.0d. Gloster Aircraft and Hele-Shaw Beecham variable pitch propellors had patents on licence in 30 countries including Argentina, India, Russia and Japan.

Glosters continued to produce many fine R.A.F. service fighters, such as the Gauntlet and the better known Gladiator, and later the Meteor and Javelin. The first jet plane to fly for the Allies was Gloster designed and built. Designated the E 28/39, it was designed by George Carter with the close collaboration of Frank Whittle and first flew on 15th May 1941. R.E.G. Sayer, Gloster's chief test pilot, flew E28/39 in the initial trial flights but was tragically killed on 21st October when his Typhoon crashed into the sea off Northumberland. Michael Daunt was able to carry on the trials on E 28/39 as fortunately Sayer had kept him closely informed of progress.

Flying prototypes is always hazardous, as can be seen from the records of Gloster test pilots. The early pilots, however, must rank as special pioneers in the art of flying. Their first job was not to test but to find out if the aircraft would fly at all.

John James was Gloster's first test pilot from 1919 to 1923 and successfully flew the Mars I Bamel to victory in the Aerial Derby on 17th July 1921 and 7th August 1922. He also set the British Air Speed Record of 196.4 mph on 12th December 1921. He was the first in a line of extraordinary men who flew for Glosters. Larry Carter, who worked for the company from 1923 to 1926, won the Aerial Derby in the Bamel on 6th August 1923, and also in 1923 won the Kings Cup Air Race flying a Grebe, GEBHA. He died in 1926 15 months after sustaining serious head injuries when in June 1925 at Cranwell Aerodrome he crashed a Gloster II making a forced landing. At his funeral Maurice Piercey flew a Gamecock in circles high above the cemetery as a mark of respect to a great flyer.

L.L. Carter, test pilot for Glosters, died Spetember 1926 aged 28 years.

Gloster II at Felixstowe. 1924 trials.

Gloster III at Cranwell, 1924, prior to speed trials flight and subsequent crash.

British Schneider Trophy team on the way to Baltimore on board the S.S. Minnewaska 1925.

Gloster III trial flight Baltimore 1925.

Piercey was test pilot for Glosters from 1926 to 1927, followed by Howard Saint, from 1927 to 1935; he probably flew more Gloster types than any other pilot, fourteen in all, from Grebes and Gamecocks to Gauntlets and Gladiators. The names of Gloster's test pilots are many, thirty or more, a special breed of men of rare talent and courage.

One of the many new skills which were quickly learnt by Martyns craftsmen was the making of wooden propellers. From the early days of the first world war through to the change from wood to metal and the formation of V.P. Airscrews Ltd. prior to the 1939-1945 war, wooden propellers were made in their hundreds, probably thousands, at Martyns. I must here thank Mr. Kenneth Brookes, who has given me so much help on every aspect of this book, not least with his marvellous memory, in finding rare photographs and information and in providing technical paintings of Gloster aircraft types which he produced himself. The authentic colours are well researched and in most cases unique, there being no colour photographs of the older types. He has also written technical material for me.

Ken Brookes had a long association with Martyns and Glosters which began with his own father's employment at Martyns. Fred Brookes started in the early 1900's in the High Street as storeman, and later became chief time-keeper and interviewer of prospective employees at Sunningend. Today he would be called a personnel manager and he was with the company for 43 years. Through Fred Brookes' position in the company he was able to take his son Ken, at the age of 12, into the factory to see the Gloster IV, the 1926 Schneider racing seaplane, painted and ready in her racing trim, a unique and exciting sight. The impression this made on Ken Brookes was dramatic. He has since had a lasting love of aircraft and a keen determination that this great piece of Cheltenham's history should not be forgotten. His enthusiasm has been a spur to me.

Ken joined Martyns early in 1928 as an apprentice cabinet joiner. However, his first job was helping to make ribs for Grebe and Gamecock aircraft wings, then on to their assembly and propeller making, moving from department to department as the work dictated. He also worked on ship interiors, his first assignment being staircases, panelling, columns and furniture for the Orontes. He also produced ecclesiastical work, including choirstalls, pulpits and screens. Almost his first job was on Westminster Cathedral choir stalls, made in Austrian Oak, which was considered the best wood, having a closer grain than other oaks.

Glosters' move to Hucclecote, which began in 1925 and was complete by 1930, meant that work ceased in Cheltenham on aircraft. Art work also fell off as the Depression began to bite. When not busy, the men made tools for their own and company use and carvers would work on Gibbons style of carving. In 1934 Maples took over Martyns and the men, Ken Brookes remembers, were at the time working on the Preston and Barnsley Civic Centre, and also on furniture and fittings for the P & O liner Queen Mary. Maples' interest in taking over Martyns was probably prompted by the prospect of getting a foot into the shipping side of the business, which was now considerable. The take-over was not popular with the men.

In 1939 Ken Brookes moved to G.A.C. Brockworth working on Gladiators, Henleys, and Hurricanes as an aircraft woodworker. He was involved with the Gloster/Whittle E 28/39 and later the Meteor as toolroom inspector and with Javelins as design office draftsman. Ken's sight of his first plane back in the 1920s led him into a fascinating career, both as a craftsman in wood and at the drawing board. A draughtsman who could actually form a wooden propeller must be rare indeed. He described the making of propellers in wood to me:— "Having established the length and width of the propeller required the timber is then one of the most important items to be considered. During the War 1914—1918 and also in the 1920s and early 1930s, Honduras mahogany was used. On some occasions 1″ thick French walnut boards alternated with mahogany. Only first class selected wood was used. It was very straight grained and beautiful to work. The

Landing stage area Schneider Trophy Race day, Bayshore Park, Baltimore 1925, illustrationg some of the chaos after storms.

preparation for forming then started. These boards approximately 1″ thick which were previously planed were toothed with a toothing plane to form a key. Having taken out any bumps or hollows on the surface of these boards they were then 'sized' with diluted very thin glue. This was to retard the hot glue penetrating the grain. When this 'size' had dried hard it was then ready for glueing and pressing. The glue used was a special aircraft glue called 'Croid'. The boards had to be kept warm to allow the glue to run while being pressed. The press at H.H. Martyns in the 1920s was a bit primitive compared to the present day electrically operated press. It was all done by hand and clamped down by huge spanners. Having left these staggered boards overnight, (roughly the shape of the propeller) the glue was allowed to set hard for approximately two days. It was then ready for shaping. A hole the diameter of the driving shaft of the engine was drilled exactly in the centre of the block outline. This hole was also used to fix the block to a bench for working. Along this bench at 9″ stations out from the centre hole each way to the tip of the blade was a mark where the templates were positioned for shaping below the datum line or almost flat surface side of the propeller.

"Careful shaping was required at this stage to ensure accuracy. When all of these templates of varying sizes had been finally shaped into position, using half round rasps and files, the surplus timber would be roughed off by a 1″ wood chisel and mallet, down to the shapes previously made. Small block planes and spokeshaves were then used to clean up the under face of the blade and finally a cabinet scraper and sandpaper to bring it to a fine finish for varnishing. The propeller would then be turned over and the above datum surface similarly treated to form a perfect aerofoil. The length marked equally from the centre line of hub to tip was determined by a line on the bench surface and cut to length. The tip shape was also made by a template to the necessary requirement.

"Finally, after being brought up to a fine finish and then varnished, around five or six 3/8″ diameter holes were drilled with a drill jig to accommodate the bolts for fixing on to the driving shaft."

It was aircraft production which probably saved Martyns at the outbreak of war in 1914 by providing work for men and machinery but it was almost its downfall as well. At the end of the 1914-1918 war the Government was quick to cancel orders placed for aircraft and also frequently changed specifications. The Ministry had on 21st November 1918 switched its order of 16th October 1918 to supply 300 Sopwith Snipe machines, to 300 Nieuport Nighthawks. Unfortunately the Sopwith A.B.C. Dragon Fly engines were not suitable for the Nighthawks. At the time the Ministry of Munitions of War, Air Group, said in a letter dated 1st October 1918:— "Please note that the Sopwith Snipe is considered one of the most important machines in the field today." By November 1918 the Sopwith was being fitted with the B.R.2. engine, and fortunately the Nieuport Nighthawks required the same engine. David Longden's report on the affair states:— "On 11th September 1919 and before we had completed a single machine, and without any previous information whatsoever, we received a telegram from the Liquidation of Aircraft Contracts Committee to the effect that "your contract for the Nighthawk aeroplanes was cancelled and that all work is to cease and in view of the signing of the Armistice you are to transfer from war to peace industries at the earliest possible moment. With a view to avoiding waste material, Mr. Churchill instructs me to give you two month's notice .... 20th September 1919 .... take stock .... and submit your claim for compensation." On 12th September a further telegram reduced the contract to 50 machines; the 11th September's telegram was sent in error. So from 300 in the original contract the order was reduced to 50 machines.

David Longden met General Alexander, chairman of the Liquidation of Aircraft Contracts Committee in London, to explain that the company had laid out £160,000 to £180,000 for components

Propeller making at Sunningend Works during the first world war.

Propeller finishing and balancing at Sunningend. A.I.D. Inspector in uniform, centre.

Flight section and erecting, G.A.C. Brockworth parade in front of a 1924 Gamecock.
Front row from left — H. Austin in charge of flight; P. Fielding, inspector; Larry Carter, pilot; L. Chapel, Siddeley mechanic; Bert Brice, erector.

Gloster Gamecock II 1927, airborne.

and because of repeated modifications required by the Ministry to their design, no aircraft had been completed or paid for. There was a serious difference of opinion over the "fair and reasonable price." The Committee figure was £825 per machine, based on the first design without modifications. After modifications, Glosters' figure was £1,050 per machine. At a further meeting on 26th September 1919 in London with General Alexander, chairman; Mr. Morley Mower, secretary; Mr. George Hoare, assistant to the General; David Longden was informed that they did not now require the 50 Nighthawks completed either!

The cancellation of contracts for planes and spares meant that claims had to be made urgently by the company for compensation; for components bought, work started and the general disruption caused. The long and difficult negotiation with government officials which ensued caused cash flow to become desperate. The banks would not help, since they doubted if the Government would ever pay. A.W. Martyn spent weeks trying in all quarters to raise cash. The company was within days of being unable to pay its workforce and of being forced into liquidation when fortunately cash was found by A.W. Martyn to tide the company over.

The claim for the cancelled Nighthawk contract dragged on from 1919 to 1921. The cash problem was exacerbated by the action of Mr. E. Hartland in 1917. Hartland, of Hardwick Court, Chepstow, had been a useful source of capital for expansion from the early days of Martyns in the High Street. He was known by the workmen as 'Money Bags', made frequent visits to the company offices and while necessary, was not an easy man to deal with. A letter written by A.W. Martyn to his father H.H. from Maisemore, near Gloucester, on January 13th 1917 indicates this. "Under the most favourable circumstances there will be no dividend not even pref. in the next two or three years as Mr. Hartland requires £46,000 to be paid off before any dividend is paid and he is in a position to force this, at any rate at present . . ." (A final document on 30th October 1928 sets out that all repayments had now been made to Mr. Hartland and was signed by his wife Amy and himself. Mr. Hartland signed a document on 21st November 1929, still as a director of H.H. Martyn & Co. Ltd. agreeing to the lease of H.H. Martyn's floor space to Glosters at Sunningend).

On top of Mr. Hartland's request for £46,000 the cancelled Ministry contract was a great blow. £112,500 was paid by the Ministry to the company in September/October 1919 but this did not cover the losses incurred through disturbance of business arising from delays in delivery of materials.

In respect of construction work actually carried out, a further claim of £74,297 was outstanding. However, as part of the settlement of the affair the company purchased from the Air Board a considerable quantity of Nighthawk components which were no longer required by the Ministry. Later these components became the foundation of many aircraft types, including the early racing machines, and also permitted completion of an order for 50 finished Nighthawks and 40 sets of components for assembly in Japan for the Imperial Japanese Air Force.

The purchase of the spare components showed considerable courage and foresight on the part of the G.A.C. board, particularly A.W. Martyn and David Longden, who set up the deal. However, a cash settlement for the remaining claim was still urgent. Add £74,297 to Mr. Hartland's figure of £46,000 and the scale of the problem can be imagined, £120,000 in 1920 being a considerable sum.

The company's solicitors, Joynson-Hicks & Company, London, took out a Petition of Right in the High Court of Justice, King's Bench Division, in April 1921. On 30th July 1921 Sir Gordon Hewart, Attorney General, was delivered the Petition of Right and filed the Crown's answer. In April 1922 the Nieuport Co made a claim against the Gloucestershire Aircraft Co for some infringement on their machines, which compounded an already difficult problem.

When the Petition of Right was down for hearing, Joynson-Hicks Hunt stated that the Treasury Solicitors had made no approach with a view to settlement of the claim. On October 20th 1921 the Treasury Solicitor suggested some compromise and Joynson-Hicks Hunt advised:— "Undoubtedly it will be a great saving of expense and, if the court holds that there was a definite warranty we do not think there would be any difficulty afterwards in agreeing the damages with the Treasury."

On October 25th 1921 A.W. Martyn and David Longden met Joynson-Hicks Hunt at 12 noon at Lennox House, Strand, W.C.2. for discussions. The Treasury Solicitors had been busy at the Air Ministry to 'try to work up a case' but they had been generally advised to settle; an offer was expected to follow.

On December 29th 1921 the case was still due to go to court. Joynson-Hicks Hunt suggested Sir John Simon or Mr. Douglas Hogg "would do the case exceedingly well but would want a 500 guinea fee for the brief. Mr. Stewart Bevan, K.C. would be very able for a smaller fee."

On Friday 22nd March 1922 A.W. Martyn and David Longden again visited Joynson-Hicks Hunt in London for further discussions on the Draft of Evidence. Eventually, some months later, the claim was satisfactorily settled together with a claim for 'excess profits' tax. The Nieuport affair also was satisfactorily concluded without going to court. The correspondence shows how ably David Longden, backed by A.W. Martyn, had brought the lengthy and worrying affair to a satisfactory conclusion.

Another important member of the board of directors of H.H. Martyn and Glosters was Hugh Burroughes, who figured prominently from his original meeting with A.W. Martyn which resulted in the first airframe contracts and the start of aircraft manufacture in Cheltenham. Hugh Burroughes left the board in 1919 for a few years to look after a small engineering company he owned, Chelsea Precision Tools, but he continued his connection with both Glosters and Martyns by representing them in London. A.W. Martyn invited him to rejoin the Board in 1921, recognising his undoubted abilities and the contribution he could make to both companies.

Hugh Burroughes remained a director of both companies until 1958. He and David Longden bought A.W. Martyn's shares in 1927. Hugh Burroughes expressed to me when we met in Cheltenham in 1979 a feeling of self reproach at his and Longden's act in ousting A.W. Martyn, as the price for the shares was pretty low, with payment spread over a number of years. However, good contracts for aircraft came along more quickly than expected and they were both able to pay in full within the year.

The break seemed to have been agreed owing to boardroom differences in which the two younger members were in agreement, and A.W. Martyn felt he should leave and let the younger men run things their way. He was a saddened man at the prospect. However, his original confidence in the capabilities and qualities of David Longden and Hugh Burroughes was borne out, as both companies continued to thrive.

My 1979 meeting with Hugh Burroughes took place at the Queen's Hotel in Cheltenham. He was then about 96 years of age, eyesight undimmed, hand steady, able to write a fine neat script and still with a boundless energy for business. He was just forming a company in Norfolk in the new technology of heat exchange.

A later member of the Gloster Aircraft Co. Board was Brig. General Festing of Hyde House, Chalford, who was originally appointed to the sales staff of H.H. Martyn & Co. on 22nd April 1931 at a salary of £150 per annum, only to relinquish the post on 16th August, 1931, 16 months later "in view of your appointment to the Directorate of the Gloster Aircraft Co. Ltd.," a meteoric rise!

The Gloster Aircraft Co. continued producing fine aircraft for the R.A.F. and Fleet Air Arm, but the story parts from its close connections with H.H. Martyn at the Sunningend works and Cheltenham when it moved to Hucclecote, Gloucester, in 1925 and when 1,000 men transferred to the new works. It was a sad day for Cheltenham but the Mayor of Gloucester was delighted to receive such an influx of potential revenue into his area. Even rail links were offered to be re-installed as a branch line to Gloucester.

In 1937 The Hawker Aircraft Co. took over control of Glosters, and H.P. Folland left to form his own company, Folland Aircraft. Hubert Martyn (nephew of A.W. Martyn) also left to join Folland in his design office. After the war, Glosters regained its independence and produced the Gloster Meteor and Javelin. Glosters was one of the companies which went to form the British Aircraft Corporation (B.A.C.) and the company conceived by A.W. Martyn in 1917 lives on as part of the nation's aircraft industry.

During the 1939—1945 war Glosters produced at Hucclecote: 200 Henleys; 2,750 Hurricanes; the pioneer jet E 28/39; 3,300 Typhoons; and over 200 Meteor Jets, the only aircraft fast enough to catch and destroy the V-I flying bombs.

Through his position as chairman of Dowty Equipment Ltd, A.W. Martyn was well informed of developments in the aircraft industry. He surprised the family early in the war, at the end of an evening meal, by saying that aircraft would soon fly without propellers, a statement which was received with disbelief and countered with arguments. A.W. Martyn just said "wait and see"! His statement was vindicated when jet planes were announced to the public some years later. It is possible that A.W. Martyn may have actually observed an early flight by the Gloster/Whittle E 28/39, which had the Dowty undercarriage fitted.

Experimental Grebe 1923 at Brockworth, Basil Fielding and H. Austin (front seat) aboard.

Just prior to the war, between 1936 and 1939, Glosters produced 228 Gauntlets and 747 Gloster Gladiators, the latter playing a respectable role at the beginning of the war in this country and an heroic one during the siege of Malta.

Two Gladiators flew almost daily throughout the war out over the North Sea at altitudes of 10,000 feet and 20,000 feet to collect weather information. Many others were used for local defence of aerodromes and as trainers. The incredible manoeuvrability of the Gladiator made it popular with pilots. Though slow, with a maximum speed of about 250 mph, it was successful against the Luftwaffe in Norway and against the German and Italian Air Forces in Malta.

The link between H.H. Martyn, Sunningend, Cheltenham and the Gloucestershire Aircraft Co./Gloster Aircraft Co. may seem to be an unlikely union between art and war but a close link there was. Business necessity, the insight of A.W. Martyn and his colleagues on the board and the ability of shop floor managers to adapt and improvise the skill of the workforce combined to produce outstanding aircraft from Mars I Bamel to the Javelin — 200 mph in 1920 to over 600 mph in the '50s.

The second world war saw the reintroduction of work on aircraft by H.H. Martyn & Co. through its associated company H.H. Martyn (Aircraft) Ltd., also at Sunningend Works. On 5th August 1941, an agreement was made for the Ministry to provide certain machine tools and install them for the production of aircraft components. The work was different from that of the 1914—1918 war; this time there was more metal work involving lathes and milling, pressing and riveting machines, all of which in 1945 were offered by the Ministry for sale to the company. The actual parts made are not listed but insurance documents show that parts worth £25,000 were sent to Chester, Blackpool, Reading and Bristol. In 1940, £50,000 worth of parts were sent to Reading over a period from March to October.

G.T.L. Summers joined Martyns in 1935 as a skilled joiner, having served his time with a company in Worcester. He remembers working under foreman Bert Brown on the portico for the palace of King Carol of Rumania. He also remembers re-making the portico as the ship which was carrying the original one was sunk.

In 1939 Summers was seconded to H.H. Martyn (Aircraft) Ltd., then under Reg Parrot as foreman. Parts were made for aircraft and even boats in wood, Martyns' traditional material; Mosquito tail units, which took skilled men about 120 hours to make; cockpits for Horsa Gliders I and II, used in the landing of troops at Arnhem and on D Day; and the bridges of MTBs and rescue boats, which were transported to Southampton for fitting. H.H. Martyn (Aircraft) Ltd. made wings for the Armstrong Whitworth Albermarle, which was used for towing gliders, wings and rudder fins for Miles Magister and Miles Master training aircraft and bomb racks for Wellingtons. Women were also back, engaged in the old skills of covering airframes with Medapelin canvas and applying dope, and even making camouflage netting.

As in the first world war, Martyns was again called upon to turn its skills to war work, a job it did admirably. What a disaster for the workforce that there was no latter-day A.W. Martyn to build on new skills and contacts to create yet more industry for the area — boat building, perhaps.

T.A. Miller, who joined Martyns as chief surveyor in 1947 after returning from work in India, was given the job of closing down H.H. Martyn (Aircraft) Ltd, which at the time had been engaged in making parts for Mosquito aircraft. Later Mr. Miller was appointed contracts director, a position he held until the final closedown. One of his early projects was the making of floors for the 'pre-fabs' which were so vital for the rehousing of the nation after the war. This was a useful contract and another new product for the versatile workforce.

G.A.C. drawing office 1926. George Dowty, later Sir George Dowty, third on the left looking up.

Gloster A.5.31 air survey plane, 1931 — two built.

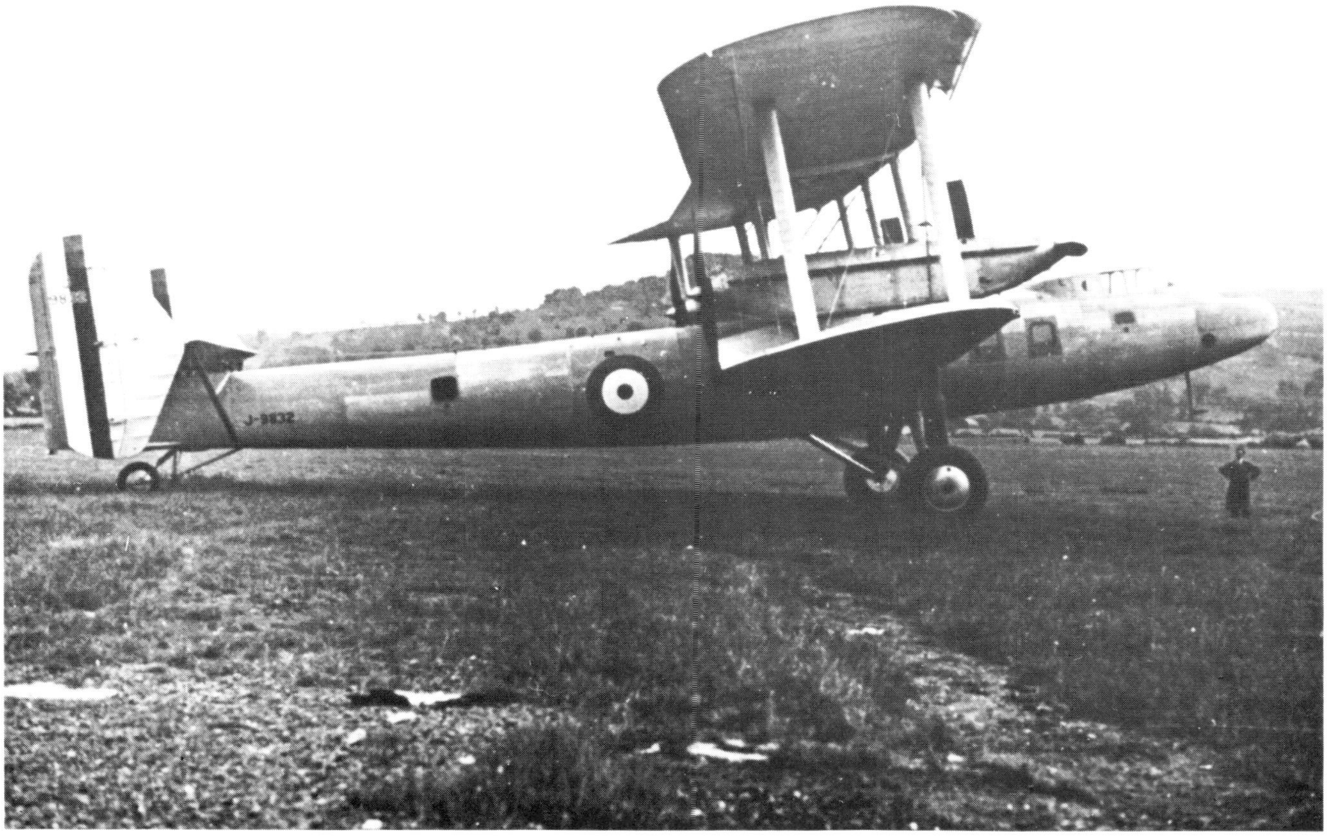

T.C.33 Troop carrier, 1931, the largest aircraft built by Glosters.

Gloster Gladiator in flight over Gloucester.

Gloster S.S.19.B. 'Multigun' (prototype Gauntlet).

Gloster Javelin T.MK.3.

Telegrams: "Glosaircra. Phone, Gloucester."
" Piccy, London.

Station: Gloucester { L.M.& S.R. / G.W.R.

Codes
A.B.C. 5th. Ed. & Bentley's.
Telephones:
Barnwood 6294-5-6-7.

GLOSTER AIRCRAFT Co. Ltd.
GLOSTER WORKS & AERODROME
HUCCLECOTE
GLOS.

Contractors to The British Air Ministry and Foreign Governments.

CHAIRMAN:
F. S. SPRIGGS, F.I.S.A.

JOINT MANAGING DIRECTORS:
T.O.M. SOPWITH, C.B.E., F.R.Ae.S.
F. SIGRIST, M.B.E., F.R.Ae.S.

SUBSIDIARY COMPANY:
STEEL WING CO. LTD.

DIRECTORS:
H. BURROUGHES.
F. I. BENNETT.
D. LONGDEN.

REFERENCE HB/ER.

LONDON OFFICE: 3, ST. JAMES'S SQUARE, LONDON, S.W.1.
(Telephone: WHITEHALL 5081)
All communications to be addressed to the firm and not to Individuals.

PLEASE REPLY TO THE LONDON OFFICE

12th August 1938.

Gloster Aircraft letterhead, 1938.

Gloster Meteors MK.F.8.

H.H. Martyn, who lived until 1937, must have observed the quite incredible growth of the Gloster Aircraft Co. and Martyns with some wonder and at least a little pride in the fact that a company founded on his skills as a carver and subsequently as a businessman should have risen to such immense success and international prestige. It was indeed a far cry from his poverty-stricken childhood and early youth. His son, A.W., must also have taken satisfaction in the continued progress of his 'baby', as Dowty supplied the undercarriages for the Gloster types and the Gloster-built Hurricanes.

Stained glass window, Hognaston Church, Derbyshire.

Chapter 8

STAINED GLASS

To add yet further to the range of services offered to architects and other clients, the stained glass department was started soon after the first world war. As with other departments the best artists and managers were sought to ensure that only the finest would be produced for the cream of clients now seeking work from Martyns. Victorian stained glass was generally poor and had lost its lively quality and artistic interest with mass production. However, the man who was recruited by Martyns to run the stained glass department, Sidney H. Meteyard, had the determination and skill to raise the standard of glass work from its Victorian decline back to its former art and glory. Hours would be spent selecting the right shade of glass for the particular piece in the picture to give tone, light and colour gradations. Even the lead pattern was important and the designs striking.

Sydney Meteyard was a teacher at the Birmingham School of Art and it was in this capacity that he first met B.P. Arnold and saw his drawings. The stained glass department was well-established in October 1919 when B.P. Arnold joined Martyns as a skilled worker in stained glass. Arnold had been at the Birmingham School of Art for a spell after he was discharged from the Army. He had served in France in the R.A.M.C. as stretcher bearer, was gassed and as a consequence of his service was awarded the Military Medal. His artistic talents began to emerge while his feet were in the mud of the Western Front, where he drew and sketched his comrades and his surroundings. It was these drawings which came to the notice of the staff of the Birmingham School of Art, in particular Sydney Meteyard, who encouraged him and started him on his artistic career.

Those working in the stained glass department at the outset were a small and select team. Sydney Meteyard, who had retained his own studios in Birmingham, was in charge. He was a designer and artist of the highest order. Wallace Beck was another, already skilled in the art, having had his own stained glass business in Cheltenham for many years before he joined Martyns' stained glass department when it opened. Beck's work can be seen in most of the churches in Cheltenham and the surrounding area. He started his own business up again when Martyns closed the department after less than ten years. It was a great blow to all concerned when the department closed, but insufficient work could be found to keep it going. Mr. Muckley, another member of the team, was a specialist in producing the effects in the glass for the heads, hands and faces of the figures.

Several young men were recruited from the Birmingham School and trained in the various aspects of the craft, each member of the team producing his part of the whole. First, Sydney Meteyard would produce scale drawings 1″ to 1′, elaborately coloured, showing his interpretation of the suggested subject. When these had been approved by the client and/or architect he would then produce a full size cartoon, a beautiful drawing showing accurately all details of faces, hands, drapery, ornaments and accessories and architectural features. The team at Sunningend then set to work to translate this drawing into glass.

The glass available was of high quality and of a wide variety of types to obtain the various effects required. Density and thickness varied so that at times two pieces might be sandwiched together to obtain a subtle colour or effect. Flashed glass was produced as required in the kiln. Flashing consisted of 'veneering' coloured glass on to a clear or white glass which could then be modified by grinding or by etching with hydrofluoric acid to reveal the white base, a useful procedure for showing pearls on vestments and in heraldic work. The other type of glass was known as pot-metal, in which the colour persists all through.

Beautiful colour and accidental variations of great charm could be found. A yellow silverstain ranging from pale lemon to deep orange was used and the resultant tone varied according to the temperature of the firing of the kiln. Other colours were obtained by firing various mixtures of iron oxide and flux, looking much like ground chocolate, to give effect to the folds of drapery, details of scrolls and inscriptions. Two firings were often required as some density could be lost when the two elements first fused together.

Once selected, the glass had to be cut to shape and size allowing for the intervening strip of lead, a very skilled part of the work as if the correct allowances were not made the finished work would be much too big for the available space. The lead was of 'H' section and once the glass was fitted the final job would be to coax some fat, suet or black-lead into the joints and edges of the lead to keep out the rain or damp. Bernard Arnold, now in his 90s, kindly described to me his impressions and memories of Martyns' stained glass department in 1919:

"The studio itself had been opened some little time before I arrived, and I was disappointed not to have been there at the very beginning of things for all the appointments were quite perfect and much time and money must have been spent on assembling and equipment. The rooms were on the top floor of the works, where maximum daylight was available. The glass was of the highest quality, and the other accessories such as the kilns for firing the glass when painted, and benches for cutting and leading and general finishing, all in perfect position and order. These conditions did not change or deteriorate during the whole time I was there and it was a sad day when we had to leave them."

Following the war, memorial windows were in great demand all over the country. Mr. Arnold remembers the first piece entrusted to him, an armoured knight, St. Michael, for a window in Troon, Ayrshire. There followed a large window in Scarborough and others in Stow-on-the-Wold, Glos., and Petersfield, Hampshire. Many more were produced but their whereabouts now are not known. Wally Beck, Bernard Arnold and Sidney Meteyard all became life-long friends, but they went their separate ways after the closedown.

Bernard Arnold joined the man who found him his position at Martyns, sculptor and architect Walter Gilbert, founder of the Bromsgrove Guild in 1890 (closed 1953), a man whose name and reputation crop up again and again in connection with Martyns. An agreement made on 12th October 1918 shows how close was Walter Henry Gilbert's association with Martyns. At this time he was living at 8 Calthorpe Road, Edgbaston, Birmingham, and was appointed assistant manager of the company for five years at a salary of £450 per annum rising to £600 plus expenses. Within one month of his appointment Walter Gilbert was made art managing director, but without a seat on the board. He was to have the opportunity to go to the United States if the company extended its interests there. His main brief was to obtain orders, see clients, advise on pricing and supervise all work secured by him and carried out in the company's studios. Walter Gilbert remained a staunch, able and loyal employee and good friend of the company for years.

Bernard Arnold continues his artistic career at 90, painting, some of his work still being influenced by his fascination with stained glass.

Few of the venues where Martyns stained glass now resides have been located. I hope that in time, through interest generated by these notes, more people will come forward with information.

Venues known apart from those in the text are:

Ship decorative work
Hognaston Church, Derbyshire
Newlands Church, Langside, Scotland — Victory window
Harwood Parish Church, Bolton

Victory window, Newlands Church, Landside, Scotland. Architect: Clifford and Lunan.

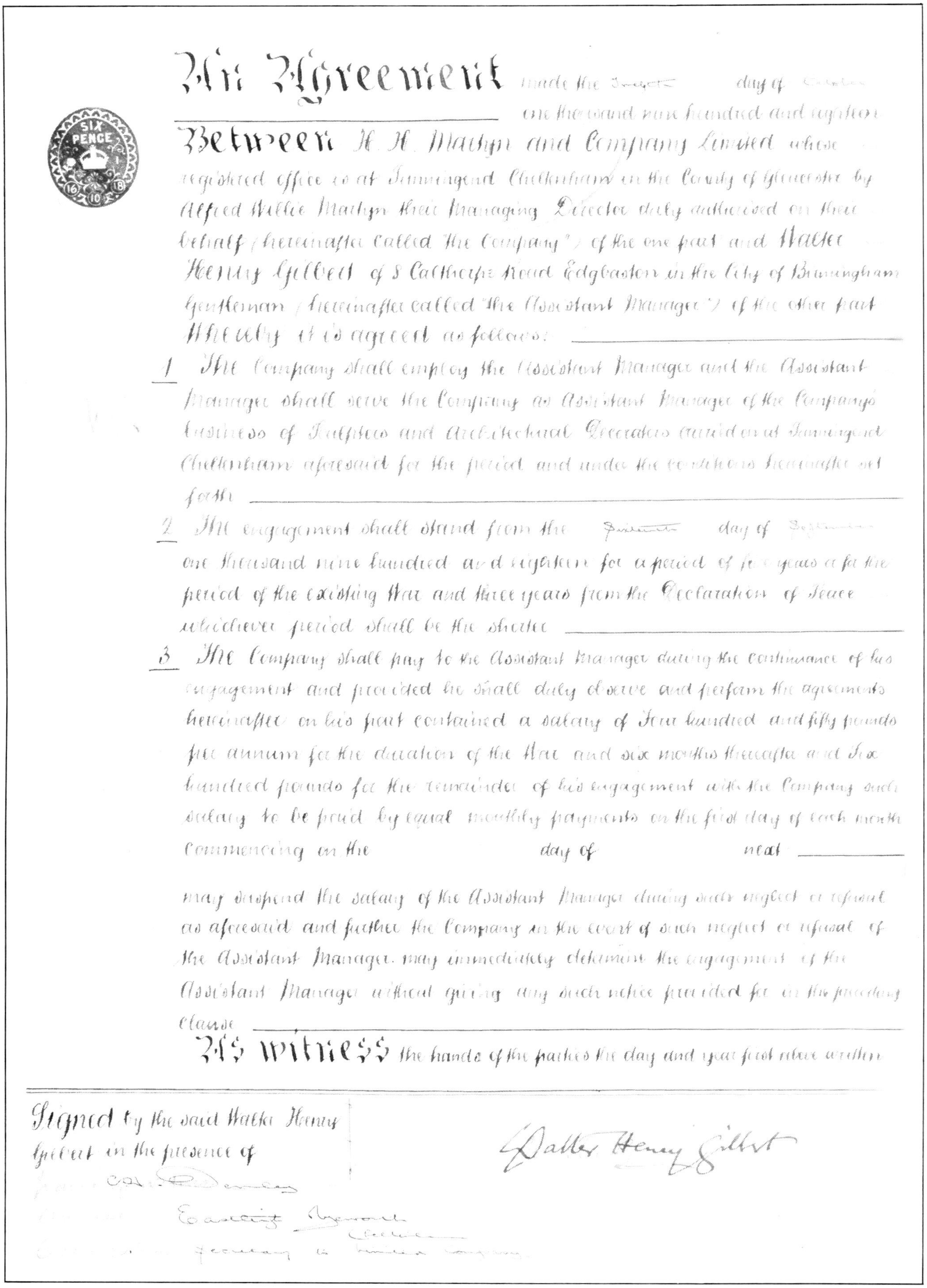

An Agreement made the [illegible] day of October one thousand nine hundred and eighteen

Between H. H. Martyn and Company Limited whose registered office is at Sunningend Cheltenham in the County of Gloucester by Alfred Willis Martyn their Managing Director duly authorised on their behalf (hereinafter called "the Company") of the one part and Walter Henry Gilbert of 8 Calthorpe Road Edgbaston in the City of Birmingham Gentleman (hereinafter called "the Assistant Manager") of the other part

Whereby it is agreed as follows:

1 The Company shall employ the Assistant Manager and the Assistant Manager shall serve the Company as Assistant Manager of the Company's business of Sculptors and Architectural Decorators carried on at Sunningend Cheltenham aforesaid for the period and under the conditions hereinafter set forth

2 The engagement shall stand from the [illegible] day of September one thousand nine hundred and eighteen for a period of [illegible] years or for the period of the existing War and three years from the Declaration of Peace whichever period shall be the shorter

3 The Company shall pay to the Assistant Manager during the continuance of his engagement and provided he shall duly observe and perform the agreements hereinafter on his part contained a salary of Four hundred and fifty pounds per annum for the duration of the War and six months thereafter and Six hundred pounds for the remainder of his engagement with the Company such salary to be paid by equal monthly payments on the first day of each month commencing on the day of next

may suspend the salary of the Assistant Manager during such neglect or refusal as aforesaid and further the Company in the event of such neglect or refusal of the Assistant Manager may immediately determine the engagement of the Assistant Manager without giving any such notice provided for in the preceding clause

As witness the hands of the parties the day and year first above written

Signed by the said Walter Henry Gilbert in the presence of

[illegible]

Walter Henry Gilbert

Walter Henry Gilbert's agreement dated October 1918.

Stained glass windows, Harwood Parish Church, Bolton (east window). Artist: Sidney H. Meteyard.

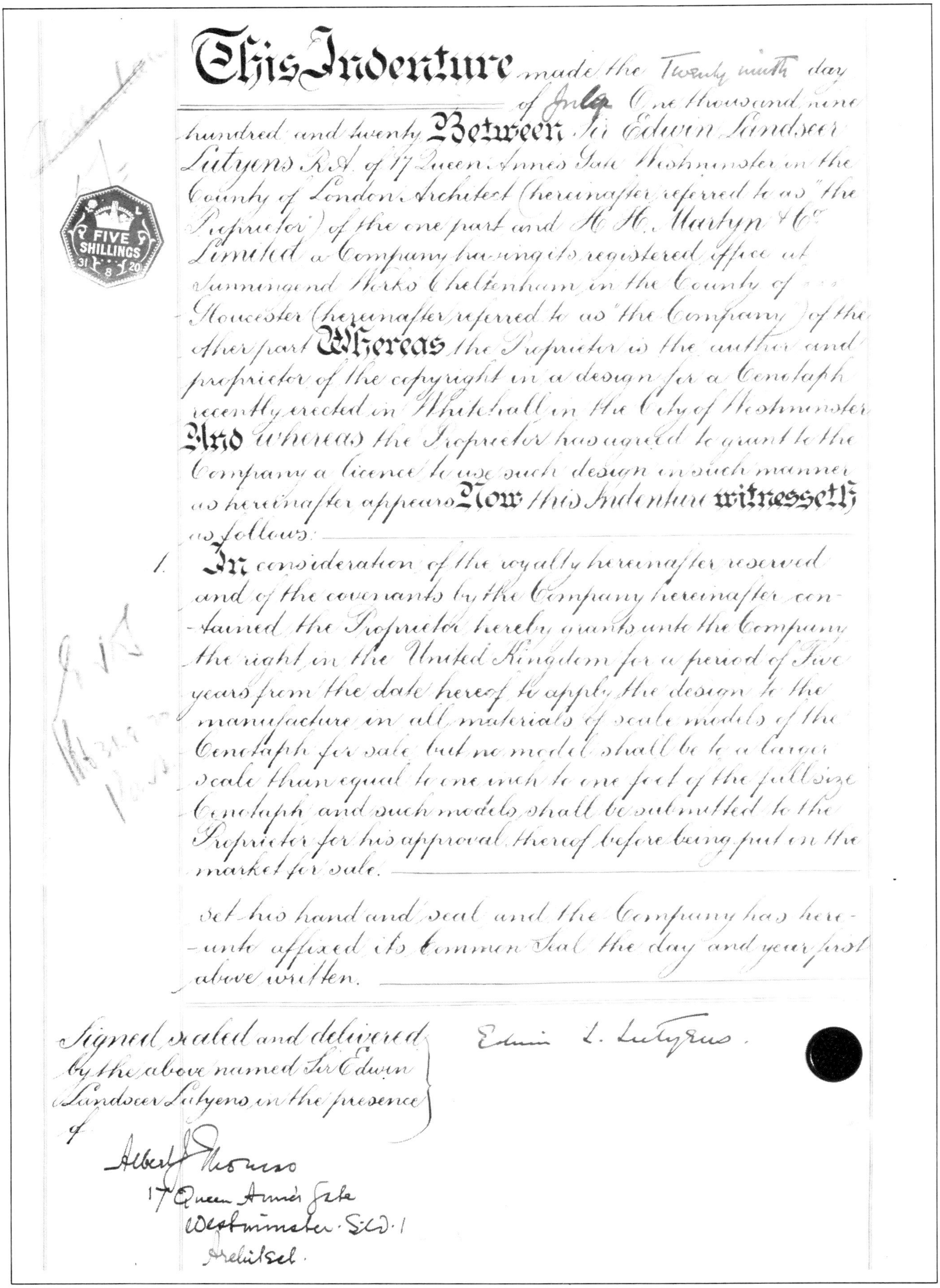

This Indenture made the Twenty ninth day of July One thousand nine hundred and twenty **Between** Sir Edwin Landseer Lutyens R.A. of 17 Queen Annes Gate Westminster in the County of London Architect (hereinafter referred to as "the Proprietor") of the one part and H. H. Martyn & Co. Limited a Company having its registered office at Sunningend Works Cheltenham in the County of Gloucester (hereinafter referred to as "the Company") of the other part **Whereas** the Proprietor is the author and proprietor of the copyright in a design for a Cenotaph recently erected in Whitehall in the City of Westminster **And** whereas the Proprietor has agreed to grant to the Company a licence to use such design in such manner as hereinafter appears **Now** this Indenture **witnesseth** as follows:

1. **In** consideration of the royalty hereinafter reserved and of the covenants by the Company hereinafter contained the Proprietor hereby grants unto the Company the right in the United Kingdom for a period of Five years from the date hereof to apply the design to the manufacture in all materials of scale models of the Cenotaph for sale but no model shall be to a larger scale than equal to one inch to one foot of the full size Cenotaph and such models shall be submitted to the Proprietor for his approval thereof before being put on the market for sale.

set his hand and seal and the Company has hereunto affixed its Common Seal the day and year first above written.

Signed sealed and delivered by the above named Sir Edwin Landseer Lutyens in the presence of

Edwin L. Lutyens.

Albert J. Thomas
17 Queen Anne's Gate
Westminster S.W. 1
Architect.

Sir Edwin Landseer Lutyens' Licence.

Chapter 9

SUPPORTING DOCUMENTS

Few documents of Martyns relating to contracts for work and employees have survived. The bomb which fell on the night of 11th December 1940 and destroyed the tool and spares store also gutted the office, and with it the 1888 to 1940 records.

A.H. Nottingham, foreman in the foundry, heard the sound of the bomb shrieking just before it struck. He was approaching the door to the store from the foundry and just had time to take cover against the wall to the side. The door was blown out and shattered, and Alf Nottingham was struck in the face by a metal splinter which ricocheted from the opposite wall. He was fortunate not to have remained in front of the door. His injury affected him for many years and was part of the reason for his leaving the company in 1946 to set up his own transport business.

Bert Norris tragically lost his life when the bomb fell. He was a joiner and also a member of the company fire service, which may have accounted for his being on duty at the works that night. The fire which raged through both office and store was the more difficult to control as the bomb had holed the water tower. A.W. Martyn heard within the hour of the fire at Sunningend. He was not then any part of the company but he stood in the cold December air outside his daughter's home at Southam where he lived throughout the war and from where the flames and glow of the fire could be clearly seen. He was obviously greatly shocked and moved at the sight as he stood for a long time with most of his family. Hardly a word was spoken but fears for his old colleagues must have raced through his mind. Fortunately there were few casualties among the work force.

When Maples closed the works in 1971, it seemed that there was a purge ordered by management, who wished the name and records of Martyns to disappear for ever. Records, artifacts, mouldings and carvings for plaster casts were burnt and irreplaceable information and patterns were destroyed. Men who had worked for Martyns for many years asked if the destruction could be stopped and were told to carry on and burn the past, 'as it was of no interest'. However, some items survived, souvenirs were kept, carvings were saved and of course no-one could destroy memories in the minds of the men.

Maples also held an auction and the rest of the company's history went far and wide and has proved largely untraceable. The borough unfortunately failed to buy any item for the Town. A mirror beautifully carved by Harry Dean would have been a gem for the Town to retain.

Items of great interest have however turned up after years in basements and cupboards, such as H.H. Martyn's own record of his early life in two exercise books found after lying 60 years in a cellar of a house which belonged to Mr. Denley, the company secretary, in London Road, Cheltenham. A large metal deed box came to light at the Old Sunningend Works, Lansdown, rescued by Mr. John Heapey, the financial director of Schindler Lifts, which now occupies the premises, just as its contents were about to be thrown out. It contains many interesting documents dating from 1920 almost up to the final years of the company, including the minutes of meetings held during the 1926 General Strike, detailing the arrangements for a return to work. Signatures of the men's leaders from each section of the works appear on a scrap of paper.

Industrial relations throughout the history of the company were good, the only strike being that of 1926 which began on about 1st May, the men remaining out for almost two weeks. The strike ended on 12th May and the following records show the process which took place to re-start the works, and the goodwill which persisted in spite of the problems of resuming work.

A difficult period in the company's history was the deep depression in the early 1930s. A few documents relating to this period show how the management and staff co-operated to help the company weather the difficulties. The shop floor took a cut of ½d. per hour in their wages.

On 17th March 1932 the directors decided, owing to the present economic conditions generally prevailing, to cut the salaries of managers of departments, but to divide proportionately 10% of the company's profits between them at the end of the year.

F.P. Edmond's salary was cut to £360.0s.0d. per annum and he received on 31st July 1933 £82.0s.0d. share of profit. A.H.F. Spurr, manager of the plaster, stone and woodcarving department, was also cut to £360.0s.0d. per annum but because presumably the proportion of profit attributable to the department was less he received only £40.0s.0d. profit share. H. Johnstone's salary was cut to £500 and he received £72.0s.0d. The salary of W. Beveridge, manager of woodworking departments was cut on 17th March 1932 to £546.0s.0d. per annum. He received £145.0s.0d. on 31st July 1932 as his share. W.J. Davidson, chief surveyor and estimator, previously general manager, had his salary cut to £900 per annum and he received £100. According to Mr. Davidson's letter the salary cut was a 'large reduction'. However, all managers seem to have accepted the cut as unavoidable in the circumstances.

In spite of the depression orders were still coming in and on 1st February 1933 Mr. R. Young was taken on as works contract superintendent at £750 per annum plus discretionary bonus and two weeks' holiday per annum.

On 31st October 1930 J. Parker of St. Lukes, Cheltenham was given a voluntary payment of £1.0s.0d. per week in appreciation of 'loyal services to the firm in the past'. The directors had learned that he felt unable to return to work and wished him a 'well earned rest and peace and quietness'.

The Company was not without some compassion, it seems, and though the figure seems very low at £1.00, in today's terms it would equal probably £10.00 which as a voluntary payment would seem quite generous.

The company was on the King's National Roll, that is it pledged to employ not less than 5% of its staff from disabled ex-service men. A document dated 7th January 1937 shows that in one department H.H. Martyn & Co. employed 396 men and 15 women, of which 22 were disabled ex-servicemen.

Some other documents which relate to the pay and conditions are unfortunately fragmentary and only cover a short period so no overall picture can be gained but they indicate that wages did not rise annually and even fell back in the depression in 1932.

Rates of pay and conditions were reviewed from time to time. In 1927 an outside foreman on metal work received 1s.5d. (7p) per hour. In 1931 an agreement shows that fitters in the art metal department should receive 1s.1½d. (5½p) per hour minimum rate and others 1s.4d. (6¾p). In 1936 the minimum rate for fitters in the same department had *fallen* by ½d. to 1s.1d. (5p) per hour and others to 1s.3½d. (6½p). In 1939 fitter's rates had risen again as the National Association's terms suggest. At this time income tax was 5s.6d. in the £ (27½p).

Other comparable employers at the time were paying fitters:

R.E. & C. Marshall	1s. 6½d. an hour (8p)
The Birmingham Guild	1s.10½d. an hour (9p)
Bromsgrove Guild	1s.5d. — 1s.7d an hour (7½p — 8½p)

An idea can be gained of the company's policy by the agents appointed in various parts of the world. Over the years a large number of representatives were taken on, mainly on commission only, usually 4% or 5% of the profit on a contract. Many were men with their own existing contacts in the field, or with showrooms for architectural work.

On 8th May 1922 Edmund Michael James was appointed agent in Johannesburg, South Africa, on 7% commission.

On 10th September 1935 Castor J. Love took over the agency for South Africa.

On 30th May 1922 Ogilric Braid, Sydney, Australia, agency for Australia and New Zealand on 5% on cash actually received.

On 1st January, 1928 agency for Hong Kong and China awarded to The Associated Agencies (Far East) Ltd. at 5%.

The foregoing are the only details of agents to come to light; there were many more but the records are lost.

TO THE EMPLOYEES OF SUNNINGEND

The Directors and Management feel that it is their moral duty to issue a statement as to the situation created at Sunningend in connection with the General Strike, in view of the unfortunate condition in which it places all associated with the Works.

They deeply regret that the employees of Sunningend have been called out, and for the benefit of all, let us reconsider the position at the earliest possible moment.

THEY TRUST YOU WILL URGE YOUR EXECUTIVES TO AGREE TO YOUR IMMEDIATE RETURN, AS THEY (THE DIRECTORS AND MANAGEMENT) ARE PREPARED TO ARRANGE FOR THE COMPLETE RESUMPTION OF WORK ON THE OLD BASIS AND UNCONDITIONALLY.

It is the sincere desire of all to have peace and understanding and bring this regrettable business to an end by resuming a constructive policy.

SIGNED ON BEHALF OF THE DIRECTORS AND MANAGEMENT OF

H. H. MARTYN & CO., LTD.
and
THE GLOUCESTERSHIRE AIRCRAFT CO., LTD.

MANAGING DIRECTOR

RECORD OF NEGOTIATIONS FOR RESUMING WORK AT SUNNINGEND WORKS, CHELTENHAM.

13th May, 1926.

In view of the unusual circumstances, it is important that we make a clear issue, free from misunderstanding and friction, and that each and all of our employees are acquainted with every detail of what takes place at our meetings.

Negotiations were inaugurated through our announcement in the Echo of May 11th. To this announcement the Management received no reply, either directly or indirectly.

The General Strike was called off on Wednesday night, May 12th. No deputation from the men approached us on Wednesday night to consult with regard to the necessary arrangements for starting.

At 7.30 on Thursday morning, May 13th, several hundred men appeared at the gates to resume work. No communication, however, had been received by the Management, and the gates remained closed as usual.

MINUTES OF MEETING HELD ON THURSDAY MORNING,

MAY 13TH, 1926.

There was no deputation received from the men until 11 o&clock on Thursday morning. This deputation consisted of Mr. Stevens and Mr. Burrows, representing all trades of both Companies, viz. The Gloucestershire Aircraft Co. Ltd. and H.H.Martyn & Co. Ltd., and they were met by Mr. Longden and Mr. Denley, Secretary.

They stated that the men arrived at 7.30 on Thursday morning, May 13th, to start work, and found the gates closed, and it was then explained to them that the gates had been closed for s fortnight and that the Management had received no intimation as to when all the men would be available to return to work, as it was clearly stated in the Press that each executive had to await their instructions before returning to work. As there are a large number of trades represented in these Works it was obvious to the deputation that the Management could not possibly arrange to resume work until theywere satisfied that the whole of the

Works could resume operations. The deputation appreciated that they ought to have advised the firm when they were all in a position to make a start.

The Management then informed the deputation that no new conditions would be made and that they would be prepared to meet a deputation of the whole of the organization immediately they were in a position to inform the Management that all sections had received their instructions to return, and the Management would then be in a position to make the necessary arrangements for re-instating all. No qualification was made, no new understanding was asked for, no new conditions were imposed and the old basis was being adopted entirely.

For the purpose of re-instating, however, the question of how best arrangements could be made for the men to return was dealt with and the question of some form of re-engagement was mentioned.

The Management would like, here, to make it clear that they have difficulties which they are anxious that the employees should fully realise, as if the men were allowed to come back without the organization being in satisfactory working order to receive them, great inconvenience would be caused, not only to the Companies but also to the individual workmen.

MINUTES OF MEETING HELD ON THURSDAY AFTERNOON,

MAY 13TH, 1926.

At 3 o'clock Mr. Longden received a telephone call from Mr. Allen of the Labour Exchange, informing him that a deputation of all the organizations was ready to meet him, and an appointment was then agreed for 3.45 p.m.

Mr. Longden received this deputation immediately and Mr. Denley, Secretary, was also present.

The deputation consisted of the following:-

A.J.Denchfield	A.E.U.
J.R.Elks	Coppersmiths
F.C.Turner	Brass & Metal Mechanics
F.J.Wyatt	Sheet Metal Workers
G.Stevens	N.A.F.T.A.
A.T.Quelch	Woodworkers
T.R.Smith	M. O. B.
T. Peers	Plaster Dept.
W.E.Budding	Moulders
J.Anderson	Plasterer
J.W.Betteridge	General Workers
E.A.Denton	Inspection Dept.
G.E.Walkling	Wood Machinists

This deputation represented the workers of both the Gloucestershire Aircraft Co. Ltd. and H.H.Martyn & Co. Ltd.

Mr. Quelch was appointed as spokesman for the deputation and informed Mr. Longden that all sections had now received their instructions and were ready and available to return immediately or at such time as the Management would name, convenient to themselves, leaving them sufficient time to make the necessary arrangements to start.

Mr. Longden informed the deputation that he was extremely pleased to hear that they had now cleared all the outstanding matters and that the Management would at once make arrangements. These arrangements were discussed.

As a number of men had gone away it was proposed and agreed that the reinstatement should be on the same lines as when the employees ceased work. This procedure was that each man, who was in the employ of the Companies when work ceased, would enter the Works, receive a slip, and in exchange, from his department, a permit to commence work. This was to enable the Staff and the Departments to arrive at the number of men who would be returning in each section, and to make adequate arrangements. After these permits had been handed out the Management would be able to state the exact time that work would commence, as each section would be able to say what necessary arrangements would require to be made. ~~This was all agreed~~. omit.

Before, however, finally making these arrangements Mr. Longden requested them to assure him that they were really all prepared to start work and to keep on working, and not go out the next day in sympathy with anyone else, as it had come to his knowledge that there was a rumour (and he amphasised that it was only a rumour and that he did not wish to take any steps) to the effect that a man had been threatened that he would be called out that night. This alleged threat was between Mr. Longden's interview receiving the deputation in the morning and the interview then in progress.

They informed Mr. Longden that they repudiated this, but stated that there was a possibility of their coming out again in sympathy if all the local men were not re-instated.

Mr. Longden then informed them that this was rather a contradiction of their statement that all had instructions to resume work and were ready and willing to return. They stated that it was their instructions from Headquarters, and Mr. Longden informed them that under these circumstances we would probably only have the Works open for a day, when they might go out again, and this most certainly could not be done, as it was impossible to keep opening and shutting up Works of this magnitude, where over a thousand men and their dependents were involved.

The original intention had, therefore, to be altered, of starting when each organization had received their instructions, as <u>there was a condition placed in these instructions which prevented them from starting and continuing if some other concern were unable to start work at the same time</u>.

Mr. Longden appreciated the way in which they met the difficulty as they immediately agreed that they would come back to him when they could give him an assurance that - in their own words - they would not "play ducks and drakes with the Companies".

Mr. Longden assured them that when such a time arrived, the Management were prepared to reinstate every man who was in work when the General Strike took place. He assured them that there would be no victimisation of any man by either firm, and no man would be allowed to be victimised by the men, and the same conditions on both sides would remain in force which existed previous to the General Strike.

David Longden

A. T. Quelch.

MINUTES OF MEETING HELD AT SUNNINGEND WORKS ON FRIDAY AFTERNOON, MAY 14TH, 1926, AT 3 O'CLOCK.

A Deputation called at 3 o'clock, consisting of the following:-

J. R. Elks	Coppersmith (Sheet Metal Dept)
F. C. Turner	Art Metal Dept.
G. Stevens	N. A. F. T. A.
A. T. Quelch	Woodworkers

T. A. Smith	Woodworkers
G. E. Walkling	Wood Machine Shop
F. G. Wyatt	Sheet Metal Dept.
W. E. Budding	Iron Moulding Dept.
J. W. Betteridge	General Workers
A. J. Denchfield	N.E.D. A.E.U.
C. F. Burrows	Experimental A.E.U.
R. Stubbs	At the request of Management
J. Anderson	Plasterer
T. Peers	Plasterer

This Deputation represented trade organizations of both Companies, viz. The Gloucestershire Aircraft Co. Ltd. and H.H.Martyn & Co. Ltd., and was met by Mr. Longden, and Mr. Denley, Secretary.

The Minutes of the previous Meetings were read and confirmed.

Mr. Longden stated that the Companies wished to bring the whole of their influence to bear in re-organizing, and he assured them that they were willing to co-operate with them and that they must all have a keen sense of their responsibility to get these Works going.

Mr. Longden then asked the Deputation if they were now in a position to resume work on the conditions existing previous to the General Strike, and that it was to be clearly understood that there was to be no victimisation of any man by either side.

Mr. Elks then informed Mr. Longden that they were now pleased to say that they had got over all their outside difficulties which had been discussed at previous meetings, and they would be able to arrange for an immediate return, and they clearly understood that the same conditions on both sides would remain in force as set out by Mr. Longden.

Mr. Longden then expressed his pleasure that the Deputation had got over all their difficulties, and arrangements were then discussed for re-starting.

The Deputation then retired to agree between themselves the question of arrangements for re-starting.

After the private meeting of the Deputation they informed Mr. Longden that they would telephone him at 5.30 to confirm these arrangements, which would enable a start to be made on Monday morning at 7.30.

Mr. Longden pointed out that should any Employee delete from his form any contribution which he had previously paid, the Management reserve the right to discharge such Employee, as they would assume that he had not complied with the spirit of good faith as agreed upon.

The meeting then terminated, and at 5.30 p.m. Mr. Longden received a telephone call confirming that the men had accepted the arrangements, which would enable a start to be made on Monday on the old basis of wages and conditions which were in existence at the time of going out, and as contained in the Minutes of Meetings with the Deputation.

Signed for and on behalf of H.H.Martyn & Co. Ltd.

DIRECTOR.

Signed for and on behalf of The Gloucestershire Aircraft Co. Ltd.

MANAGING DIRECTOR.

Signed on behalf of the Deputation

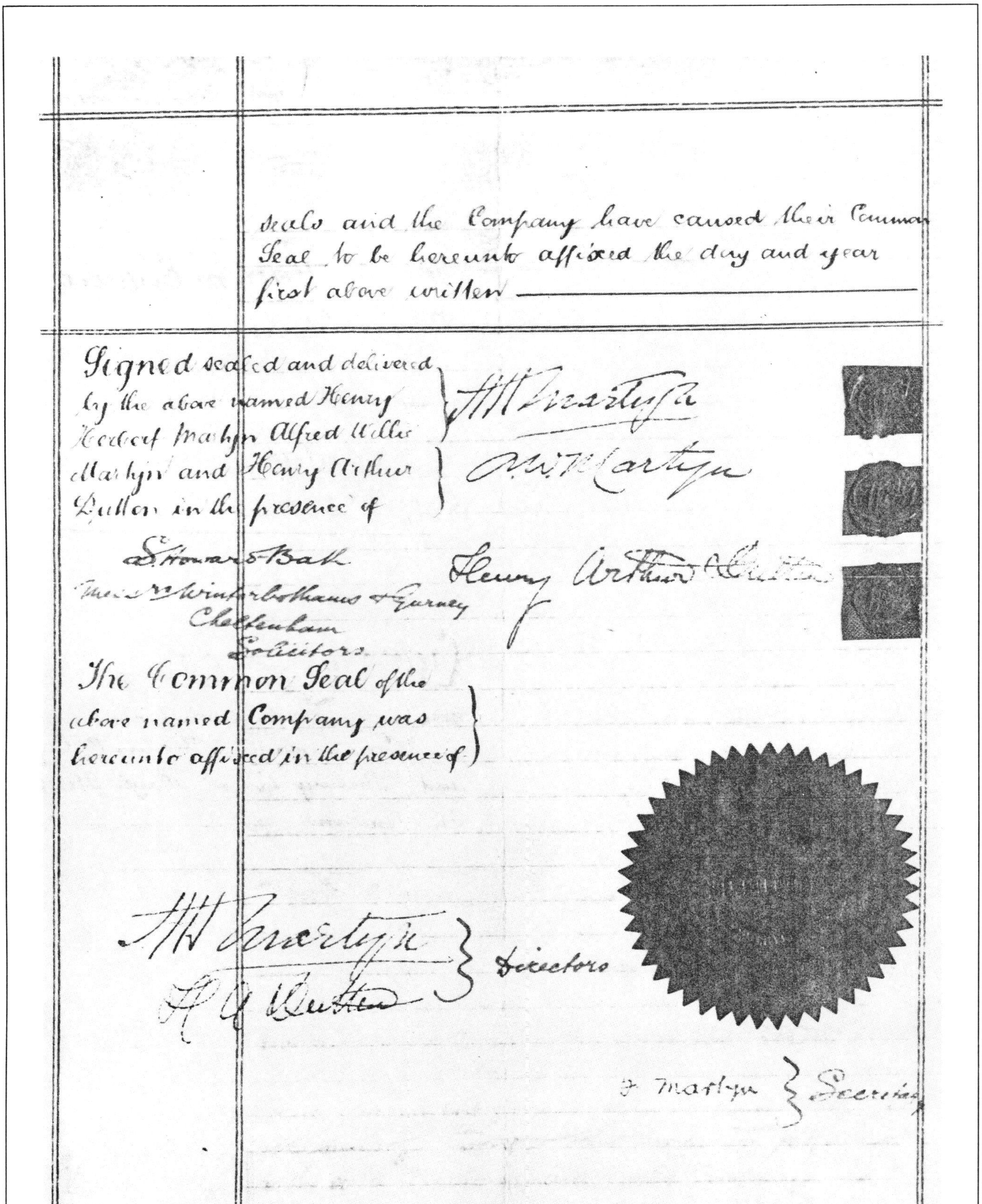
seals and the Company have caused their Common Seal to be hereunto affixed the day and year first above written

Signed sealed and delivered by the above named Henry Herbert Martyn Alfred Willis Martyn and Henry Arthur Dutton in the presence of

H H Martyn

A W Martyn

Henry Arthur Dutton

E Howard Bath
Messrs Winterbothams & Gurney
Cheltenham
Solicitors.

The Common Seal of the above named Company was hereunto affixed in the presence of

H H Martyn
H A Dutton } Directors

[illegible] Martyn } Secretary

Signatures on conveyance of freehold on Sunningend on the 28th May 1900.

H. H. MARTYN & Co. Ltd.
SCULPTORS AND
ARCHITECTURAL DECORATORS

LONDON
OFFICES AND SHOWROOMS
5, GRAFTON STREET, BOND STREET, W
TELEGRAMS "SUNNINGEND, LONDON" TELEPHONE REGENT 7355-6

MODELLING STUDIOS
192, ALBANY STREET, N.W.
TELEPHONE MUSEUM 2060

MANCHESTER.
Representative: NORMAN NEWTON.
HARDY'S BUILDINGS, CATEATON STREET.
TELEGRAMS: "ARTWURK, MANCHESTER." TELEPHONE: 4922 CENTRAL.

NEWCASTLE-ON-TYNE.
BACK ROSEDALE TERRACE, SHIELDFIELD.
TELEPHONE 2570 CENTRAL.

AND AT SYDNEY, N.S.W. (AUS.)
JOHANNESBURG (S. AFRICA), &C.
MONTREAL, QUE. (CANADA).

BY APPOINTMENT

HEAD OFFICES
Sunningend Works
CHELTENHAM

22nd March, 1928.

Please Quote Our Ref. C.H.D./...

I, Charles Harry Denley, Secretary of H. H. Martyn & Company Limited, hereby certify that at an Extraordinary General Meeting of Shareholders, duly summoned and held at the registered office of the Company on Tuesday, March 20th, 1928, the following Extraordinary Resolution was duly passed:-

That the under-mentioned properties be disposed of, as and when opportunity arises, such proceeds to be invested in Government securities in the name of the Debenture Trustees:-

"Sunningend", College Road
Nos. 1 & 2, Belle Vue Lawn
59, High Street.

Dated this Twenty second day of March, 1928.

Signed ____________________
SECRETARY

These Resolutions filed 24 Mar. 1928 at Company's office official receipt received
H. ...
29/3/28

The decision to dispose of the now old Sunningend works in College Road on the 22nd March 1928.

C A R V E R S' R U L E S.

To come into operation as from December 12th 1919.

1. Wages. -- The minimum rate of wages for Wood and Stone Carvers shall be 1/9 per hr.

2. Hours. -- The normal working week for Wood and Stone Carvers not to exceed 47 hours

3. Overtime Rates -- That all the time made after the termination of a full working day be charged for at the following rates, viz.- First two hours, time and a quarter; second two hours, time and a half; after which double time until the recognised time of starting in the morning; Saturdays, time and a half to the usual tea-time after which double time until the recognised time of starting Monday morning; Sundays, Bank Holidays, Christmas Day, double time. No overtime to be worked if any member if signing the local out-of-work book.

4. Out-of-Town Expenses -- That the sum of 3/- per day be allowed, seven days per week, on all jobs when residing away from home, tram, 'bus and railway fares in addition. All time spent in travelling to be paid at ordinary rates.

5. Foremen -- All Foreman shall receive at least 2d. per hour above the standard paid working men under them.

6. Apprentices and Improvers -- That only one apprentice or improver be allowed to every four men, the total number not to exceed six.

7. Protection from weather -- That as a protection from weather and to prevent loss of time all carvers on outdoor jobs be supplied with tarpaulins, or other suitable covering, and in the time of foggy weather artificial light shall be provided. Employers failing to comply with this rule to pay for all time lost thereby. No carvers to be required to carry tarpaulins, models, etc. of unreasonable nature.

9. Sharpening of Tools -- Employers to pay for the sharpening of all stone tools, filling of hammers, and to provide all rasps and bow-strings.

10. Alteration of Rules. -- That after these Rules have been ratified they shall be binding on employers and employed, and should either party desire an alteration six months notice be given, to terminate on May 1st. or November 1st.

REVISED Rules to remain in operation until November 1st. 1922:-

Rule 1. - Wages. The minimum rate of wages for Wood and Stone Carvers shall be 1/9d. per hour.

Rule 3. - to read after Monday morning:- Bank Holidays, time and a half for the whole day; Sundays and Christmas Day, double time. Persistent overtime not to be worked if any Member is signing the Local out-of-work Book.

Rule 4. - That the sum for out of town expenses be altered to 2/6d. per day, and no extra rate per hour.

Carver's rules and rates of pay.

COPY

192, ALBANY STREET

LONDON, N.W.1.

25th November, 1932.

Messrs. H.H.Martyn & Co. Ltd.,
Cheltenham.

Dear Mr. Denley,

Replying to yours of the 24th inst. we give below the current rates as requested, for the London area:-

Stone Carvers. Ornament 2/7d Minimum
Figure 3/3d Minimum

The above rates are at present under consideration.

Wood Carvers. Ornament 2/9d. Minimum

Plasterers. 1/8½d. per hour.

Details of how this reduction was brought about were sent you on 5th February.

Details of further reductions to bring Plasterers in line with other Building Trades were sent you on 3rd October.

Labourers. 75% of Tradesmen's Rate.

Joiners &c. 1/7½d. within a radius 12 miles of Charing Cross.
1/7d. between 12 & 15 miles of Charing Cross.

Yours faithfully,
H. H. MARTYN & CO. LTD.

(Sgd) H. M. Davies.

LONDON MASTER BUILDERS' ASSOCIATION.

13th January 1933.

Dear Sirs,

ANNUAL REVIEW OF WAGES.

For your information I give below copy of the resolution passed by the National Joint Council for the Building Industry on the 12th instant.

"That on and from the first day of February 1933 the rates of wages payable to craftsmen and labourers engaged in the Building Industry shall be DECREASED by one-half penny an hour, provided always that the rate payable to Labourers in any grade shall not be less than 75 per cent. of the Craftsmen's rate".

The rates in London will, therefore, be as follows:-

	Mechanics.	Painters.	Labourers.
Within the 12 miles radius	1/7	1/6	1/2¼
From 12-15 miles radius	1/6½	1/5½	1/2.

In connection with this it will be necessary to issue the following:-

(a) A Leaflet, copy of which Members will be requested to hand to each workman in their employ.

(b) A Notice to be posted up in shops and on jobs.

Reference will be made in the Leaflet and Notice to the agreed adjustment in Plasterers wages to take effect on the 1st prox.

WILL YOU PLEASE BE GOOD ENOUGH TO LET ME KNOW BY RETURN OF POST THE NUMBER OF COPIES OF EACH YOU WILL REQUIRE.

Yours faithfully,

W.J. RUDDERHAM.

Secretary.

COPY OF LETTER.

THE CHELTENHAM MASTER BUILDERS ASSOCIATION.

Secretary. H.F.Midwinter.

Crescent Place.
CHELTENHAM.

17th January 1933.

Dear Sirs,

Will you please note that the recent application of the Operatives to Up-grade Cheltenham, which would have had the effect of increasing wages, has failed.

Will you please also note that as and from the 1st February, owing to the fall in the cost of living figures, wages in the Building Industry will be reduced by ½d per hour, provided that Labourers do not receive less than 75% of the Craftsmens rate.

Cheltenham being a Grade A. town the wages on and after that date will be

Craftsmen	1s.4d.
Labourers	1s.0d.

Yours faithfully,

(SGD). H.F.MIDWINTER.

2nd April, 1935.

RULES GOVERNING MEN WORKING AWAY ON JOBS IN RESPECT OF PAYMENT OF FARES.

4 to 20 miles -	Fare once every week, or be conveyed to and from work.
20 to 40 miles -	Payment of fare every two weeks.
40 to 60 miles -	Payment of fare once a month
Over 60 miles -	Payment by mutual arrangement before the operative proceeds to the job.

Works outing to Gough's Caves, Cheddar, 1926.

H.H. Martyn & Co., Fire Brigade 1926. A.W. Martyn and his two daughters and granddaughter entertain the men who had beaten the brigades of both Gloucester and Cheltenham in a fire fighting competition.

Back row standing left to right: Unknown; Unknown; Jack Mills, foreman, french polisher; Bill Carr, foreman, erecting shop aircraft: Fred Wintle, wages and accounts; Unknown; Unknown; Fred Brookes, timekeeper; Reg Nutt, accounts; C. Grinham; Bert Gardner, wood machinist; Jack Turvey, foreman, wood mills; Unknown; Unknown; Jack Wortley, foreman, joiner; W. Watson, mill wright; Chris Payne, joiner; Jack Binmore, joiner; Bert Norris, joiner (killed on night of raid); W. Mills; Unknown; Unknown; Unknown; Tommy Stinchcombe, joiner.

Second row standing left to right: A.? Robertson, wood machinist; Harry Wixey, wood machinist; B. Smith; Unknown; G. Turner; Bill Littlewood, wood machinist; H. Uzzell; Unknown; Unknown; Daughter Ida with Grand-daughter Barbara on knee; Mr. A.W. Martyn, chairman and managing director; Daughter Madeline; Unknown; Wilbert Cook, foreman; W. Gibbons; Unknown; T. Weeks; Unknown; Unknown; F. Skinner; Harry Brookes, painter wing shop.

Third Row (seated) left to right: Unknown; Unknown; C. Evans; Unknown; Neville Payne, wood machinist; Chris Thompson, assistant time-keeper; George Houghton, under manager, joinery; Wilf Toms, apprentice wood machinist; A. Nottingham; Unknown; W. Ball; Charles Gisborne, woodcarver.

Martyns aircraft assembly team outside the Winter Gardens, Cheltenham, 1915.

Great Ormond Street Children's Hospital. Architects: Stanley Hall and Easton & Robertson.

Chapter 10

'MARSTEEL' PRESSED METAL

Marsteel was an offshoot of Martyns and was a pressed metal department working in the premises of Sunningend.

On 12th December 1929 H.H. Martyn & Co. purchased the business of The Gloucester Coach and Sheet Metal Company, which was owned by Mr. Caleb Davis, adding considerably to the company's ability to work in sheet metals.

In December 1936 and through to 1938 ten agencies were appointed to canvass prospective clients in the building trades, municipal authorities and elsewhere for Marsteel trims and door linings, 5% commission being payable on secured orders.

On 1st February, 1937 J. Johnson of Romford, started work as foreman in charge of the pressed steel and metal department, then about to expand, at a salary of £400 per annum. The position had been advertised in The Daily Telegraph. Mr. Johnson was 40 years old with 20 years' experience in pressed steel work.

Marsteel produced movable unit steel partitions for Great Ormond Street Children's Hospital. The Adelphi had swing fire doors made and also lavatory cubicles. The floors for the post-war pre-fabs were also made in the section, a sign of the times as pressed steel began to replace wood. The purely functional and stark appearance of the work contrasted greatly with the decorative work still being executed in the factory. Steel bins, cookers, cupboards, factory storage shelving, library shelving, picture rails even, must have jolted the sensibilities of men who had produced exquisite decorative work. The very sound of the doors of steel lockers being clanged shut must have echoed in the halls of the past. However, 'progress' was overtaking tradition, the men produced the new stark architectural requirements with the dedicated skill of Martyns, and important contracts followed.

One of the large contracts the department had was the making of lift cages for the firm of Waygood Otis. The long standing association with Otis Lifts was partly instrumental in the eventual purchase of the Sunningend factory by the Schindler (UK) Lift Company who carry on the traditions of fine workmanship in their lifts and in the 1980s still employ a large number of Martyns men in their works.

As in most departments of the company the employees often had a flair for seeing a new or better way to deal with a problem. In 1935 F.P. Edmonds of 'Stretton', Old Bath Road, Cheltenham invented an efficient weather and draught-proof construction for sliding windows and doors, also enabling large panes of glass to be used without heavy mullions (pat. no. 540698).

In 1936 F.P. Edmonds patented through H.H. Martyn & Co. an improved striking plate for door latches, pat. no. 477694. In 1932 a patent was taken out by him for an improved 'reflex' door stop, no. 14945.

Chapter 11

MARTYN/MAPLE

In 1934 Maples of Tottenham Court Road, London took over Martyns and the company became known as Maple-Martyn. The change was no more popular with the staff at Martyns than when A.W. Martyn relinquished his control in 1927, only seven years before. The staff continued to consider themselves Martyns men and some friction was evident between the men and the management appointed from Maples. The men were at times assembled to be told that they should forget Martyns and their past of which they were proud and become "Maple minded". Maple minded they could not be and the feeling even now with the 'retired', young and old, is that Martyns was the company they worked for and they could never be integrated in the Maple Organisation.

The takeover came about for several reasons. Maples were interested in acquiring ship work for their furnishings and by 1934 Martyns had built up a considerable connection and reputation in this field. The main interests of Hugh Burroughes and David Longden, principal members of the board, now lay in the Gloster Aircraft Co. rather than Martyns. There was also some commercial logic in the argument that the association of the two companies could be beneficial, with the furniture and soft furnishing of Maples complementing the comprehensive architectural decoration produced by Martyns.

Though the arrangement may have been of benefit to the corporate body, the workforce was unhappy with the association; their work they felt became less and less important in the group, though in this they were mistaken. Had they been told and known the truth, morale would have been better. In 1950 a report in the 'New Dawn' official

Chairman's office of the John James Group of Companies. Panelling, plaster ceiling, fireplace and bronze central heating grilles by the Maple Martyn Organisation. Furniture, carpets and curtains by Maple Contracts, Bristol.

London's famous Guildhall, restored after the second world war, clearly demonstrates the fine craftsmanship of Maple-Martyn. Gothic panelling and heraldic carving was carried out to the instructions of Sir Giles Scott, Son and Partners.

union magazine said "The Martyn furnishing and decorating side of this £3,000,000 business is in fact the major part of the Maple-Martyn Organisation. H.H. Martyn & Co. plays an important role in the Maple furnishing business".

Men with skills of the highest order found themselves making television cabinets, a repetitive and simple task. Interest waned. However, many large and important contracts were still executed. Castings of large dimensions were undertaken by the foundry — Churchill for the Guildhall, London, the Commando Memorial and Robert the Bruce, to mention just a few.

Maples of Tottenham Court Road, like Martyns, had built up a reputation in palaces and fine houses throughout the world, in their case, solely on furnishings. They were founded by John Maple in 1841, 47 years before H.H. Martyn founded his company and one year before his birth. A small shop in Tottenham Court Road which remained open till 9.00 p.m. daily, was the seed of its success, not dissimilar to the industrious beginnings of H.H. Martyn.

Another similarity was the way that John Maple's son took over the business and dramatically drove it to international fame and fortune just as did H.H. Martyn's son.

Furniture was Maples' business and they had branches in several major cities of the world. Their boast was that they made furniture for bed-sitters to palaces. The men who worked for them became 'Maple minded' and were encouraged to be and think that way, which explains why the partnership was so difficult for the work-force of Martyns, who did not want to lose their identity. Two of Maples' Directors closely connected to Martyns were Mr. G. Holman who was managing director for a time and Mr Allden. Mr. Morton was the last managing director.

Martyns was eventually bought from Maples by Macolland of South Wales and became the only manufacturing company in their group. They decided that its main value to them was in its premises. The irony of the sell-out was that a covenant which protected the workforce from having its sports field sold off in fact probably triggered the winding up of the company. The sports field was a vaulable asset which could only be stripped and cashed by overcoming the covenant. Once Martyns was closed down, the sports field could also be sold. There was no other reason for selling, as Mr. T.A. Miller, Maple-Martyn's contracts director, informed me that to his knowledge in 25 years of trading the company was profitable in all but two. It was always said the Martyns' profits paid Maples' dividends. So 83 years of experience and a wealth of talent and expertise and traditions were scrapped for the money in land and buildings.

Strangely though, almost like a ghostly ritual, an annual general meeting of H.H. Martyn & Co. Ltd. is held in its own old premises. The company, though not trading, still exists. Schindler Lifts (UK) Ltd., which bought the Sunningend premises, also bought the company name, and has to comply with the regulations by holding the A.G.M.

Prior to the closedown by Macollands, Martyns had reduced its workforce to only 300. Problems had faced the company as polystyrene cornices replaced plaster and fibreglass coats of arms replaced bronze. Lower standards were accepted by the architects and clients because of the high cost of **'the best'**.

The stone carvers were first to go. Most had finished in 1947 though one tenacious individual continued — in the old and original craft of cutting gravestones! Decorative wood carving was much reduced and it was a bitter blow when the foundry had to close from lack of work.

Another problem which cut into sales was that hardwood joinery, which had traditionally been the province of Martyns and similar companies, began to be undertaken by the big builders such as McAlpine and Costain. They formed their own hardwood joinery departments, no longer sub-contracting to Martyns as in the past.

Could these serious problems have been overcome? In hindsight it would seem that at least some of them could. Why not get into plastics and fibreglass and produce **'the best'**? It seems strange too that Singers of Frome, Martyns' chief competitors in foundry work, still do castings. Just look at the trials and innovations in the company's mid-history. In difficult times it kept ahead by generating new ideas and spawning new products and activities.

However, it seems that the company's premises and sports field had come too tempting a source of easy money. The sports field was an early facility covenanted to the workforce. It consisted of five tennis courts, two football pitches, a cricket ground and running track. There were two pavillions with bar recreation and changing rooms. It is believed that the land was given by Mr. H.H. Martyn, and it was a long standing tradition to drink a toast to his name at special functions.

The covenant, it is understood, stated that in the event of the field not being required it should become an asset of the Hospital. However this residual right was apparently bought off.

Offices of the Australian Mutual Provident Society, London. Panelling in mahogany, also carving in lime wood, fibrous plaster ceilings, metal work etc. Architect: Messrs. Thompson and Walford.

Chapter 12

CABINET MAKERS, FURNITURE, JOINERY AND WOOD PANELLING

Very early in the history of Martyns, before the turn of the century, furniture of the highest quality was already being produced. Cheltenham Museum has a beautiful display cabinet made in walnut, the interior lined in bird's eye maple, of magnificent proportions and very finely carved, made in the 1890s and attributed to Martyns. It is the combined work of cabinet makers and carvers.

Much of the furniture produced was copied from classical period designs. However, a great deal was made to original design for such special contracts as the Holker of Indor in 1917, the King of Rumania in 1938 and many others. One of the early problems encountered in the furniture department was matching the cost of producing to the high quality desired with the available market. Some furniture was impossible to market in the early 1920s for this reason. However, the department found answers and continued to produce furniture of all descriptions for homes, offices, ships and palaces throughout the company's history. In 1934, when Maples bought Martyns, the furniture department became an extension of the already established Maple furnishing tradition. The men continued to make furnishings for ships and offices.

In 1936 the Cheltenham Manufacturing Co. was formed, a Martyn based operation, as a separate subsidiary of Maples, dedicated to furniture manufacture. The making of radio and television cabinets became a bread and butter line given to the Cheltenham work force, a job which was tedious for men who had made fine furniture. They felt they were being given the second-rate jobs while the best and most interesting work was kept for Maples men in London. Such rivalry and discontent was not unnatural for men unable to do other than that which they were instructed.

Wood panelling was a speciality with Martyns from the beginning and some very fine examples can be seen, not least that which A.W. Martyn had put in at his home The Hearne, Charlton Kings. He also had some beautiful decorative plaster work incorporated.

A magnificent table designed and built for the Palace of King Carol of Rumania lies at the bottom of the Mediterranean with other furnishings, sunk in the hostilities of 1939.

In 1950 a richly carved dining room suite executed in English walnut, was made for despatch to Iraq.

The department carried out each process of furniture-making by hand except for the veneering, which was done on one of the largest veneering presses in the country. Even veneering in the early days was done by hand, using hot scotch glue and a mahogany veneer hammer with a brass strip. R. West, who started in 1917 as an apprentice, took charge of the veneering department, and in the course of his 36 years with the company saw the change from hand work to the big presses.

A few documents relating to staff taken on in the department are interesting, particularly as they set out the terms offered by the company at the time.

On 1st December 1933 S.P. Brewer of New Malden, Essex was taken on to 'take charge of the furniture manufacture and furniture design section' at a salary of £350.0s.0d. per annum.

On 25th February 1918 William Beverage of Liverpool, who was a joiner at that time, was taken on as manager of the joinery department. His wages were to be £10.0s.0d. per week with three weeks' holiday per year. The document shows the first suggested pay as £6.0s.0d. per week with two weeks' holiday, which he would not accept. Men's wages did not rise fast during the period after the wage cuts in 1932. William Beverage only received £12.0s.0d. per week — the percentage of his cut is not known though. Beverage proved to be an efficient manager who remained in his post for many years.

On 9th January 1933, W. Trott of Brighton was taken on 'as foreman painter (working)' at 2s. per hour; minimum of 50 hours per week. Painting and decorating was another service offered by the company, and following plaster or other major work the painters would often be required to pick out the work in colour, entailing highly skilled work on the detailed plaster mouldings. The teams travelled far and wide on decorative contracts.

An idea of quality, variety and excellence of the woodwork carried out can be imagined from the list of timber in stock in 1932 and valued by James F. Fraser & Co. Bishopsgate, London, for the company at some £12,000.

Chestnut	Caban Mahogany
Sycamore	Gaboon Mahogany
Ash	Deal
French Walnut	Laurel
American Walnut	Cherry
Borneo Cedar	Ebony
English Oak	Pear
Austrian Oak	Elm
Honduras Mahogany	Satin wood
Japanese Oak	Blackbean
American Oak	Greywood
Teak	Maple
African Walnut	Pine
Fiddle Mahogany	Russian Oak
Birch	

Main suppliers of timber were Mallinsons of London and the above timbers were probably supplied by them. The purpose of the valuation seems to have been a reduction of stock to help weather the recession of the early 1930's, involving the sale of some of the wood. This is in line with other economies, such as the cuts in wages at the same time. This is not, I am reliably informed, a complete list of the wood which the company had in stock and used over the years. Very many other woods were used.

Two views of the joinery works, Sunningend, High Street, Cheltenham, 1905.

Joinery and panelling contracts

Buckingham Palace
Joinery work.

Harewood House (for Princess Royal)
Joinery work.

Train for H.R.H. Prince of Wales — Indian Tour
Joinery work.

Palace at Bucharest for King Carol
Joinery work.

Lal Bagh Palace
Joinery work.

Royal Train for H.M. King Farouk
Joinery work.

Chichester County Offices
Joinery work to assembly hall and committee room.

Hackney Town Hall
Joinery work.

Wandsworth Administrative Buildings
Panelling to Council Chamber.

London University
Panelled dining hall.

Halifax Building Society, Coventry
Joinery work to banking hall.

Halifax Building Society, Hull
Joinery work to banking hall.

Permanent Co-operative Building Society, London
Panelled board room and suite of offices.

Leicester Permanent Building Society
Joinery work.

Stuart House, Cambridge
Oak panelling to hall, staircase, board room.

Bishops Stortford College
Memorial oak organ case.

Westminster Cathedral
Stalls in oak inlaid with mother of pearl, ivory and rare woods.

St. David's Cathedral, Cardiff
Oak choir stalls, altar, reredos and pulpit.

First Church of Christ Scientist, Boston, U.S.A.
Panelling in oak.

St. Michael's Church, Blundellsands
Chancel panelling, pulpit, book cupboards.

Martins Bank H.Q., Liverpool
Joinery.

Union Corporation, London
Suite of panelled offices.

Tanganyika Concessions Ltd., London
Board room in walnut.

Trussed Concrete Steel Co., London
Suite of offices panelled in Peroba wood.

Haig Hall, Wigan, for Earl of Crawford
Oak fittings for library.

English Speaking Union
Oak fittings to library.

Pier Hotel, Worthing
Panelling to bars.

Brunswick Inn, Hove
Panelling to bars.

Bristol Hotel, Brighton
Panelling to bars.

Whitehall Theatre, London
Black ebonised panelling to auditorium etc.

Newport Civic Centre
Joinery work.

Swansea Civic Centre
Joinery work.

Hornsea Municipal Buildings
Joinery work to assembly hall and council chamber.

Cardiff Civic Centre
Extensive contract in all mediums.

Some of the more important furnishing contracts for ships and other venues before 1934 were as follows:

Furnishings

Imperial Hotel, Torquay
London Casino
Derby Police Courts
Duchess of Richmond
Duchess of York
Orontes
Rangitata
Empress of Japan
Empress of Britain
Midland Bank Head Office
Cardiff Royal District Council
Lal Bagh Palace, Indore

Furniture

Barnsley Municipal Buildings
Council Chamber furniture.
Preston County Offices
Lal Bagh Palace, Indore

From advertisements in the Architectural Review:

1919/23 Tudor Grange, Birmingham, panelling.
1919/23 Anchor Line Buildings, Liverpool, wood panelling.
1919/23 Australian Mutual Provident Society, London offices, panelling in mahogany.
1923/29 Lexden Grange, Colchester, panelling and furniture.
1923/29 Daily Mirror Offices, London, oak panelling.
1931 First Church of Christ Scientist, Stockport, panelling and reading desks.
1923/29 Eaves Hall, Clitheroe, Lancs., all panelling and woodwork.
1929/39 Royal Bank of Canada, Lothbury, London, walnut panelling to piers, pilasters and counter fronts.
1929/39 Lancashire County Offices, panelling etc. etc.

The men employed in Martyns' Joinery Department 1914—1918:

Foreman — H. Austin

L. Price	
G. Tudge	A.R. Miller
W. Faracher	W. Henry
O.E. Miles	H. Boardwell
D.F. Sandy	R.W. Dickin
W. Carr	T.C.V. Brunsdon
A. Bowyer	W. Detheridge
H.M. Brooks	E. Saunders
E. Dowdeswell	E.G. Rogers
F.B. Horner	F. Stevenson
H. Aves	W. Ball
W. Anderton	A. Palmer
? Woodruff	W. Brown
R.A. Shorney	J. Entwistle
H.M. Smith	W. Prout
W. Kerslake	M.T. Rogers
J. Ballantine	F. Bush
M. Hooper	J. Miles
H. Bould	V. Cooper
S.O. Porter	D.T. Williams
S.T. Davies	G.W. Evans
R. Cook	W. Hooper
H. Poole	S. Walters
C. Burford	A.T. Quelch
W. Curtis	R. Graham
O. Porter	? Branchflower
A. Whittle	T. Morrow
L. Denley	E.G. Williams
H. Frankland	W.B. Bradley
A. Norton	S. Morris
W.V. Bliss	W.H. Heal

The men employed at H.H. Martyn Joinery Department 1939—1945:

Foreman — H. Austin

T. White	
O.E. Miles	H.F. Badger
A.H. Janes	? Birchley
A.E. Gregory	H. Bloor
C. Evans	S.J. Ward
S. Eeles	A.H. Brown
T. Clarkson, later manager of cabinet makers	E.A. Moss
	E. Farley
T.W. Caudle	E. Morton
F. Boughton	E.G. Baker
B.T. Barratt	F. White
R. Bowden	C.G. Yiend
W. Binmore	S. Edden

As can be seen, the joinery staff was reduced by two thirds by 1945.

A few others who have been mentioned to me were: Walter Gregory, Frank Holiday, Sid Paish, Herbert Brewer, Mr. Stinchcombe and Wilbert Cook, who invented a special edging tool for veneering, still used today by Ted Clifford in his joinery and cabinet making business.

Arthur Bush, who came from the Bath Furniture Co., was brilliant at carving and shaping the legs for chairs or tables; a few deft strokes with the draw knife and spoke shave and the beautiful shape would emerge.

One has only to see the furniture and panelling made by the men of this department to realise that each one was an artist in his own right, dedicated to produce **The Best.**

Part of the Joinery Department about 1922.

Stuart House, Cambridge. Panelling and decorative plaster work.

Design Department 1922.

Tea table made for Prince Ibrahim.

Side table.

Bookcase made for Prince Ibrahim.

Sideboard about 1934.

First Church of Christ Scientist Stockport. Architects: Arnold England. Panelling desks and rostrum in Australian oak.

Library. Greenways, North Ferriby Hull. Architects: Messrs Blackmore Sykes and Co. Chimney piece, panelling and plaster ceiling.

Trophy cabinet designed by R.W. Symonds for Lloyds Bank.

Cocktail cabinet specially made for a client.

Sideboard made for The Lebanon.

Circular veneered table about 1936.

S.S. Orvieto. Architect: A.N. Prentice. The company's first ship contract, executed 1909.

Chapter 13

SHIP CONTRACTS AND TRAINS

The first ship contract placed with Martyns was for decorative work in the Orient Line's Orvieto in 1909, just one year after the company's move to its new and extensive premises at Lansdown. David Longden joined the company to take charge of ship contracts some two years later. It was no coincidence that A.W. Martyn had taken on a man to progress this valuable business who was a qualified architect with a close connection with ship design, and a close friend of Alexander McInnes Gardner, the ship interior designer.

David Longden's background had been steeped in shipping before he joined Martyns. He was educated in Glasgow, and in 1904 was articled to James Miller in Glasgow, a company which carried out considerable ship interior design including that of the Lusitania. Alexander McInnes Gardner, who worked for James Miller at that time, was responsible for most of the Lusitania designs. Later, he founded his own company and was commissioned to carry out interior designs for the Queen of Bermuda and Monarch of Bermuda, many Canadian Pacific Ships including the Empress of Britain, the Aorangi Tiki and the Aorangi Tata, on all of which Martyns received contracts.

In 1978 the Empress of Britain and Empress of Canada, both with work by Martyns, were sailing under the names of Carnival and Mardi Gras respectively out of Miami, Florida, refurbished as fun ships but still showing their breeding in the original wood panelling. However, most of the old ships have been broken up and the work by Martyns either demolished or sold off to hotels or perhaps in some cases collectors. Others ended up on the sea bed, victims of war.

Interior fitting and furnishing of ships is a complex business as nothing is straight or square, both decks and walls curving and meeting in complex multiple angles. This complicated geometry has to be interpreted in the manufacture of the wood panelling so that it fits perfectly at all points. The decorative plaster work must have complementary curves and the pattern continue and not run-off. Pillars must look upright where deck and ceiling may curve at opposing angles. The final result should look square, so optical illusion is part of the skill.

The dedicated workforce interpreted these problems accurately. Martyns' first ship contract on the S.S. Orvieto (A.N. Prentice, architect) was the standard bearer which led to the company carrying out decorative work on well over 100 ships in the next 58 years for customers such as:

Elder Dempster, Ellerman and Bucknall, Silver Line and New Zealand Shipping Co.
Anchor Line (Henderson Bros.) Ltd.
Peninsular and Oriental Steam Navigation Company Ltd.
Cosulich Line — Blue Star Line (1920) Ltd.
Orient Line — Lamport & Holt, Ltd.
The Cunard Steamship Company Ltd.
British India Steam Navigation Company Ltd.
Canadian Pacific Steamships Ltd.
Canadian National Steamships, etc., etc.

In 1933 an account of the extensive ship interior decoration work done by Martyns appeared in the Shipbuilding and Shipping Record. The writer listed thirty-six ships on which Martyns had worked in the 24 years since they had first entered this field. He went on to say:

"With the services of the architect being more and more utilised for the design of ship interiors, it is fortunate that a firm such as H.H. Martyn & Co. (who have probably executed more complete ship interiors than any other firm in existence and have years of experience behind them) are moving with the times and are, shall we say, completely au fait with all forms of modern decoration. They have at their disposal not only well equipped workshops covering practically every branch of the industries involved, but also craftsmen and operatives with a long tradition of shipbuilding behind them, who are just as skilled in the handling of modern design as the more traditional.

S.S. Orvieto. Plaster ceiling and columns for dining room.

"The long list of ships which have been dealt with by H.H. Martyn & Co. is sufficient in its variety to show that whatever type of decoration is being used, the work and execution has been to the satisfaction of the owners. Ship decoration, particularly in the modern manner, offers no easy task to the craftsman. The straight and angular lines of the average interior on shore present problems which are simple compared with the ever curving lines of the ship interior. Accuracy in execution is almost more essential than in the most intricate cabinet making. Without perfect craftsmanship, the most skilful and attractive design is doomed to failure, and especially when an effect of simplicity is being aimed at, as is usually the case today.

"It is not possible to cover up bad joinery work with paint and putty. It will stand as it is left, a credit or otherwise to the one who has executed it. In the 'Empress of Britain' particularly this was very obvious. Practically the whole of the work carried out by H.H. Martyn & Co. relied for its effect on good workmanship and the materials used, which in this case consisted mainly of various rich timbers left more or less in their natural condition without paint or stain of any kind.

"H.H. Martyn & Co. Ltd. have a distinct advantage over some other decorators insofar as they are able in their extensive workshops, which comprise some five acres of working floor space at Cheltenham, to produce metalwork, joinery, woodcarving, fibrous plaster, stone and marblework sculpture. They are, therefore, independent of outside manufacturing assistance in any work which is placed in their hands. Results of this can be seen in the ships they have dealt with, producing a sense of harmony both in design and crafsmanship."

This harmony of craftsmanship led to contracts from practically all the leading shipping companies and eminent ship decorative architects, some of

S.S. Orvieto.

whom were: A. McInnes Gardner, Esq., F.R.I.A.S.; Messrs. Mewes & Davis (Arthur J. Davis, Esq., A.R.A., F.R.I.B.A.; Charles H. Gage, Esq., F.R.I.B.A.); A.N. Prentice, Esq., R.B.C., F.R.I.B.A.; Messrs. P.A. Staynes Roi; A.H. Jones, F.R.I.B.A.; Robert Whyte, Esq."

The making of fluted columns for ships was a complicated task involving a great many processes. The columns were designed to enclose the steel uprights and were therefore hollow. They were made up in tongued and grooved lengths, which were fixed together to form a tube. The turning of these tubes, often 15′ long, was a task entrusted to Mr. Moss, who had his workshop in the Rose and Crown Passage and in which he had fitted a home-built lathe of mammoth proportions, driven by a gas engine belonging to his neighbour Mr. Isher in the adjoining property. The complete column would be turned by Mr. Moss to a perfect finish. When returned to Sunningend the hollow column would be sawn in two lengthways, tongued and grooved, carved, french polished and sent to the ship yard for fitting round the stanchions. One of the famous ships for which Mr. Moss turned the Martyn columns was the ill-fated Titanic.

Anchor Line Building, Liverpool. Architect: James Millar. Decorative plaster work, panelling and woodcarving.

S.S. Orvieto. **Decorative ceiling, panelling and columns.**

S.S. Empress of Asia. Architect: G.A. Crawley. Dining saloon, plaster and wrought iron work.

S.S. Otranto dining saloon. Decorative work and dining furniture, similar work in first class public rooms, staircases and entrances.

S.S. Orvieto.

R.M.S. Lusitania. Architect: James Millar. This work was probably carried out during a refit.

Further work probably carried out during a refit on R.M.S. Lusitania.

French polishing of the fine woodwork in ships went on for many years as the following lists supplied by J.L. Booy shows. He started work at Martyns at the age of 14 in 1923 and became a highly proficient french polisher working on the 57 ships listed from 1947 to 1966.

Works No.	Date	Vessel	Line
945		Hinemoa	N.Z.S.
		Orion (R/C)	Orient
1400		Falaise	British Rail
1828	16- 6-47	Dwarka	B-I
707	30-10-47	Solandra	B-I
1826	30-10-47	Sirdahna	B-I
	30-10-47	Duchess of Richmond	C P S
948	1- 2-48	Accra	Elder Dempster
949	1- 2-48	Apapa	Elder Dempster
611	6- 6-48	Kampala	B-I
616	6- 6-48	Karonza	B-I
	6- 6-48	Duchess of Bedford	C P S
	6- 6-48	Stanfirth	Stanhope Line
	1- 2-48	Stanroyal	Stanhope Line
	12-12-48	Orcades (R/C)	C P S
689	12-12-48	Angola	Portuguese
	20- 1-49	Queen of Bermuda	Furness
693	3- 3-49	Port Brisbane	Port Line
	18- 5-49	Otranto (R/C)	Orient
951	22- 8-49	Himalaya	P & O
	22- 8-49	Rangitoto	New Zealand
	10- 9-49	Rangitata	New Zealand
	30- 4-50	Empress of Scotland	C P S
	8- 6-50	Chusan	P & O
119	31- 3-51	Ocean Monarch	Furness
705	11- 5-51	Port Aukland	Port Line
1884	11- 5-51	Patricia	Swedish
	11- 5-51	Oronsay	Orient
629	29- 9-51	Aureol	Elder Dempster
454	20-12-51	Normania	British Rail
636	8- 9-53	Olympia	Greek Line
675	12- 2-54	Arcadia	P & O
1021	12- 3-54	Orsova	Orient
692	1- 9-54	Saxonia	Cunard
1476	22- 9-54	Iberia	P & O
1498	1- 1-55	Southern Cross	Shaw Saville
693	30- 4-55	Ivernia	Cunard
	15- 7-55	Ocean Layer	Cable Layer
1533	29- 2-56	Reina Del Mar	Pacific Steamship
731	14- 4-56	Empress of Britain	C P S
1849	1- 6-56	Bergensfjord	Norwegian
733	1- 7-56	Nevasa	Troopship
478	20-12-56	Ann Evelyn	Yacht
1269	20-12-56	Carnatic	
155	28- 2-57	Empress of England	C P S
700	28- 5-57	Sylvania	Cunard
1061	12-11-60	Oriana	Orient
171	10- 3-61	Empress of Canada	C P S
1974	5- 5-61	Princepe Perfeito	Portuguese
1621	12- 5-61	Canberra	P & O
	15- 7-61	M.Y. Ariane	Yacht
175	20- 4-62	Northern Star	Shaw Saville
716	20- 5-65	British Confidence	Tanker
728	28- 2-66	Kungsholm	Swedish
	14- 5-66	M.Y. Chambel IV	Yacht
830	27- 5-66	Wahine	New Zealand
	— — 66	Britannia	Swedish

S.S. Orford. Decorative bronze panel 9 ft. 2 ins. long.

S.S. Vandyck. Plaster work decorations to the dome.

The main areas in which Martyns worked were the first class lounges and foyers, staircases, smoking rooms and swimming pools. Work ranged however from the Queen liners to troop ships.

An important contract in 1950 was for the new Southampton Passenger Terminal Ocean Dock, specified as:— 'taking over the whole of the public spaces and providing wall treatment, ceilings, decorations, partitions, lighting, heating, air conditioning, plumbing, flooring, electrical installation, sanitary fittings, kitchen equipment, loud speakers, furniture and furnishings.'

Martyns was also called upon to do refits for liners and in the late 1940s carried out refurnishing and redecoration to the Queen Mary, Empress of France, Queen of Bermuda, Orcades, Empress of Scotland, Orontes and Rangitata. These post-war refits were carried out on a cost-plus basis, a favourable arrangement for the company since no contract could lose money.

The Canadian Pacific ships also came in for refits. Unfortunately all the old 'Empress' ships of this line were sunk during the war, taking with them many men and much of the work of earlier Martyns craftsmen. However, many 'Duchess' ships were re-fitted by Martyns on their return from troop service.

Work was offered the company by P & O when they built replacements for those lost through enemy action, two of which were the Orcades and the Oronsay in the 1950s.

Arnold Edwards, manager of the foundry, had become a great favourite over the years with Cunard, and when it came to the contract for the Green Goddess every single item of metal work was produced by him in the Martyn foundry.

The very last shipping contract was the reconditioning of the Ocean Monarch at Cammell Laird, Birkenhead, this contractor being dogged by union problems.

In 1961 Martyns worked on the new Canadian Pacific liner, Empress of Canada. Doors of silver bronze, finely figured willow veneer panelling for the walls and many other decorative features were produced and fitted for the Windsor Lounge and the Canada Room, the main social centre of the ship. The same year saw work on the P & O liner Canberra, in which the first class entrance halls and stairways and a unique spiral staircase were Martyn made and decorated. Just prior to these, work had been completed on the Portugese liner Princepe Perfeito in numerous public rooms and the swimming baths.

S.S. Vandyck. Lounge, decorative plaster work, ceiling, walls and columns.

In 1967 Martyns signed a contract for £¼ million for work on the Cunard liner Queen Elizabeth II, to provide panelling, ceilings and all the fittings in the after part of the ship.

T.A. Miller, Martyns contracts director from 1947, described to me some of the aspects of the Queen Elizabeth II work:— "On the Q.E.II. contract we sweated for quite a time; six firms had tendered, five contracts had been awarded and we still had not been selected. Martyns, however, was awarded the last one and Jack Wallace, Cunard's architect, said he singled Martyns out because the work required was so varied and was a wide contract in terms of materials. The contract was for the aft staircase, conference room, after bar, through deck room (double room), main lounge and stage.

"Curved glass was required for the staircase, curved in plan and raking in elevation, (made of armoured glass by Pilkingtons for Martyns). The fitting at the butt joints had to be perfect.

"There was slow progress on fixing the panelling and plasterwork. Scottish joiners were used at the Scott Lithgow shipyard to fix the items made at Martyns in Cheltenham. Union trouble was a considerable problem, Jimmy Reid at the time being chairman of the shop stewards. Eventually the ship was moved to the Terminal Dock, Southampton and the Scottish joiners were no longer involved and also, fortunately, a troublesome ringleader was dropped. However, I needed men to finish the work on time or we would incur penalties. I obtained ten joiners from local builders and 80 from the Naval Docks at Portsmouth, so work progressed well. Because of engine problems we found ourselves with extra time and successfully completed the work ready for the trials."

F.A. Glover spent 49 years with Martyns, mainly in charge of outside contracts engaged in assembly and fitting at the shipyards. The first ship he worked on was the S.S. Empress of Asia for the Canadian Pacific Steamship Co. in 1914 and his first in total charge of the work was the Oronsay for Orient Line in 1924. He applied his expertise to over 100 ships in his 49 years with Martyns.

On 17th April 1935 a contract with the Orient Steam Navigation Co. Ltd. was drawn up for work on S.S. Orion, to cost £4616.10s.3d., to be carried out as follows: decorations for the various tourist class saloons, entrances etc. constructing the forward and after staircases, electric light fittings and accessories on the following decks:

P & O Steam Ship Maloja. Dining saloon, plaster work and panelling.

Tourist Class Dining Saloon 'F' Deck, Tourist Class Cafe 'E' Deck, Tourist Class Lounge 'F' Deck, Children's Tourist Class Nursery 'E' Deck.

Lighting, including fixed or occasional standard or table lamps were a line much to the fore from the early days. Quite a number of trains were fitted out by Martyns, including the train used for the Prince of Wales' tour of India in 1920, King Farouk's train and also trains of the Canadian Pacific Railway, for which table lamps of classic design were made, incorporating rams' heads. A.W. Martyn bought in some of the excess examples of these Canadian Pacific Railway lamps for his home in Charlton Kings. Similar work was also done for the Canadian Pacific Railway Hotel in Vancouver. A.W. Martyn personally supervised the making of terra-cotta heads of various animals at Doulton's factory for the hotel. The animal heads were set high on the exterior of the building.

In 1938 a further contract was received from John Brown for the Cunard White Star Co. for work on ship 552, (Queen Elizabeth), to include the tourist main staircase, decorative work, walls and ceilings, tourist main staircase and entrances, all at a cost of £11,465.0s.0d.

Some of the work produced in 1935 for the Queen Mary included the electrical fittings, of which detailed accounts are available. Light fittings in silver bronze to various designs from trough lighting to pilot lights were produced. The contract was for 272 lights for the Music Practice Room, First Class Main Staircase, 'C' Deck Entrance, 'B' Deck Entrance, 'A' Deck Entrance and Main Deck Entrance. A typical specification was:- silver bronze with silver bronze fittings, decorative glass, stoved white enamel copper reflectors all fitted and wired, at a contract price of £4710.7s.0d. The Queen Mary is now a tourist attraction, permanently moored off Long Beach, California. Other work by Martyns which can still be seen in all its splendour is plasterwork, joinery and metal-work in the main foyers, staircases and First Class public rooms.

The following ships all had work by Martyn craftsmen in them but records are minimal and though mention is made in some instances of a particular room it may not be that it was the only contract on that ship. Where no location of work is given the records are incomplete. Many of the shipping companies had their records destroyed by bombs during the war.

S.S. Vandyck. Music room decorative work.

Carmenia

Canberra
Spiral staircase and entrance halls in Australian walnut (Design by Hugh Casson).

Franconia

Ivernia

Kungsholme

Northern Star

Southern Star

Driana
Music Lounge.

Saxonia

S.S. Awatea
Dining Saloon First Class.

S.S. Western Prince
Smoke Room.

S.S. Empress of Scotland
Dining Room.

S.S. Seucia

S.S. Western Prince
Main Stairway.

S.S. Oronsay
Smoking Room First Class.

S.S. Fort Amherst
Dining Saloon.

The Architectural Review mentions Martyns in connection with the following ships only:

The Empress of Russia, the smoking room of Jacobean character in toned oak. Also in 1914 the Orama, carved woodwork and plaster ceilings.

T.S.S. Orama. Dining Saloon (first class).
Architect: A.N. Prentice, Esq., F.R.I.B.A.

S.S. Empress of Asia. Sussex Room.

A list from a Martyns Brochure:

Ships

S.S. Queen Elizabeth — Cunard Steamship Co., Ltd.
Staircases, Foyers and Entrances.
G. Grey Wornum, Esq., F.R.I.B.A.

S.S. Queen Mary — Cunard Steamship Co., Ltd.
Staircases, Foyers and Entrances.
Messrs. Mewes & Davis.

S.S. Empress of Britain — Canadian Pacific Steamship Co., Ltd.
First-Class Public Rooms, Foyers and Entrances.
Messrs. Staynes & Jones.

S.S. Empress of Japan — Canadian Pacific Steamship Co., Ltd.
First-Class Public Rooms, Foyers and Entrances.
Messrs. Staynes & Jones.

S.S. Duchess of Bedford — Canadian Pacific Steamship Co., Ltd.
First-Class Public Rooms, Foyers and Entrances.
Messrs Staynes & Jones.

S.S. Duchess of Athol — Canadian Pacific Steamship Co., Ltd.
First-Class Public Rooms, Foyers and Entrances.
Messrs Staynes & Jones.

S.S. Duchess of Richmond — Canadian Pacific Steamship Co., Ltd.
First-Class Public Rooms, Foyers and Entrances.
Messrs. Staynes & Jones.

S.S. Duchess of York — Canadian Pacific Steamship Co., Ltd.
First-Class Public Rooms, Foyers and Entrances.
Messrs. Staynes & Jones.

S.S. Monarch of Bermuda
First-Class Public Rooms.
Messrs. A. McInnes, Gardner & Partners.

S.S. Queen of Bermuda
Vestibules.
Messrs. A. McInnes, Gardner & Partners.

S.S. Lady Nelson — Canadian National Steamship Co.
First-Class Public Rooms, Foyers and Entrances.
Robert Whyte, Esq.

S.S. Lady Drake — Canadian National Steamship Co.
First-Class Public Rooms, Foyers and Entrances.
Robert Whyte, Esq.

S.S. Lady Hawkins — Canadian National Steamship Co.
First-Class Public Rooms, Foyers and Entrances.
Robert Whyte, Esq.

S.S. Otranto. Architect: A.N. Prentice. Lounge, decorative work.

S.S. Lady Rodney — Canadian National Steamship Co.
First-Class Public Rooms, Foyers and Entrances.
Robert Whyte, Esq.

T.S.S. Orama — Orient Steamship Navigation Co.
First-Class Public Rooms, Foyers, Staircase and Entrances.
A.N. Prentice, Esq., F.R.I.B.A.

T.S.S. Oronsay — Orient Steamship Navigation Co.
First-Class Public Rooms, Foyers and Entrances.
A.N. Prentice, Esq., F.R.I.B.A.

T.S.S. Ormond — Orient Steamship Navigation Co.
First-Class Public Rooms, Foyers and Entrances.
A.N. Prentice, Esq., F.R.I.B.A.

T.S.S. Orontes — Orient Steamship Navigation Co.
First-Class Public Rooms, Foyers and Entrances.
A.N. Prentice, Esq., F.R.I.B.A.

T.S.S. Otranto — Orient Steamship Navigation Co.
First-Class Public Rooms, Foyers, Entrances, Smoke Room and cedar wood panelling.
A.N. Prentice, Esq., F.R.I.B.A.

T.S.S. Orford — Orient Steamship Navigation Co.
First-Class Public Rooms, Foyers and Entrances.
A.N. Prentice, Esq., F.R.I.B.A.

T.S.S. Orcades — Orient Steamship Navigation Co.
First-Class Public Rooms, Foyers and Entrances.
Brian O'Rorke, Esq., M.A., F.R.I.B.A.

T.S.S. Orion — Orient Steamship Navigation Co.
Cabins de Luxe, Tourist Class Public Rooms, Entrances and Staircases.
Brian O'Rorke, Esq., M.A., F.R.I.B.A.

Metal castings for The Queen Mary.

Each photograph was signed on the back. "To my friend and collaborator A. Edwards from Walter Gilbert. Feb. 1936.
The Queen Mary, similar metal work.

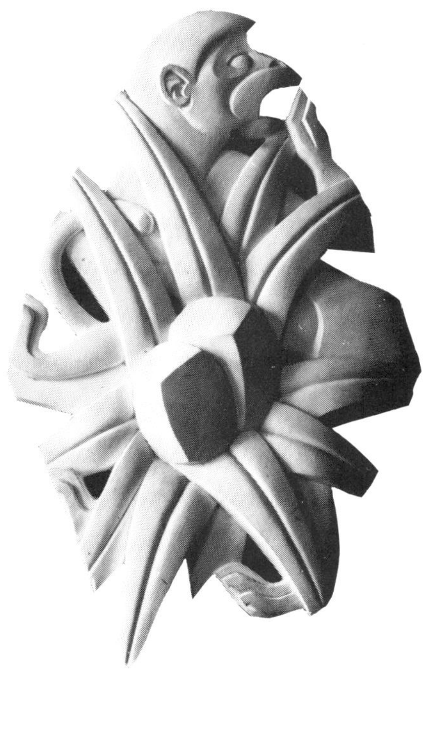

The Queen Mary. Carved wood paterns for casting shown in photograph.

Martyns work is to be seen in the First-Class Public Rooms of numerous large liners including the following, pre-1934:

Maloja	Orford
Vandyke	Vulcania
Vauban	Toloa
Lancastrian	Princess Kathleen
Cameronia	Duchess of Bedford
Moldavia	Duchess of Atholl
Empress of Asia	Duchess of Richmond
Empress of Russia	Duchess of York
Telma	Lady Nelson
Ulna	Lady Hawkins
Indarra	Lady Drake
Princess Marguerite	Lady Rodney
Orvieto	Orontes
Otranto	Rangitata
Orama	Rangitane
Ormonde	Empress of Japan
Oronsay	Empress of Britain

The Queen Mary, similar metal work.

War time amenity ships and leave ships for men and women serving in the Far East stations were decorated economically.

Menetheseus
Officers' ward room, Wrens' mess, Petty Officers' Recreations room.

Yachts

Fort Townsend
Upper deck.

M.Y. Nimet Allah
Owner deck cabin/dining room.

C.P.S. Liner Duchess of Bedford. Architects: Staynes and Jones.

For the Royal Barge, Martyns was commissioned by the Admiralty to carve the fine figurehead.

The Shaw Savill Lines vessel Ocean Monarch was probably the last of the incredible number of liners luxuriously fitted out by Martyns. The Empress of Japan contract was perhaps the most extensive. Many others may have included as much work but records are no longer available.

On the Empress of Japan an advertisement in the Architectural Review includes the following copy:

'Shipbuilders:- Fairfield Shipbuilding & Engineering Co., Govan, Scotland.

Architects:- Messrs. Stains & Jones.

Martyns decorative work:- The whole of the decorative furniture, carpets, electric fittings etc. to:- First Class Dining Saloon, Private Dining Saloon, Verandah Café, Smoke Room, Lounge, Card Room, Writing Room, Palm Court, Swimming Bath, Entrance to Swimming Bath. Also to the Deluxe Suites, Entrance Halls, Bedrooms, Sitting Rooms and Verandahs etc.'

From Advertisements in the Architectural Review:

1919/23	S.S. Orvieto, lounge.
1919/23	Empress of Asia, Suffolk Room.
1919/23	Empress of Asia, Dining Saloon.
1919/23	S.S. Ormonde, First Class Lounge.
1923/29	R.M.S. Orford, the lounge.
1923/29	S.S. Otranto, Lounge, Writing Room, Dining Saloon, First Class Public Rooms, Staircases etc.
1932	Monarch of Bermuda, Smoking Room, Writing Rooms, Library, Lounge, Wing Cafes, Verandah Cafe, Midship Entrances, Sun and 'A' Decks, Forward Entrances and Gymnasium.

Although Martyns shipwork contracts were probably its most extensive activity and incorporated some of its finest work, research has proved to be difficult because of the short life of many of the ships owing to the war, and also because few records survive. In many cases, even where records exist, only the architect and not the company or the men producing the work is mentioned. The chapter is therefore far shorter than it should be.

It is also sad that, although at one time in the offices at Cheltenhan there was an extensive library of photographs showing the work the company had done on every ship, it would seem that these too, like many of the ships, have disappeared without trace.

The interior fitting out of first class railway carriages was another prestigious business for the company.

The known work on the Royal Trains for the Prince of Wales Tour and King Farouk have already been mentioned, as have the Canadian Pacific Railway rolling stock, but at the time of going to press it has proved impossible to find photographs or further details of the work. Therefore this important part of the company's work must remain undocumented for the present.

S.S. Empress of Scotland. Architects: Messrs. P.A. Staynes, R.O.I. and A.H. Jones, F.R.I.B.A.

S.S. Monarch of Bermuda. Smoking room. Architects: Messrs. A. McInnes, Gardner & Partners.

S.S. Western Prince. Main stairway. Architects: Messrs. A. McInnes, Gardner & Partners.

T.S.S. Gothic. Nickel silverwork, 1948.

S.S. Orontes. Lounge (first class). Architect: A.N. Prentice, Esq., F.R.I.B.A.

S.S. Empress of Britain. "D" Deck. Entrance fireplace. Architects: Messrs. P.A. Staynes, R.O.I. & A.H. Jones, F.R.I.B.A.

Spiral staircase — B Deck entrance. S.S. Canberra designed by the Casson Conder Partnership.

Saloon — Continental Pullman cars. Martyns carried out the whole of the interior decoration including panelling, marqueterie work, furniture and fittings.

S.S. Orontes. Nickel silver castings, typical of work carried out on many ships.

Fred Arkell — at work carving for St. Paul's Cathedral pulpit.

Chapter 14

WORK IN LONDON AND OTHER MAJOR CITIES OF THE WORLD

It seems fitting that the work of an Englishman born in Worcester, 'The Faithful City', so named for its royal allegiance to Charles II, who by hard work and bulldog-like — or more aptly for his stature, terrier-like, tenacity — fought his way from poverty to success, should eventually, through the company he founded, be so widely represented in the important buildings of the capital city of his country and indeed world wide.

H.H. Martyn & Co.'s work is to be seen in the splendour of the finest halls, where the nation honours its most illustrious visitors — in the corridors of Government, in the financial centre of the City, in the Courts of Justice, in the religious heart. In fact in the fabric of society of the very core of our land the supreme Martyn craftsmanship exhibits a parallel in its excellence to the highest institutions, professions, and nobility with which it is associated.

Martyns work is to be found not only in these lofty courts of London but in the everyday surroundings of its citizens; its craftsmanship can be seen adorning their paths, gateways, shops, and monuments, embellishments of rich carvings and columns, enhancing the surroundings which most people take for granted but which if removed, would bring a starkness to the city. It is often said that if people looked up instead of at the pavement or into shop windows they would see the splendour of the city. The fine concepts of architects and artists, made real by the worker in wood, stone, marble, plaster and metal, should be seen and admired as a legacy unlikely to be repeated in such abundance or in such excellence again.

On a journey through London in search of Martyns work, it seems fitting to begin in Whitehall at the Cenotaph, a memorial in strong contrast to the intricate skills of carving and decoration for which the company is famed. Pure of line, the Cenotaph designed by Sir Edwin Landseer Lutyens is in its simplicity profound. Entrusting H.H. Martyn & Co. to cut, shape and erect the form and carve the simple wreaths was an honour for the company, the culminating height of all the many memorials to the men who died in the first world war, for which the company had become already famous and was later in the second world war to be called upon to create again.

The Speaker's Chair for the House of Commons, in the Sunningend Works.

From the Cenotaph, the focus of the nation's respect for those lost in two world wars, it is a short distance to the Houses of Parliament, the centre of government, and thence to the very centre of that institution, the Speaker's Chair. Carved of Australian black bean wood, a gift from Australia, and designed by Sir Giles Gilbert Scott, O.M., R.A., F.R.I.B.A. to resemble the previous chair destroyed in the Blitz, it stands on its platform at a height of 13′ 6″. Much of the work on the chair, in particular the canopy and coat of arms, was carved by Charles Gisborne, who had been with the company since the 1900s and retired soon after carving this, his last great work. He was honoured with the B.E.M. for his contribution to this and his many other works of art carving. T.A. Miller, Martyns contracts director, told me that the company was very keen to get the contract for the Speakers Chair, in fact his instructions were "at all costs get it!" However, when the gift of black bean wood arrived from Australia, it was not a good sample and in the end Mallinsons supplied the wood, which satisfied the craftsmen. The Australian gift is not lessened by this; they perhaps had not met perfectionists like Martyns before. Others who were involved in the carving with Charlie Gisborne were Sam Bourne, Lashford Spinks, Fred Arkell and Les Timms.

Still in the House of Commons, there are the impressive Dispatch Boxes which were also designed by Sir Giles, and blend Gothic and Tudor traditions. A gift from New Zealand, they were made by Martyns of purruri wood, which has a satin-like finish. The boxes are enriched with finely cast and chased bronze clasps, locks and decorative pierced work, all of which was burnished until it looked like silver. The whole is lined with vaumol hide — the green leather used throughout the House. The great table on which the Dispatch Boxes stand was also made by Martyns.

About the House of Commons are 500 cast bronze grilles and many other beautifully modelled grilles in the doors of the chamber, as well as 'armour bright' steel dog grates for the Prime Minister's conference room and the division lobbies. The gallery rails are also Martyn-made, as is the special wood carving which only the senior craftsmen from Martyns were skilled enough to execute, so intricate was the work to match the old carvings with which it intermingles.

One of those who worked in the House of Commons was G.F. Turner, whose carving in the free style of Gibbons won him a place of excellence among the excellent at Martyns. His name appears from the early 1900s. He was manager of the Arts Department for many years, but later left to form

Charlie Gisborne B.E.M. working on the carving for the House of Commons, Speaker's Chair.

One of the pair of House of Commons Despatch Boxes made in purri wood embellished with burnished bronze.

Les Timms carving a section of the Royal Coat of Arms for the front of the Speaker's Chair.

his own company in Bolton, Lancs, a successful enterprise in a similar field. Turner's father, Arthur, was a Martyns craftsman also and it was through him that his son became an early apprentice of Martyns. The names of others who worked on this historic building are unfortunately unrecorded but their work will testify for many years to their skill.

In 1953 restoration work in the finest tradition and equal to the work of past master carvers was done by the company's own craftsmen in the restorative work in the Guildhall, where Gothic panelling and heraldic carving was carried out for Sir Giles Scott, Son & Partners. Again only the older, more highly skilled men were equal to the original craftsmen. Sir Giles was delighted with the oak panelling and the Crown with supporting Lions. Also in the Guildhall stands Oscar Nemon's seated figure of Winston Churchill, cast in Martyns' foundry and weighing half a ton.

Central Hall, Westminster, also has Martyns joinery, wood carving and fibrous plaster work faithfully restored to its original glory.

An early patron of Martyns was Queen Victoria, who commissioned decorative work by the company. Later, King George V used the company's services, for which in 1917 it was awarded the Royal Warrant. Windsor Castle has Martyn joinery and woodcarving, including the altar rail in St. George's Chapel. In Buckingham Palace there are joinery, fibrous plaster and decorations, one venue being the Long Gallery. Other work records at the Palace are not available, but it is known that the lift interiors of the Queen's apartments were refurnished every year by Martyns, having been originally made by the company for Otis Lifts.

More recently work was carried out in St. Paul's Cathedral. In 1964 the company, under the direction of Mr. Paul Paget, R.S.A., F.R.I.B.A., made the magnificent pulpit, including the stairs leading to it and the great canopy over it, all exquisitly carved and fashioned.

Westminster Cathedral has work produced at an earlier time in the company's history, about 1904. The Canon's Stalls are made in oak inlaid with veneers and also mother of pearl, ivory and rare woods. A fine example of great skill, they are situated on either side of the altar sanctuary and are worth close examination.

Westminster Abbey has only one example of Martyns work, The Queen Alexandra's Memorial, on which Harry Breckin, according to his daughter, was working at the time of the General Strike in 1926.

David Holford and others of the team assembling part of St. Paul's Cathedral pulpit.

Foreman carver M. Norman working on acanthus leaf design for St. Paul's Cathedral pulpit.

Ted Large at work on a section of St. Paul's Cathedral pulpit.

Left to Right — Harold Guest and Tom Bridges on final assembly of St. Paul's Cathedral pulpit.

Left to Right — R. Davidson, David Holford and Walter Gregory, foreman, at work on St. Paul's Cathedral pulpit.

Other smaller places of worship in London where work can be seen are: St. Paul's Church, Wilton Place, joinery and wood carving; All Saints Church, Highgate, bronze memorial with design of soldiers and horses by Robert Lindsey Clark; Third Church of Christ Scientist, fibrous plaster work; St. Andrew's Church, Holborn Viaduct, particularly fine fibrous plaster work and panelling; Notre Dame, Wilton Place, London; Church of St. John Baptist, Kensington, pulpit in stone; St. Paul's Church, Knightsbridge, finely carved Bishop's Throne and surround. Wood carving was executed in the following churches before 1905: St. Simon's, Paddington; St. Lawrence, Old Jewry; St. Saviour's, Ealing; Holy Trinity, Roehampton, stone screen of fine proportions; St. Peter's, South Tottenham; St. James, Muswell Hill.

Some fine gates at Marble Arch, mentioned previously in the chapter on bronze casting (Chapter V) have since been removed. Other work will in the course of years have been destroyed by bombing or dismantled in the interest of progress, so some mentioned in this book may inevitably have gone.

Bureaucracies too can boast of work by Martyns, the doors of the New Government Offices in Whitehall Gardens having two doors cast in aluminium 22′9″ high 16′ wide at a cost of £13,000. These were installed in 1951. Dowty Auto Units installed the electro-hydraulic system which operates the doors, which weigh several tons each.

Panelling, carving and plasterwork for the Mercers Hall was another contract won by the company. Instrumental in obtaining this notable contract was the expertise of H.J. Johnson, a marvellous draughtsman and head of the drawing office. He had an amazing ability to draw in detail from fragments of old plasterwork. Craftsmen in the carving shop worked from the intricate drawings to produce mouldings of a plaster carving which now is fixed high over a door in the rebuilt hall of the Mercers Company in the City.

Messrs. Selfridges & Co. Ltd. above main entrance in Oxford Street. The whole work in cast iron, to the design of Messrs. Graham, Anderson, Probst and White.

The men who carved are nameless but they gave deeply of their personal effort and skill. Carved fruit and flowers, leaves transparently thin, stems, inlaid panels, new balustrades, carved capitols, all had to be made to match the product of one of the greatest examples of eighteenth century craftsmanship. They succeeded triumphantly and proved that the industrial age had not extinguished English skill.

Some of the country's finest old buildings which were severely damaged or in some cases totally gutted by fire in the blitz were lovingly restored by Martyns craftsmen.

The comprehensive service offered by the company was popular with top architects engaged in this restorative work. In 1947 Martyns had fifteen of the country's finest woodcarvers, many with over 50 years of experience preceded by a comprehensive and full apprenticeship with highly skilled working teachers. This ensured that Martyns were required to work on the halls of all the liveried companies of the City which were damaged. The Mercers Hall was the most extensive contract. All the bronze, plaster, iron and carving work was done by Martyns, Maples being responsible for the soft furnishing and the chandeliers. The Guildhall contract was also extensive, and included panelling, tracery, heads and griffins carved by Les Timms and designed to hold a pole and flag on special occasions.

The T.U.C. building has bookcases and joinery work by Martyns. The Co-operative Building Society has a panelled boardroom and suite of offices. Cable House has bronze entrance doors, balconies and fan lights. The Australian Mutual Provident Society and the General Assurance office both have joinery and woodcarving by the company. The Phoenix Assurance Company has fibrous plaster work. The London and Manchester Assurance Company has stone carving and wrought iron grilles, in its main entrance. The Liverpool Victoria Friendly Society received metal work and entrance doors, and The British General Assurance Company, Cheapside has a Martyns main entrance.

The Bank of England contract was won against competition from Singers, the Bromsgrove and Birmingham Guilds, and others. Mr. Leslie Kerns was the manager at Martyns London office — a well respected man who circulated among the architects seeking work for the company. He succeeded in getting on the short list for the big Bank of England contract. However, an unusual test was set up by the Bank and its architects. In competition with others, Fred Taylor and his equivalent outside foremen were required to set up a big bronze door in the basement of the bank, which had to swing and fit perfectly to the wall to the finest tolerances. Fred Taylor had made his own needle tool for such work and his fit at all

Court Number 1, Old Bailey, London W.I. Carving, wood panelling and furnishing.

Lancashire County Offices, Preston. The chairman's bench and dais together with the panelling, seating, furniture, benches and tables, bronze radiator grilles, electric light fittings etc. In the county hall, assembly hall, committee rooms, county mess room, ladies' retiring room, private committee room, chairman's room, county architect's office and gentlemens' retiring room were carried out by H.H. Martyn & Co. about 1935.

points was perfect. His fit was the best by far, so not for the first time the team of Kerns and Taylor ensured that work came Martyns' way. At the time Martyns was doing this work another company was shoring up the sinking building by replacing oak piles with poured concrete. Fred Taylor remembers that some of the oak piles were good as new and others rotten.

Some of the bank contracts carried out by Martyns craftsmen:

Banks

Bank of England, Threadneedle Street
Bronze figure of Ariel on dome, inner bronze doors.

Martins Bank, Lombard Street
Main entrance, bronze counter grilles.

Midland Bank H.Q., Poultry
Woodcarving and joinery, stone carving, bronze doors, bronze staircases, wrought iron work, bronze windows.

Midland Bank, Oxford Street
Entrance doors in staybright steel.

Lloyds Bank H.Q.
Bronze windows.

Eastern Bank
Stone carving.

Hong Kong & Shanghai Banking Corporation, Queen Street
Metal work, doors in bronze.

Glyn Mills Bank, Lombard Street
Counter screens, entrance interior.

Bank of Canada, Cockspur Street
Counter screens.

Bank of Canada, Lothbury
Entrance counter screen.

Bank of Australasia

Standard Bank of South Africa
Joinery and woodcarving.

Midland Bank, Alpha Square
Metal work.

National Provincial Bank, Drapers Garden
American walnut panelling with stainless steel trims, fibrous plaster ceiling, American walnut table.

Sculptural groups and monuments have unfortunately not been well documented but the following are known:

In Queen Mary's Garden, Regents Park, there is a fountain group sculpted by W. McMillan R.A. and cast in the Cheltenham Foundry in 1950.

The Stag cast in aluminium for the Old Brewery Site, Victoria, London, being assembled.
Left to Right — John Hortley (Apprentice) and Alf Merrett welding.

The Stag receiving its finishing touches.
Left to right — Tom Weekes, Mr. Reed (foundry manager), Alf Merrett, Harold Cook (colourer).

Later in 1962, the 20′ high stag by F. Brainbridge-Copnall, President of the Royal Society of Sculptors, was set on the site of the Old Stag Brewery in Victoria. The sculptor stated: "It was a credit to Martyns of Cheltenham as it was probably the biggest piece of aluminium ever to be cast". He had tried everywhere to get the piece cast but only Martyns gave him the confidence. He was sure it would become a London landmark.

Some of the hotels in the City with excellent decorative work are listed. However, modernisation has often meant the destruction of fine plaster work and panelling etc. as in the case of the Cumberland Hotel, Marble Arch, where the octagonal entrance lounge and cast metal doors have made way for 'up to date' materials. A set of 12 unusual mirrors with ornate frames and peach coloured glass, to make the onlooker seem bronzed and healthy, was broken up by hammer when the 'Gentlemen's' was modernised.

The Strand Palace Hotel had the restaurant and Winter Gardens ornamented with fibrous plaster work, and the Park Lane Hotel has fibrous plaster decorative work. The Churchill Hotel, London, was one of the company's last contracts. The work was woodwork, plaster and decorations in all the public rooms and Churchill Bar.

Whitehall Theatre, London. Architects: E.A. Stone and Partners. Ebonised panelling and the complete fibrous plaster decorations.

The Stag being lifted ready for despatch.

Theatres

London Casino
Decorations and furnishings.

Saville Theatre
Decorative plaster work to auditorium stalls, bar etc.

Whitehall Theatre
Black ebonised panelling to auditorium, staircase, entrance hall, stalls, foyer and bar. Circle bar, ladies room. All decorative plaster work.

In the Royal Festival Hall in 1954 Martyns supplied the console case for the organ. It was made of veneer mahogany with ebonised ends and black inlaid lines at the top and front. When the National Theatre was opened the trowel and mallet used by the Queen were made by Martyns, as was the ornamental casket, of polished English walnut, which contained them.

Cinemas

Granada Cinema, Woolwich
Decorative plasterwork.

Regal Cinema, Marble Arch
Decorative plasterwork.

Education and Allied

Kings College for Women, Campden Hill
Stone carving.

London University
Panelled dining hall, wrought iron railings.

Science Museum, South Kensington
Showcases.

Finsbury Library
Exterior lamps etc.

Geological Museum, Kensington
Stone carving, lead facia and guttering.

Shops

Derry & Toms Ltd.
Complete restaurant, barber's shop, light fronts and walnut doors and metalwork.

Selfridges
Bronze and cast iron main entrance doors etc. and windows.

Shoreditch Electricity Show Rooms
Oak board room and showroom.

Robert Lewis, 19 St. James Street
Shopfront in Honduras mahogany.

Town Investment, 61 St. James Street
Shopfront in cast bronze.

No. 9 St. James Street, Piccadilly
Main entrance and cast lead drainpipes.

Simpson, Jermyn Street
Main entrance.

Residences

Many residences were decorated with fine plaster, panelling, wood carving and metal work. The following is a list from brochures produced by the company:

Buckingham Palace
Windsor Castle
Harewood House
Cardiff Castle
Lal Bagh Palace, Indore
Ashgate Lodge, Chesterfield
Ascot Place, Berkshire
Briery Close, Windermere
Eaves Hall, Clitheroe
Guisborough Hall
Greenways, North Ferriby
Hill Grove, Kidderminster
Horsley Park
Hyde Park Terrace
Lanwades, near Newmarket
Lexden Grange
Marsden Manor
New Court, Cheltenham
Redlands, Glasgow
Tudor Grange
11 Hill Street, Mayfair
Thornton Manor
Drovers, Singleton
Kedleston Hall, Derby
Hursley Park, Winchester
Marsh Court, Stockbridge
Cowley Manor, Cheltenham
Shugborough Hall, Stafford
Compton Castle, Somerset
Hinchingbrooke, Huntingdon
Pylewell Park, Lymington

Country Houses

Sledmere Hall, Yorks.
Joinery work, plasterwork and decorations.
Messrs. Brierley & Rutherford.

Benacre Hall
Panelling and decorations.
Messrs. Lister Lee & Sons

Notgrove Manor
Panelled hall, dining room and plaster ceiling.
A.N. Prentice, Esq., F.R.I.B.A.

Restoration of ceilings and fireplaces, fitments to bedroom.
Brian O'Rorke, Esq., M.A., F.R.I.B.A.

The Grange, Bampton
Panelling and carving to library.
Thomas Rayson, Esq., A.R.I.B.A.

Winfield House, Regent's Park
Wrought iron entrance gates, grilles, etc.
Messrs. Wimperis, Simpson & Guthrie.

Other contracts mentioned in various brochures are as follows:

A FEW

DECORATIVE CONTRACTS

CARRIED OUT BY

H·H·MARTYN & CO

LIMITED

OF

CHELTENHAM

5, GRAFTON STREET
OLD BOND STREET
LONDON · W.1 · ENGLAND

Workshops and Foundry: CHELTENHAM

Telephone: EUSTON 7000 (Extension 140)
Telegrams: SUNNINGEND · LONDON
Code: A.B.C. Fifth Edition.

ROYAL COMMISSIONS

BUCKINGHAM PALACE.
Joinery work, Fibrous Plaster and Decorations.
His Majesty's Office of Works.

HAREWOOD HOUSE, for H.R.H. The Princess Royal.
Joinery work, Plaster work and Decorations.
* *Messrs. Brierley, Rutherford & Syme.*

TRAIN FOR H.R.H. THE PRINCE OF WALES, for his Indian Tour.
Joinery work, etc.
Metropolitan-Cammell Carriage and Wagon Co. Ltd.

PALACE AT BUCHAREST for King Carol of Roumania.
Carving, Joinery work and Bronzework (Furniture by Maples).
* *F. Lorenz, Esq.*, Bucharest.

LAL BAGH PALACE, for the Maharajah (Holkar) of Indore.
Joinery work, Fibrous Plaster, Decorations and Furniture.
* *Bernard Triggs, Esq., F.R.I.B.A.*

ROYAL TRAIN FOR H.M. KING FAROUK of Egypt.
Joinery work.
Metropolitan-Cammell Carriage and Wagon Co. Ltd.

PUBLIC BUILDINGS AND TOWN HALLS

ULSTER PARLIAMENT BUILDINGS.
Stone Carving, Plasterwork and Wrought Iron.
* *Sir Arnold Thornley, F.R.I.B.A.*

NOTTINGHAM EXCHANGE.
Stone Carving, Joinery work, Fibrous Plaster, Decorations and Bronzework.
* *T. C. Howitt, Esq., F.R.I.B.A.*

BIRMINGHAM CIVIC CENTRE.
Stone Carving, Bronzework.
* *T. C. Howitt, Esq., F.R.I.B.A.*

NEWPORT CIVIC CENTRE.
Joinery work, Plasterwork, Bronzework and Decorations.
* *T. C. Howitt, Esq., F.R.I.B.A.*

SWANSEA CIVIC CENTRE.
Stone Carving, Joinery work, Plasterwork, Bronzework, Electric light fittings and Decorations.
* *Messrs. Ivor Jones & Percy Thomas.*

HORNSEY MUNICIPAL BUILDINGS.
Joinery work to Assembly Hall and Council Chamber, Bronzework to Exterior.
* *Reginald H. Uren, Esq., A.R.I.B.A.*

GEOLOGICAL MUSEUM, Kensington.
Stone Carving, Lead Fascia and Guttering.
His Majesty's Office of Works.

DERBY POLICE COURTS.
Stone Carving, Court Furnishings, Plasterwork and Metalwork.
* *C. H. Aslin, Esq., F.R.I.B.A., M.I. Struct.E.*

BARNSLEY MUNICIPAL BUILDINGS.
Council Chamber Furniture and Metalwork.
* *Messrs. Briggs & Thornley.*

PRESTON COUNTY OFFICES, Extension.
Council Chamber, Dining Rooms and Committee Rooms.
* *Stephen Wilkinson, Esq., F.R.I.B.A.*

CHICHESTER COUNTY OFFICES.
Bronze Doors and Screens, Joinery work to Assembly Hall and Committee Room.
* *C. G. Stillman, Esq., F.R.I.B.A.*

HACKNEY TOWN HALL.
Joinery work and Metalwork.
* *Messrs. Lanchester, Lodge & Davis.*

WANDSWORTH ADMINISTRATIVE BUILDINGS.
Panelling and Seating to Council Chamber and Bronze Fountain.
* *Messrs. William & Edward Hunt.*

Stockport Town Hall. Panelling and Grinling Gibbons style carving to the seating and Mayor's dias.

MANCHESTER TOWN HALL, Extension.
Bronze work to Bridges, Balustrades and Showcases, etc.
* *E. Vincent Harris, Esq.,* R.*A.*

RANGOON COURTS OF JUSTICE.
Bronze Gates.
* *Director General, India Stores Dept.*

WILTSHIRE COUNTY OFFICES, Trowbridge.
Fibrous Plasterwork.
* *P. D. Hepworth, Esq., F.R.I.B.A.*

UNIVERSITIES AND SCHOOLS

LONDON UNIVERSITY.
Panelled Dining Hall and Wrought Iron Railings.
* *Messrs. Adams, Holden & Pearson.*

STUART HOUSE, Cambridge.
Oak panelled Hall, Staircase, Board Room, Entrance Doors and Carved Tympanum.
* *Messrs. Geo. Hubbard & Son.*

CLARE COLLEGE, Cambridge.
Wrought Iron work.
* *Sir Giles Gilbert Scott,* R.*A.*

BISHOPS STORTFORD COLLEGE MEMORIAL.
Oak Organ Case.
* *Clough Williams-Ellis, Esq., M.C.,* J.P., *F.R.I.B.A.*

SOMERVILLE COLLEGE, Oxford.
Carving (after Grinling Gibbons) to Organ Case.
* *Messrs. Courtney Theobald & Dean Skurry.*

ST. JOHN'S COLLEGE, Cambridge.
Wrought Iron Entrance Gates and Railings
* *Edward Maufe, Esq., A.R.A.*
(Fixing delayed on account of War).

CATHEDRALS AND CHURCHES

WESTMINSTER CATHEDRAL.
Canons Stalls in Oak inlaid with Mother-of-Pearl, Ivory and rare woods.
* *Messrs. Norris & Shattock.*

ST. DAVID'S CATHEDRAL, Cardiff.
Oak Choir Stalls, Altar and Reredos, Pulpit and Sanctuary Lamp.
* *Messrs. Grant & Goodchild.*

WORCESTER CATHEDRAL.
Carved Mahogany Reredos and Stone Screen for Jesus Chapel.
* R. *A. Briggs, Esq., F.R.I.B.A.*

KIBWORTH CHURCH.
Carved Oak Screen.
* *W. H. Bidlake, Esq., F.R.I.B.A.*

LUTTERWORTH PARISH CHURCH.
Carved Oak Chancel Screens.
* *W. H. Bidlake, Esq., F.R.I.B.A.*

THE FIRST CHURCH OF CHRIST SCIENTIST, in Boston, U.S.A.
Panelling in Oak.
* *Chester Lindsay Churchill, Esq.*

HOLY TRINITY CHURCH, Hereford.
Chancel Screens.
* *Messrs. Nicholson & Clarke.*

BOURNVILLE CHURCH.
Pulpit in Alabaster.
* *Messrs. Harvey & Wicks.*

ST. MICHAEL'S CHURCH, Blundellsands.
Oak Choir Stalls, Reredos, Chancel panelling, Pulpit and Book Cupboards.
* *Messrs. Quiggen & Gee.*

MALVERN COLLEGE.
Carved Stone Reredos.
* *Sir Reginald Blomfield,* R.*A.*

SYNAGOGUE

LEEDS SYNAGOGUE.
Bronzework.
* *J. Stanley Wright, Esq.,* L.R.*I.B.A.*

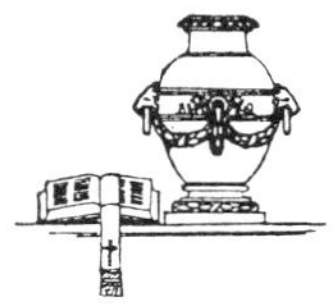

CREMATORIUMS

GOLDER'S GREEN CREMATORIUM.
Oak Seating inlaid with Ebony and Book of Memory Stand.
* *Messrs. Mitchell &* Bri*dgwater.*

CITY OF LONDON CREMATORIUM.
Panelling in Oak and Catafalque.
E. E. Finch, Esq., M.I.C.E.

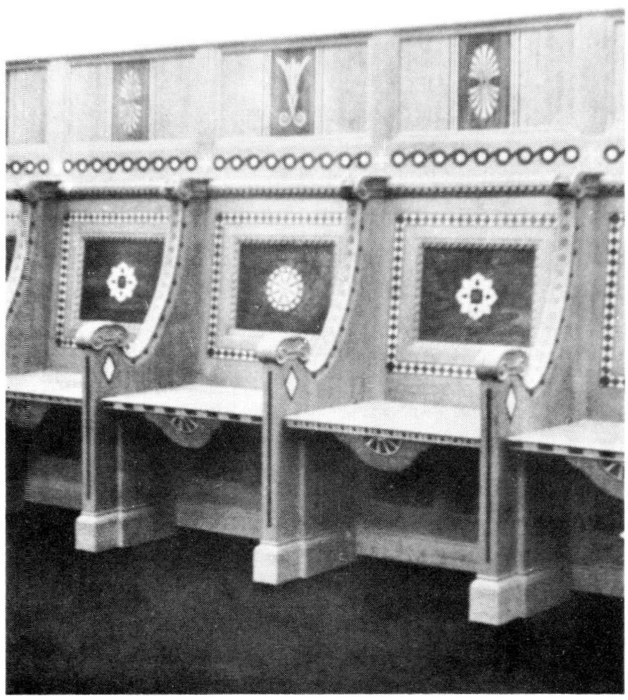

Westminster Cathedral. A portion of the Sanctuary seating inlaid with ivory and rare woods.

Union Bank of Scotland, Cornhill, exterior stone work.

BANKS

BANK OF ENGLAND, London.
Internal Bronze Doors, Bronze Figure of Ariel on Dome.
* *Sir Herbert Baker, K.C.I.E., R.A., and A. T. Scott, Esq., F.R.I.B.A.*

BANK OF ENGLAND, Southampton.
Bronze Entrance Doors, Wrought Ironwork.
* *Victor Heal, Esq., F.R.I.B.A.*
(Job suspended on account of the War).

MARTIN'S BANK, Headquarters, Liverpool.
Stone Carving, Joinery work, Plaster work, Cast Bronzework and Wrought Ironwork.
* *Herbert J. Rowse, Esq., F.R.I.B.A.*

MARTIN'S BANK, Lombard Street.
Bronze Counter Grilles.
* *Sir Herbert Baker, K.C.I.E., R.A., and A. T. Scott, Esq., F.R.I.B.A.*

MARTIN'S BANK, Branches.
Bank Fittings and Interior Decorations.
* *E. C. Aldridge, Esq., A.R.I.B.A.*

MIDLAND BANK, H.Q., Poultry.
Stone Carving, Bronze Doors, Bronze Staircases, Wrought Ironwork.
* *Laurence M. Gotch, F.R.I.B.A., with Sir Edwin Lutyens, P.P.R.A., K.C.I.E.*

LLOYDS BANK, H.Q., London.
Bronze Windows.
* *Sir John Burnet, Tait & Lorne*

HONG KONG & SHANGHAI BANK, Hong Kong.
Bronze Entrance Doors, Lift Doors.
* *Palmer & Turner, G. L. Wilson, F.R.I.B.A.*

BIRMINGHAM MUNICIPAL BANK.
Balustrades, Metalwork to Safe Deposit.
* *T. C. Howitt, Esq., F.R.I.B.A.*

EDINBURGH SAVINGS BANK.
Plasterwork, Bronze Counter Screens and Bronze Lanterns.
* *Messrs. Oldrieve Bell & Patterson.*

OFFICES

BUSH HOUSE, London.
Bronze Entrance Screens and Doors, Bronze Staircase and W.I. Staircase.
* *Messrs. Corbett, Harrison and McMurray.*

INDIA BUILDINGS, Liverpool.
Plasterwork, Bronzework.
* *Messrs. Briggs, Thornley and H. J. Rowse.*

VICTORIA HOUSE, London, W.C.1.
Bronze work and Lead work.
* *C. W. Long, Esq., F.R.I.B.A.*

UNION CORPORATION, London, E.C.
Suite of Panelled Offices
* *John Hodges, Esq., A.R.I.B.A.*

TANGANYIKA CONCESSIONS LTD., London, E.C.
Board Room in Walnut.
* *Messrs. Angell & Curtis.*

LONDON & MANCHESTER ASSURANCE CO., London.
Stone Carving and Wrought Iron Grilles.
* *A. C. Burlingham, Esq., F.R.I.B.A.*

TRUSSED CONCRETE STEEL CO., LTD., London.
Suite of Offices panelled in Peroba and Metalwork.
* *Messrs. Adie Button & Partners.*

HALIFAX BUILDING SOCIETY, Coventry.
Joinery work to Banking Hall and Bronze work.
* *Messrs. T. R. Meakin & Son.*

HALIFAX BUILDING SOCIETY, Hull.
Joinery work to Banking Hall and Bronze work.
* *W. B. Blanchard, Esq., F.R.I.B.A.*

PERMANENT CO-OPERATIVE BUILDING SOCIETY, London.
Panelled Board Room and Suite of Offices.
* *E. P. Morrey, Esq., F.R.I.B.A.*

LEICESTER PERMANENT BUILDING SOCIETY.
Joinery work, etc.
* *Messrs. G. Lawton Brown, & P. C. Jones.*

CABLE HOUSE, London.
Bronze Entrance Doors, Balconies and Fanlights.
* *Sir Herbert Baker, K.C.I.E., R.A., and A. T. Scott, Esq., F.R.I.B.A.*

ROLLS ROYCE LTD., Crewe.
Main Staircase in Bronze.
* *W. G. Phillips & Partners.*

North British Mercantile Insurance Company, showing exterior stone work to facing and capitols.

Carved stonework. Luton library.

COUNTRY HOUSES

SLEDMERE HALL, Yorks.
Joinery work, Plasterwork and Decorations.
* *Messrs. Brierley & Rutherford.*

BENACRE HALL.
Panelling and Decorations.
* *Messrs. Lister Lee & Sons.*

NOTGROVE MANOR.
Panelled Hall, Dining Room and Plaster Ceiling.
* *A. N. Prentice, Esq., F.R.I.B.A.*
Restoration of Ceilings and Fireplaces, Fitments to Bedroom.
* *Brian O'Rorke, Esq., M.A., F.R.I.B.A.*

THE GRANGE, Bampton.
Panelling and Carving to Library.
* *Thomas Rayson, Esq., A.R.I.B.A.*

WINFIELD HOUSE, Regent's Park.
Wrought Iron Entrance Gates, Grilles, etc.
* *Messrs. Wimperis, Simpson & Guthrie.*

LIBRARIES

UNIVERSITY LIBRARY, Cambridge.
Bronze Entrances, Aluminium Bronze Screens.
* *Sir Giles Gilbert Scott, R.A.*

BODLEAN LIBRARY, Oxford.
Stone Carving.
* *Sir Giles Gilbert Scott, R.A.*

BROTHERTON LIBRARY, Leeds University.
Plaster work.
* *Messrs. Lanchester & Lodge & Davis.*

NATIONAL LIBRARY OF WALES, Aberystwyth.
Wrought Iron Balconies, Lamp Standards, etc.
* *Messrs. Adams, Holden & Pearson.*

HAIG HALL, Wigan, for the Earl of Crawford.
Oak Fittings to Library.

ENGLISH SPEAKING UNION.
Oak Fittings to Library.
* *Clough Williams-Ellis, Esq., M.C., J.P., F.R.I.B.A.*

NATIONAL CENTRAL LIBRARY.
Wrought Iron work.
* *Hugh Gold, Esq., F.R.I.B.A.*

HOTELS

THE CUMBERLAND HOTEL.
Octagonal Entrance Lounge and Cast Metal Doors.
* *Oliver P. Bernard, Esq., O.B.E., M.C., F.R.I.B.A.*

THE STRAND PALACE HOTEL.
Restaurant and Winter Gardens.
* *Oliver P. Bernard, Esq., O.B.E., M.C., F.R.I.B.A.*

THE IMPERIAL HOTEL, Torquay.
Lounge Entrance Hall, Furnishings, etc.
* *Messrs. Watson & Watson.*

THE MIDLAND HOTEL, Manchester.
Decorations to Cocktail Bar and Canopy.
* *H. J. Connal, Esq., F.R.I.B.A. (L.M.S. Railway Co.).*

THE PIER HOTEL, Worthing.
Panelling and Fittings to Saloon and Public Bar.
* *Messrs. Stewart & Hendry.*

THE BRUNSWICK INN, Hove.
Panelling and Fittings to Saloon and Public Bar.
* *Messrs. Stewart & Hendry.*

THE BRISTOL HOTEL, Brighton.
Panelling and Fittings to Saloon Bar.
* *Messrs. J. L. Denman & Son.*

THEATRES

THE LONDON CASINO.
Decorations and Furnishings.
* *Messrs. E. A. Stone & Partners.*

SAVILLE THEATRE.
Plaster work and Decorations to Auditorium, Stalls, Bar, etc.
* *Messrs. T. P. Bennett & Son.*

WHITEHALL THEATRE.
Black Ebonized panelling to Auditorium, etc.
* *E. A. Stone, Esq., F.S.I. (Messrs. E. A. Stone & Partners).*

PHILHARMONIC, Liverpool.
Lead Cresting and Metalwork.
* *Herbert J. Rowse, Esq., F.R.I.B.A.*

CINEMAS

THE GRANADA, Manchester.
Fibrous Plaster work and Decorations.
* *Benslyn & Morrison, F./A.R.I.B.A.*

THE GRANADA, Woolwich.
Fibrous Plaster work and Decorations.
* *Cecil Masey, Esq., F.R.I.B.A.*

THE GRANADA, Bedford.
Fibrous Plaster work and Decorations.
* *Benslyn & Morrison, F./A.R.I.B.A.*

THE REGAL CINEMA, Brighton.
Fibrous Plaster work and Decorations.
* *W. R. Glen, Esq., F.R.I.A.S.*

THE REGAL, Birmingham.
Fibrous Plaster work and Decorations.
* *W. R. Glen, Esq., F.R.I.A.S.*

THE REGAL CINEMA, Liverpool.
Fibrous Plaster work and Decorations.
* *W. R. Glen, Esq., F.R.I.A.S.*

THE REGAL CINEMA, Marble Arch.
Decorations and Seating.
* *Clifford Aish, Esq, F.R.I.B.A.*

THE REGAL CINEMA, Cheltenham.
Fibrous Plaster work and Decorations.
* *Leslie C. Norton, Esq., L.R.I.B.A.*

SHOPS

MESSRS. DERRY & TOMS, LTD., London.
Restaurant complete, Barber's Shop, Lift Fronts and Walnut Doors.
* *Bernard George, Esq., A.R.I.B.A.*

MESSRS. SELFRIDGES, LTD., London.
Main Entrance Doors in Bronze and Cast Iron Windows.
* Messrs. Graham Anderson, Probst and White.

SHOREDITCH ELECTRICITY SHOWROOMS.
Oak Board Room and Showrooms.
* *Messrs. Yates Cook & Darbyshire.*

MESSRS. ROBERT LEWIS, 19, St. James Street, London.
Shopfront in Honduras Mahogany.
* *George Vernon, Esq., F.R.I.B.A.*

TOWN INVESTMENTS, LTD., 61, St. James Street, London.
Shopfront in Cast Bronze.
* *William Walcot, Esq., F.R.I.B.A.*

Middlesex Guildhall. Architects: Messrs Gibson, Skipworth and Gordon.

Sledmere House, decorative plaster work.

Institution of Civil Engineers. Great George Street, Westminster.

Institution of Civil Engineers. Great George Street, Westminster. Committee room.

Sample of decorative plaster panel.

A council chamber.

Sample of decorative plaster panel.

Martins Bank, Liverpool, showing cast supports for tables, counter grille and decorative plaster work to ceiling.

Barnsley Municipal Building, plaster and bronze work.

Various Other Contracts

Town Halls

Public Offices, Westminster S.W.
Conference room, modelled plaster work. *Architect Sir Henry Tanner.*

Lambeth
Stone carving etc.

Woolwich
Joinery, woodcarving and stone carving.

Holborn
Decorative work.

Wandsworth Administration Building
Panelling and seating of council chamber and bronze fountain.

Municipal Baths
Fibrous plaster.

Westminster Ophthalmic Hospital
Stone carving.

Guys Hospital
Stone carving.

Central Collegiate Building W.I.
Modern work in entrance, screen swing doors and windows in calcolour aluminium.

Golders Green Crematorium
Oak seating inlaid with ebony. Book of Memory stand.

City of London Crematorium
Panelling in oak and cataphalque.

Bush House, Aldwych
Bronze entrance screens and doors, bronze staircase and W.I. staircase.

Victoria House, Southampton Row, W.C.1.
Bronze work, lead work, bronze entrance door.

Union Corporation E.C.
Suite of panelled offices.

Tanganyika Concessions Ltd. E.C.
Board room in walnut.

Trussed Concrete Steel Co.
Suite of offices in peroba and metal work.

Australia House
Stone carving.

India House
Metal work.

Regent Arcade House, Argyll Street and Regent Street
Bronze entrance doors.

Caird Hall, Dundee, decorative plaster work.

Civil Service Supply
Interior work.

Unilever House, Blackfriars
Large bronze entrance gates, etc.

South Africa House

Government of N. Ireland House, 13 Lower Regent Street
Main entrance and 'Ulster' sign.

Electra House, Victoria Embankment
Main entrance.

Lambeth Bridge
Pineapples with gold leaf, weighing 18 cwt. each, fixed in position by Mr. F. Taylor, who assures me one is leaning slightly!

Slazenger Trust, Albermarle Street
Decorative work.

Thomas House, Thomas Street
Stone carving over entrance and interior work.

Soho Post Office
Decorative work.

Luton Library
Stone carving etc.

Cardiff Empire. Interior decorative work.

Some Particularly Interesting Contracts

Barbara Hutton's Residence, Regents Park
Decorative work.

Law Courts, Strand
Large Gothic cast iron features to tower.

Old Bailey Law Courts, Nos. 1 and 2 Courts
Complete fittings and carving work, the coats of arms. Joinery and metal work in other court rooms and corridors.

The Masonic Shrine, Great Queen Street
Bronze doors, lamps and altar, particularly fine casting of Walter Gilbert's work.

Stock Exchange
Interior work at various periods.

Pre 1905

Metropolitan Fire Office, Moorgate Street
Decorative work.

Stock Exchange (Extension)
Decorative work.

Lloyds Advertising Office
Decorative work.

Aldford House
A particularly fine wrought front entrance gate.

Later work can be seen in the following:

Daily Telegraph Offices
Metal partitions.

Queen Elizabeth Hall, South Bank
Textured cast aluminium windows, doors and other metal work.

Royal Thames Yacht Club
Joinery and panelling in exotic woods, furniture and metal work.

Woolgate House
Metal work.

Other major cities of the world have work produced by Martyns at Cheltenham which had to be packed and shipped out at no small cost. In many cases men from the Cheltenham works travelled out to assemble the work on site, considered worthwhile regardless of expense by clients and architects requiring **the best.**

The esteem with which architects held the company's ability to produce extremely fine work is demonstrated by the demand for work as far afield as Burma, Australia, South Africa, South America and Canada, as well as in European countries, with their own traditions of excellence in architectural carvings. In Ireland, stone carving, plaster work and wrought iron, bronze and marble work was produced for the Ulster Parliament Buildings for Sir Arnold Thornley, F.R.I.B.A., in Belfast Town Hall, stone carving, and in Stormont Castle, Belfast, plasterwork.

Bronze entrance doors, inner and lift doors were made for the Hong Kong and Shanghai Bank, Hong Kong in co-operation with Walter Jenkins & Co., who did the marble work there, and other work of a decorative nature was executed. According to verbal information a second set of doors had to be cast after the war as the Japanese had melted the original ones down during the Occupation to use the bronze for their war effort. The Bromsgrove Guild cast the second much smaller set.

Particularly fine entrance gates were made for the Courts of Justice, and wrought bronze work for the National Bank of India in Rangoon, Burma. On the other side of the globe, in Boston, U.S.A., oak panelling to the design of Chester Lindsey Churchill, architect, was produced for the First Church of Christ Scientist. In Europe, carving, joinery, bronze and furniture was made for King Carol of Rumania's Palace at Bucharest, the work being executed to the instruction of F. Lorenz of Bucharest, architect. The King's crown jewel cases in silver bronze were also made by Martyn craftsmen. A quantity of the work was unfortunately lost when the vessel carrying some of the furniture was sunk in the Mediterranean at the beginning of the 1939 war.

Martyns carried out work in India for Bernard Triggs, F.R.I.B.A. on Lal Bagh Palace for the Maharajah (Holkar) of Indor, including joinery, fibrous plaster, decoration, furniture, wrought and cast bronze work and silver bronze. Also in India is the fine Queen Victoria Memorial in Calcutta, where the 16′ bronze figure of Victory stands high overlooking the city, with the figures in marble beautifully carved by Robert Lindsey Clark in their lovely simplicity at ground level for all to appreciate. Other wrought and cast bronze work was also produced for the memorial. King Farouk of Egypt ordered a Royal Train, from the Metropolitan-Cammell Carriage & Waggon Co. and featuring Martyns joinery and decorative work.

In South Africa, stone carving was produced for Johannesburg Town Hall, and an incredibly fine piece of wood carving for the Civic Hall in Johannesburg in 1916. This was the organ case, made in mahogany in Cheltenham and assembled around the organ on site. Work in Canada includes the gates for the University of Saskatchewan, the gates for the Royal Canadian Air Force Memorial at Trenton, Ontario, joinery, woodcarving and terra cotta for the Vancouver Hotel, Vancouver, and cast occasional table lamps for the Canadian Pacific Railway. A carving of the Lord's Supper was executed in grand proportions for a memorial to be set in a Toronto church.

In Rio de Janeiro the British Embassy gates caused great local interest when they were erected, so fine were they considered. Gates were a speciality of the company and were supplied to various Embassies, but records are sparse as to individual venues. Wood carving by Henry Arthur Dean was supplied to Buenos Aires in about 1920 but so far the exact location is not known. The spire and cross for the cathedral at Debra Libanos in Ethiopia was cast in 1962 in aluminium. Some of those who worked on it were: G. Hancock, A.G. Merrett, H. Dickenson, C. Twinning, manager G.W. Reid and assistant manager H. Lewis. The height of the spire and cross was 54′. Also in Ethiopia the throne and footstool for the Emperor Haile Selassie and mirror frames for his daughter's boudoir were carved in wood by David Hill which were made by Martyns. In 1957 the Royal Palace at Baghdad was supplied with fibrous plaster decorations, bronze grills, doors and fittings. The work for the Baghdad contract was fraught with problems and produced no profit for the company in spite of a second opportunity to quote after the sinking of the ship Seastan loaded with fibrous plaster panelling and carving destined for the Crown Prince's villa just outside Bagdhad. Half way through the contract the King was assassinated and the Royal Palace became the Presidential Palace. Fortunately, irrevocable letters of credit had been obtained, so the company had no worry about payment. Ted Claridge, manager of the Fibrous Plaster Department, was sent out to Baghdad to oversee the fixing of the plaster work.

One fortuitous element of the Baghdad contract was that two massive and very beautiful bronze doors were required and Martyns had two such doors which had been in store in London since 1939. They had been destined for the palace of King Carol of Rumania when war prevented their delivery. After 18 years the doors could at last be seen in all their splendour in a suitable venue.

In 1960 the U.S. Embassy in Baghdad was supplied with a special carving of the Great Seal of America. The carving was done by H.W. Foster in perspex, with great skill, working in the reverse and only on the back of the perspex, to leave the front smooth and clear. After deep carving on the reverse, where one slip of the tool would have ruined the whole, the emblem was painted in acrylic paints, achieving a striking effect. It took Huie Foster six weeks to complete the work, which is about 4′ in diameter. Huie had carved for Martyns since 1910, and perspex was a new medium for him after 50 years' working with wood, with its variety of grain and individuality. His work must exist in numberless venues. The designer of the emblem was J. Brian Cooper F.R.I.B.A. of Birmingham, for whom Martyns also carried out contracts in the Baghdad Presidential Palace and in the parliament buildings in Iraq.

For Australia, a marble pulpit was made for Brisbane Cathedral and a reredos in stone and glass mosaic for Melbourne.

In 1924 the Architectural Review carried an extensive account of the Great Reredos of Liverpool Cathedral and H.H. Martyn & Co.'s major role in the carving of this great work of architecturally applied sculpture. Sir Giles Gilbert Scott R.A. was the architect, Walter Gilbert, art managing director of Martyns, was one of the principal sculptors and Louis Weingartner the other. The main stone carvings were first made in clay, and the whole structure and the individual sculptural figures and groups were then cut from Wooler sandstone under the personal supervision of Sir Giles Gilbert Scott by Arthur Turner and his talented team of stone carvers from the studios of Martyns: W. Davis; M. Hoyle; J. Phillips; W. Meadows; H.G. Radcliffe and E. Steel. The

H.W. Foster with his carving of the Great Seal of America in perspex.

Carved stone figure of "The Word" for Liverpool Cathedral.

entire reredos is an impressive spectacle in its fine and delicately rendered carving, which took five years to complete. It is a grand structure too, being 64′ high and 48′ wide, and represents beautifully the spirit of worship in the small figure over The Last Supper, "The Word", the Crucifixion (12′ x 6′), The Commandments, The Nativity, The Resurrection and many others. It also stands testimony to the great skill of Mr. Turner and the other Martyn carvers.

Sammy Tomlin was another figure carver who worked on Liverpool Cathedral both before and after the second world war, maintaining the Martyn connection with the area.

In Europe in the very heart of finery and architectural excellence, Martyns' work in all forms of decoration work can be seen, proving that the craftsmen of this island can take their place beside the work of the best in Europe.

An interesting European commission granted to the company just prior to the first world war is best told in H.H. Martyn's own words:

> *Some little time before the outbreak of war in 1914 we had received instructions to carry out some important work for the Prince Imperial of Germany, who was having a house built upon English Tudor lines. The craftsmen had all their tools packed and preparations made to go to Potsdam, but fortunately the firm was awaiting a final wire to start; of course the only wire we received was the declaration of war.*
>
> *We had already executed an important commission for a house next to the Imperial Palace at Potsdam for Siemens, the electicial magnate. There was an amusing incident in connection with this contract which illustrated the old saw 'fools and children should never see unfinished work'. The English architect of the work told me that Siemens had written him a sharp letter in which he spoke severely*

Model in clay fifteen feet long of the Last Supper. One of the many groups for the reredos of Liverpool Cathedral carved by the team of stone carvers from Martyns.

The reredos of Liverpool Anglican Cathedral carved in Caen stone.

of the work, having seen it when being unpacked and before it was fixed in position, but that he would see it in situ before final condemnation.

Needless to say this information made me crestfallen, but smiling at my very apparent discomforture, he continued: 'a few days later I received this,' and he handed a letter to me which was as laudatory as the other had been abusive. 'The effect when fixed', wrote Siemens, 'is splendid and I must compliment and thank you and the artists for the unique work you sent me'.

Unfortunately, the work produced for Herr Siemens is not itemised and its whereabouts after two world wars to say the least uncertain.

The Showering family were particularly good customers following the great success of 'Babycham'. An enormous amount of work was done by Martyns for the three Showering borthers. Ralph Showering was an architect and had also been an engineer in India, a similar background to that of T.A. Miller, the contracts director. Ralph's house, Fearbed Copse, had extensive renovation work by Martyns. Francis Showering, who is reputed to have put the bubbles in Babycham, had his home in Shepton Mallet entirely furnished and decorated by Martyns, and magazines featured it as 'Home of the Year'. Herbert Showering's Compton Castle was also fitted out by Martyns, even to the kitchens.

In 1951 The Stratford Memorial Theatre had alterations carried out at a cost of £80,000 designed by Brian O'Rorke, architect. Martyns did all the redecorations and refurnishing including new plaster and joinery work, new drapery and new seating.

The Adelphi Hotel, Liverpool, 1914

Sefton dining room. The modelled fibrous plaster ceiling, the oak and gold enriched panelling of walls, furnishing, carpeting and decorations. *Architect, Frank Atkinson.*

The Savoy, Brighton, 1914

The whole of the decorative work to the auditorium, entrances, restaurants, cafes etc. *Architect, W.R. Glen.*

Capital for Parliament Buildings, Victoria, British Columbia. Architect: F.M. Rattenbury.

Reredos in Caen stone with panel in mosaic for Melbourne, Australia. Architect: R.H. Alsop.

Balliol College, Oxford, woodcarving and panelling.

Victoria Institute, Leicester.

Wrought and hammered bronze electrolier for Middlesex Guild Hall.

Terra-cotta animal heads for the Canadian Pacific Railway Hotel, Vancouver, British Columbia. Part of an extensive contract for the hotel. A.W. Martyn personally supervised the terra-cotta heads which were made by Daltons.

Bronze figure of Ariel on the dome of the Bank of England, Threadneedle Street.

Lloyds Bank, Liverpool.

Chapter 15

DETAILS OF VARIOUS CONTRACTS

The following lists of works was compiled from a few records which survived in a metal deed box at the old works at Lansdown and was rescued by Mr. Heapey, the Financial Director of Schindler Lifts Ltd., who took over the premises following the closure of Martyns. The list should not be taken as a complete record of work carried out by Martyns at any one venue or for the years recorded, but it is interesting to note the variety of work done during only a few years, ranging from extensive castings in bronze for banks to the simple dado rails for a London house. The prices will also be of interest in retrospect. It is sad that more records did not survive the bombs of the war and the final destruction by Maples, so that identification and recording for future interest could have been more complete. Thousands of works of artistic merit will go down as 'anon', though the expert in certain fields may be able to read the signs of particular craftsmen from the company through reference to those known.

Plaza Cinema, Gloucester, 1935
Fibrous plaster £873

Theatre Royal, Dublin, 1935
Decorative work £2,830

Savoy Cinema, Limerick, 1935
Decorative work £1,947

Regal Cinema, Cheltenham, 1938
Plaster, lights, steel work, special decoration £3,000

Henleaze Cinema, Bristol, 1938
Fibrous plaster £2,246
Painting and decorating £445

Odeon Cinema, Bury St. Edmunds, 1936
Fibrous plaster to auditorium £1,375
Decorative work £620

Rayleigh Senior School, Essex, 1936
Fibrous plaster £58

Bodleian Library Extension, Oxford, 1937
Stone carving £1,161
Stone carving £1,819
Models £247

School of Transport, Derby, 1938
Balustrading £248

University of London, 1936
Superstructure of Senate House. Block wall lining and panelling to staff refectory and ante-room ....

Birmingham Medical School, 1936
Plaster work, moulded cross banded frieze, square paterae, fluted caps £160

Gloucester Technical College, 1936
Bronze and iron metalwork to doors, decorative panels, staircase window and balustrading, grilles to windows ... £999

Imperial Hotel, Torquay, 10th September 1928
Decorative work in plaster to entrance hall and lounge £5,728

Imperial Hotel, Torquay, 1934
Decorative work £5,497
Decorative work to garden entrance and staircase £912

Longcliffe Hotel, Nanpanton, 1935
Fibrous plaster for lounge £176

Punch Bowl Hotel, Hoylake, Cheshire, 1935
Fibrous plaster for lounge — lounge parlour, service and smoke room £157

New Civic Hall, Swansea, 1931
Stone carving to coffers in archway to main entrance, stone carving to capitals, columns and enrichments in Bath stone to ante-room .... £307.10s.0d.

Wolverhampton Municipal Halls, 1937
Conductor's rostrum £83
Two settees for ground floor promenade and four for large hall foyer, plinths of solid mahogany, ebonised side panels veneered in Indian white mahogany, pale grey leather upholstery £233

Greenwich Town Hall & Municipal Buildings, 1939
Furniture for principal offices £832
Metal grilles £244

Wembley Town Hall, 1938
Ornamental iron work £1,820

Wembley Town Hall, 1939
Cast bronze coat of arms £75

Hinkley Police Station, 1937
Court fittings £1,043

River Trent Catchment Board New Offices, Birmingham, 1935
Furniture and other fittings for boardroom ....

Preston New Dock Offices, 1935
Panelling in committee room £345

County Offices, Preston, 1938
Alteration to seating £1,272

Manchester Town Hall, 1936
Supplying and fixing two bridges cast in bronze £9,735

Wiltshire County Office, Trowbridge, 1940
Fibrous plaster work £812

Huddersfield Corporation Administration Block of trolleybus dept.
No details given as to the work

Hornsey Town Hall, Middlesex, 1934 £7,590
Extensive bronze fibrous plaster and woodwork, comprising ....
Bronze metal gates, grilles, canopies, balcony rails etc. £1,269
Fibrous plaster ceilings to assembly hall £787
Fibrous plaster to council chamber £228
Woodwork finishings to council chamber £2,217
Woodwork finishings to assembly hall ... £3,054
Bronze frames to lighting over main hall £35

Chichester County Offices, 1935
Panelling for council chamber and retiring room £1,624
Pair of cast bronze entrance doors and one internal screen £422

Stoke Newington Town Hall, 1937
Fibrous plaster to library and assembly hall £281

Newcastle-on-Tyne, 1933
Offices and extensions ....

Midland Bank, Poultry, London, 1936
Carving in Portland stone £2,893
Bronze moulded handrail and wrought iron balustrade .... £2.11s.0d. per foot run also glazing.

Bank of England Sec III, 1925/36
Bronze doors and frames £3,494
17 doors as follows with polished plate glass in some:

Doors
Two west wall main west corridors ground floor £220
Two east and west walls corridors ground floor £163
One main south corridor £148
One Princess St. entrance hall west wall £935
Two Princess St. entrance hall north and south walls £640
One Princess St. lift lobby £320
Two Princess St. entrance hall doors to porter and rear room £100
Two Princess St. entrance hall doors to telephone boxes £100
One drawing office telephone box £50
Two main south corridor £700
One main west corridor ground floor .. £81
Bronze screens glazed complete £369

Bank of England Sec II, 1931/32
19 bronze doors and glazing £3,784

Doors
One main south corridor £385
Two from main east and south corridors to war stock offices £288
One from main corridor to experts' entrance hall £102
Two to semi-circular stair £282
One to north end of eastern corridor .. £160
One from lift lobby £162
One in main east corridor £362
One in main south corridor £192
One in main east corridor £188
One to semi-circular stair £148
One to stock transfer office £192
Two Inner Treasury to main corridor .. £436
Two Inner Treasury to main staircase .. £436
One door frame for semi-circular staircase at ground floor £118
One plus screen and frame between main stairs and lobby £335

Hong Kong and Shanghai Bank, Des Voeux Rd. and Queens Rd., London, Jan. 1935
Cast bronze doors.
'A' Revolving doors with solid panels and two pairs of swing doors £1,534
'B' Main ground floor Queens Road entrance to Banking Hall lobby, cast bronze screen and three swing doors £1,158
'C' Entrance gates from Queens Road, main ground floor, one pair of doors enrichment back and front with three figures above transome at front £1,337
'D' Entrance to lift lobby from Queens Road, main ground floor, cast bronze revolving doors £940
'E' Entrance to public space from Queens Road, revolving door £940
'F' Entrance from Des Voeux Road, lower ground floor, three doors enriched to front £973

Hong Kong and Shanghai Bank, Hong Kong, Jan. 1935
Cast bronze screens.
Lower ground floor two cast bronze screens.
Main ground floor one cast bronze screen.
Total £2,743
Cast bronze doors.
Theme *'Man'*
Main ground floor six single cast doors.

Main ground floor one pair double swing doors cast bronze.
Main ground floor four cast bronze single folding doors.
Main ground floor one pair cast bronze double doors.
Main ground floor one pair cast bronze double swing doors.
Total £1,707
Theme '*Vision*'
Lower ground floor three pairs of cast bronze doors £560
Theme '*BOA*'
Mezzanine floor one pair of cast bronze folding doors £270

Martins Bank, High Street, Coventry, 1938
Internal Woodwork.
Joinery £641
Other work £510

Martins Bank Ltd., Bruton Street, London, 1940
Bronze windows, bronze grilles, night safe surround and postal plate £342

Martins Bank Ltd., Bath, July 1937
Fibrous plaster ceilings £425

Municipal Bank, Head Office, Birmingham, Sept. 1937
Alterations to entrance hall £124

National Provincial Bank, Gloucester, 1939
Bronze and iron metalwork £200

"The Times", Vanway Extension, Feb. 1939
Glazed steel partitions £2,070

Remington Typewriter Co. Ltd., Oxford St., London W, May 1939
Metal partitions £785

Cottesbrooke Hall, Notts., 1938
Fibrous plaster work, 15 groined bays, 2 barrelled bays, 1 special bay over landing, 18 plain ribs elliptical, 36 plain pilasters £320

St. Marks Hospital, London, Feb. 1938
Panelling to recreation room of nurses' home £330

Kingston House Ltd., Kensington Rd., S.W.7., Jan. 1939
Bronze entrance doors and canopy £363
Four pilasters £220
Casings for pipes £48
Windows £90
Lamplights £83

Athenaeum Court, Piccadilly, W.1., 1935
Polished white metal lettering "Athenaeum Court" £96

Northern Aluminium Co., Banbury, Oxon., 1936
Main and inner doors in wood, laylight to lanterns £571

Pilkington Ltd., Head Office Extension St. Helens, Aug. 1939
Two clock dials for clock tower £50

Block of Flats and Shops, 17/20 Arlington St., S.W.1., Dec. 1935
Anodised aluminium surrounds to lift doors £511

Philips House, Shaftsbury Ave., London, 1938
Entrance door ....

Leeds Railway Station, L.M.S. Railway, 1938
Cast bronze protection bars .... £135.5s.6d.

70/71 Ennismore Gardens, April 1938
Bronze entrance doors, window grilles, supports etc. £466

Berkeley Square House, 1938
Metal dado rail ....

Leibigs boardroom, London. Architect: Collcutt and Hamish

War Memorial at Eccleston Park, Liverpool. The combined sculpture of Walter Gilbert and Louis Weingartner.

Chapter 16

THE MEMORIAL TRADITION

It is not surprising that memorials should have held such a major role in the company's work following the wars in which this nation was involved with such tragic loss of life.

The company was founded on the traditional work of the stone carver, that of gravestones, in memory of individuals, simple in shape and inscription or elaborate with finely carved angels, anchors, books or objects to denote the trade or profession of the departed.

It was not a big step for the company to produce work on a larger scale when whole communities wished to have memorials erected to the many who had not returned to the village, town, city or even nation which they had left to fight a war. H.H. Martyn had carved grave stones himself with E.A. Emms in the 1860s and 1870s and continued in memorial work after the formation of the company in 1888. However, he now began to offer a wider choice, advertising work in gun metal and bronze, both mediums far more lasting than stone. And of course stained glass, with its lovely changing lights, was offered by the company after the first world war.

It is no wonder that memorials epitomise the work of the company so eloquently. Each must be executed with care, even reverence, and painstaking accuracy with names, sometimes by the hundred and thousand, each of which must be perfect, with no slight blemish on any single letter. That one name is the only name for the family who visits to search among the many. The carved emblem, be it angel, crest of the regiment, ship or squadron, must be designed and executed with skill so that it represents Society's aspirations of excellence.

Martyns succeeded in all these aspects and was asked to make memorials by the thousand, from the simple village cross with names inscribed in stone, to the National Centre of Remembrance,

Conservative Club, Glasgow, memorial tablet.

Bronze casting for West Jesmond War Memorial, figures in the round.

the Cenotaph. Scale models of the Cenotaph were later made on licence by Martyns.

Probably the first large scale war memorial was that made for Cheltenham College. The Eleanor Cross to the 54 Old Cheltonians who died in the Boer war, was unveiled on 26th June 1903.

From the Boer war to the first world war with its devastating loss of life, the company was called upon to make many monuments, mostly cast in bronze but also involving stone work, often as a base for bronze. Robert Lindsey Clark's hand can be seen in many of the fine sculptural works incorporated in the memorials produced in the foundry at Martyns. One of particular note is that of Smethwick War Memorial, unveiled on 15th April 1926. On the sides of the base are panels sculptured by Robert Lindsey Clark depicting the Navy, Army and Air Force, very fine active works of art showing many aspects of the war. Particularly notable is the way the horses are being quietened by the soldiers controlling them. It is reminiscent of his superb 'Broken Limber'. His delicate treatment of the figure of Peace with the olive branch has the air of human resolve in the face of a young woman and is beautifully sculptured.

Walter Gilbert of Martyns and Louis Weingartner collaborated on the sculpture of the War Memorial at Eccleston Park, Liverpool, which was cast in bronze in the Martyn foundry. Although the soldier is standing conventionally on top of the plinth, the memorial has a novel feature in his mother, who is shown apparently mounting the steps below him to place a garland of laurels at his feet. It is inscribed:— 'The laurels of the sons are watered from the hearts of the mothers'.

Another memorial by the same sculptors and cast in the Cheltenham foundry is the Liverpool Masonic War Memorial. Mentioned in connection with the Masonic memorial is stained glass by S.H. Meteyard, and it is therefore fairly certain that his design was executed at Martyns' stained glass department, which was at its peak at this time under his management.

The University of Manchester has a long tablet with the names of members who fell between 1914 and 1919. It is a simple but superbly cast bronze work with classic design for the surround and with two cherub-like figures holding a shield at centre. A smaller tablet with an angel in bas relief holding a standard, together making an enfolding form on one side and top, commemorates the names of 56 men of the West Docks.

Many other companies, clubs and institutions, large and small, had tablets made. Just a few at random are the Birkenhead Constitutional Club, Liverpool Exchange Newsroom, Raleigh Cycle Co., Institute of Accountants and Actuaries, Clydesdale Bank Ltd., Charterhouse School, Clyde Trust Navigation Co., Conservative Club, Glasgow, Moss Steamship Co., Liverpool, the Glengarnock Works of David Colville & Sons Ltd., who lost 93 employees in the 1914—1919 war, and Salisbury war memorial.

Bronze tablet for Clyde Trust and Navigation Company.

Smethwick War Memorial, sculptured by Robert Lindsey Clark, R.S.B.S. Central figure.

Side panel for Smethwick War Memorial depicting The Navy and The Royal Flying Corps.

Smethwick War Memorial panel depicting The Army.

Typical memorial tablet.

Birmingham Post and Mail bronze tablet.

Part of the Gloucester War Memorial 1914—1918.

Model for War Memorial.

Woodcarved model for a First World War Memorial.

Memorial in Marble.

Memorial in Marble.

An unusual design was executed for the Birmingham Post & Mail, being circular in shape, surmounted by the figure of Peace and with two figures representing Art and Commerce at the base. The inscription lists twenty men who fell in 1914—1918.

Another fine piece of sculpture designed by Walter Gilbert was the memorial for Jesmond Dene, Newcastle-on-Tyne. The figures are symbolical, delicately sculptured and expertly cast in the round, each one a work of art in its own right, from the mother holding her child in her lap to the soldier in attentive stance, looking towards Christ on the Cross (see photograph at beginning of chapter). Larger memorials for city centres were cast, such as the 10′ high 26 cwt. figure of Britannia for Crewe, erected in 1924. The elaborate memorial for Liverpool Exchange is surmounted by Britannia in protective stance with an arm about a child, below which troops are poised vigilantly around a field gun. To the side, a nurse supports the head of a wounded soldier. The whole is a masterpiece of the art of bronze casting and the ability of sculptor and foundryman to work together to produce lasting memorials of the age.

Figure for Crewe War Memorial 1924, 10 ft. high.

Memorial to the founder of the Boys' Brigade.

The Sixteenth Fifth Lancers Memorial 1939—1945.

A similar figure of Brittania, 10 ft. high weighing 26 cwts, cast for Troon, Ayrshire.

Viscount Gladstone Bronze Memorial.

Church Memorial in bronze.

War Memorial.

Pair of bronze doors for the North Wales War Memorial.

The Royal Scots Fuseliers Memorial, Ayr, Scotland. Cast in bronze from a model by C.d'O. Pilkington Jackson, A.R.S.A., F.R.B.S., F.R.S.A.

The Black Watch Memorial unveiled by the Queen Mother.

The Cenotaph, focus of the nation's respect for those who died in defence of freedom.

The memorial at Bournemouth is less spectacular but nonetheless a fine piece of work, being a glass-fronted cabinet of large proportions with crest and flags in colour, the whole enclosing an inscribed Roll of Honour. Colchester's memorial is a similar cabinet enshrining the Roll of Honour. Troon, Argyllshire, had a 10′ cast figure of Britannia, weighing 26 cwt.

Dundee war memorial, situated high overlooking the Tay Bridge, is surmounted by a brazier with the names of the men who fell all cast in lasting bronze tablets.

The North Wales memorial consists of a particularly fine bronze door in a wrought bronze frame, the 36 panels having coats of arms in bas relief.

Many regiments commissioned Martyns for their own memorials to their comrades who died in the various campaigns. The 1/4 Battalion, The Border Regiment had tablets cast in bronze to name the fallen in India, Mesopotamia and Burma during 1914 to 1919.

The 1/5th Battalion of the Gloucesters features a sphinx guarding a tablet with some 500 names inscribed on it.

The Sixteenth Fifth Lancers had an inscribed tablet with insignia, flags and crown in a scroll. The Black Watch commissioned a bronze cast figure of a Black Watch kilted soldier.

The Australian National War Memorial, Villers Bretonneux, France, was designed by Sir E.L. Lutyens R.A.

The Chatham Merchant Naval Memorial stituated at Tower Hill, London, has 133 large bronze panels bearing the names of 25,000 merchant seamen who died on war service. The man who had most to do with the preparing of the quarter of a million letters on the plates was F.W. Abbey. He and Martyns' director J.F. Allden were invited by the Imperial War Graves Commission to attend the unveiling by the Queen. The American memorials include the cemetery at Cambridge, where the bronze base and top of the flagpole were cast at Martyns. The stone carving had to be sub-contracted out because by this time Martyns were without stone carvers, most of whom had gone by 1947.

The Caen Memorial in Normandy was an extensive contract for Martyns which included stone, and marble work. The memorial, built soon after the war, was specially dedicated to commemorate the men who fell on the beaches and bridgeheads of the Normandy landings on D Day 1944 and the days following.

Memorials to individuals were frequently commissioned. A particularly interesting one is the entrance gate to the Mausoleum of Earl Lloyd George on the banks of the River Dwyfor.

Viscount Gladstone's bronze memorial is in the form of a raised enclosure for a grave or vault elaborately moulded with stylised oak trees, figures and emblems. A protective dove at the head spreads its wings while at the feet are clasped hands.

Sir William Alexander Smith, founder of the Boys' Brigade, has a cast bronze tablet by Martyns placed to his memory in Glasgow Cathedral.

In the parish church of Newmarket is a wrought iron screen, a memorial to Lt. Hammond. A letter at the time of its delivery on 22nd August 1919 states: "It is a gem of the iron-worker's art and reflects the highest credit on your firm. It will stand, I hope for centuries, in our old parish church and will testify to all succeeding generations that whatever troubles Great Britain went through in the Great War, its excellence in the fine arts was in no way diminished." Signed, Henry B. Young, Rector.

The list of memorials is sadly incomplete and would no doubt fill volumes if records could be found since it was a speciality in which the company excelled in its sympathetic treatment.

The Naval Memorial at Plymouth to 15,600 men whose only known grave is the sea. **(See description on page 117).**

Architectural Review March 1913, first pictorial advertisement in this journal.

ADVERTISING

H.H. Martyn believed in publicity and as soon as he set up his own company and new work premises, he began advertising. His first small and simple advertisement, comprising copy only, appeared on 31st March, 1888 in the local paper, The Looker On. It is fortunate that later advertisements appeared in much larger sizes with good illustrations of recent work. This enabled the researcher to relate the time, place and object produced with great accuracy. It is sad indeed that no signature, stamp or emblem was ever attached to wood, stone, bronze or any other work, which is surprising, since in the days of the Martyn and Emms partnership the memorials at least had the name inscribed, usually in lead inlaid letters. Some later work of Martyns, such as the Commando Memorial, certainly has notice of its place of manufacture, but the vast majority has none. The opinion at the time was that the standard of excellence was its own signature. At the time, it is true, those concerned certainly know of the origins, but once they have dispersed or died, no record remains.

This chapter must be pictorial in the main and in view of its subject should be self-explanatory and illustrative of the company's work and progress over the years. The pattern of advertising shows the steady progress of the Company and marks certain events along its path.

When A.W. Martyn and H.A. Dutton became partners with H.H. Martyn in 1898, a change soon followed, more than doubling the spaces and adding Art Joinery to the list of the company's activities.

Soon after the partnership became a limited company, advertising was started in the Architectural Review, using copy-only quarter pages. In 1913 the first illustrated advertisement appeared in the Architectural Review and a similar move to illustration followed in the Cheltenham Looker On much later, in 1919.

Prior to this in the Looker On, on 6th January, 1916, the company increased the size to quarter pages and included for the first time the Royal Warrant. The main competitors in the town, Boultons, were still buying spaces no larger than Martyns' 1888 advertisements. This must have been satisfying to H.H. Martyn as an ex-employee of Boultons.

Advertising continued in illustrative form for many years, ending in the Architectural Review in 1939 and earlier than this in the local paper. It is surprising that in spite of the fact that some competitors continued to advertise throughout the war Martyns seem not even to have re-started after the war ended. Could this have been one of the reasons for its decline and eventual fall, as contemporary architects had no opportunity to become acquainted with the company's work in their own professional publication?

HOSIERS, GLOVERS,
Shirtmakers & Outfitters,
IMPERIAL CIRCUS, PROMENADE,
CHELTENHAM.
5 PER CENT. DISCOUNT FOR READY MONEY.

H. H. MARTYN,
ARCHITECTURAL & MONUMENTAL SCULPTOR,
SUNNINGEND,
(Corner of College Road), High Street.
Estimates for Sculpture, Carving, Masonry, and Chimney Pieces of all descriptions.

THE SHEEPBRIDGE COAL AND IRON COMPANY LIMITED.
Paid up Capital - - - - - - £659,586
FIVE PER CENT. DEBENTURES.
THE DIRECTORS are prepared to receive

Martyns' first advertisement as it appeared on 31st March 1888 in the Cheltenham Looker On.

4, SUFFOLK ROAD, CHELTENHAM.
FOOTBALL, FOOTBALL,
DUMB BELLS, INDIAN CLUBS,
And every
Article connected with Gymnastics,
Kept in Stock.
PRICE LISTS FREE.

H. H. MARTYN,
ARCHITECTURAL & MONUMENTAL SCULPTOR,
SUNNINGEND,
(Corner of College Road), High Street.
ESTIMATES FREE.

SHIRER & HADDON,
TAILORS & HABIT MAKERS.
HOSIERS, GLOVERS,
Shirtmakers & Outfitters

The second advertisement one week later as it appeared slightly changed. It continued in this form until June 1897.

"The healthiest and most invigorating Watering Place in the West."
THE GRAND ATLANTIC is the principal and leading HOTEL, facing the Sea. 130 sumptuously appointed Rooms, delightful Public Room; hydraulic lift; every modern comfort. Nearest to Golf Links and Railway Station; own Model Farm. Apply, MANAGER. Telegraphic address, "Atlantic." Telephone, No. 11.

H. H. MARTYN,
ARCHITECTURAL & MONUMENTAL SCULPTOR,
SUNNINGEND,
(Corner of College Road), High Street.
ESTIMATES FREE.

Australia, New Zealand, Tasmania.
Orient Line. Fortnightly Mail Service.
THE following STEAMSHIPS will Leave LONDON as under, PLYMOUTH one day later, NAPLES nine days later, for ALBANY, ADELAIDE, MELBOURNE, and SYDNEY, with Her Majesty's Mails, calling at Colombo, and taking Passengers for all Ports in Australasia:—
Tons H.P.

June 1897 advertisement.

Specialité—
Gun Metal, Bronze, Marble, and Brass Memorial Tablets.
H. H. MARTYN & CO.,
Architectural
and
Monumental Sculptors,
SUNNINGEND,
(Corner College Road).
ART JOINERY WORKS, 59, High St.
Telephone No. 298.

4th December 1899. Advertising increased in size just prior to the formation of the limited company from the partnership of H.H. and A.W. Martyn and H.A. Dutton.

BATH PARADE, BATH ROAD, and GRATTON ROAD.
TELEPHONE 215.

Specialité—
Gun Metal, Bronze, Marble, and Brass Memorial Tablets.
H. H. MARTYN & CO., LTD
Architectural
and
Monumental Sculptors,
WORKS.
SUNNINGEND,
LANSDOWN.
MONUMENTAL DEPARTMENT:
59, HIGH STREET,
Telephone No. 798, 799.

5th June 1909. There was a change in the type face and address.

H. H. MARTYN & Co., Ltd.,
"SUNNINGEND," HIGH STREET, CHELTENHAM.

BY APPOINTMENT

MONUMENTS
OF ALL DESCRIPTIONS.
EXECUTED AND FORWARDED TO ALL PARTS OF THE WORLD.
BY ROYAL WARRANT ARCHITECTURAL DECORATORS TO HIS MAJESTY THE KING.

April 8th 1916. A considerable increase in size.

H. H. MARTYN & Co., Ltd.,

ARCHITECTURAL DECORATORS, H. H. M., KING GEORGE V.

MONUMENTS, MEMORIALS, CALVARIES,

AND

STAINED GLASS.

EXECUTED AND FORWARDED TO ALL PARTS OF THE WORLD.

"SUNNINGEND," HIGH STREET, CHELTENHAM.

Telephone No. 283.

14th December 1918.

6 THE LOOKER-ON.

H. H. Martyn & Co

LIMITED

ARCHITECTURAL DECORATORS to H. M., KING GEORGE V.

MONUMENTS,
MEMORIALS,
CALVARIES,
AND STAINED GLASS
WINDOWS

EXECUTED AND FORWARDED TO ALL PARTS OF THE WORLD.

"SUNNINGEND," HIGH ST., CHELTENHAM.

Telegrams: "Sunningend, Cheltenham." Telephone No. 283.

1919. The first quarter page heralded a new approach with different wording and style each week. (Copy only advertising had appeared in the Architectural Review from January 1904 with the first picture appearing in March 1913).

6 THE LOOKER-ON.

H. H. MARTYN & Co. LTD

CHELTENHAM.

ARCHITECTURAL DECORATORS to H. M. KING GEORGE V.

MONUMENTS, MEMORIALS, CALVARIES

and

STAINED GLASS WINDOWS,

February 1919. An early pictorial advertisement. With few exceptions, future advertisements carried illustrations.

WAR MEMORIALS EXHIBITION

VICTORIA AND ALBERT MUSEUM

At the above Exhibition, Memorials executed by

H. H. MARTYN & CO., LTD.,

received the following special mention.

"Among the many wall tablets a plaster model of a Cartouche designed by Mr. Ambrose Poynter, and Mr. George H. Wenyon and executed by Messrs. H. H. Martyn & Co., Ltd. is to be particularly commended."

"A Mural Tablet designed by Mr. R. Lindsay Clark, and executed by Messrs. H. H. Martyn & Co., Ltd. is an admirable example of a happy combination of originality tempered by scholarship and executed with restraint." *Architects' Journal, July 16th.*

Messrs. H. H. MARTYN & Co., Ltd. place the Services of their Staff of Experts at your disposal, and respectfully invite enquiries for Designs and Estimates.

Head Offices & Works - Sunningend, Lansdown.
Show Rooms - - Sunningend, High Street.

1919. Words only.

H. H. MARTYN & Co.,

LIMITED

CHELTENHAM.

ARCHITECTURAL DECORATORS TO H. M. THE KING.

H. H. MARTYN & Co., Ltd.

will gladly give advice and submit designs for

MEMORIALS, CALVARIES
STAINED GLASS WINDOWS

AND ALL

ECCLESIASTICAL DECORATION

No Enquiry too Simple or too Extensive.

HEAD OFFICES & WORKS - SUNNINGEND, LANSDOWN
SHOW ROOMS - - - - SUNNINGEND, HIGH ST.

1919

H. H. MARTYN & Co., Ltd.,

SUNNINGEND WORKS,
CHELTENHAM.

Craftsmen in Metals.

1919

PLEASE NOTE.

H. H. MARTYN & Co. Ltd.,

are shortly opening a Showroom at their Sunningend, High St. address for all kinds of

ELECTRICAL FITTINGS.

Contracts undertaken for the COMPLETE INSTALLATION of

ELECTRIC LIGHT HEAT POWER

Estimates Free.

Enquiries for all things Electrical to:—

H. H. MARTYN & Co., Ltd.
Sunningend, High Street.,
: CHELTENHAM. :

January 17th 1920 announcing a new service to customers.

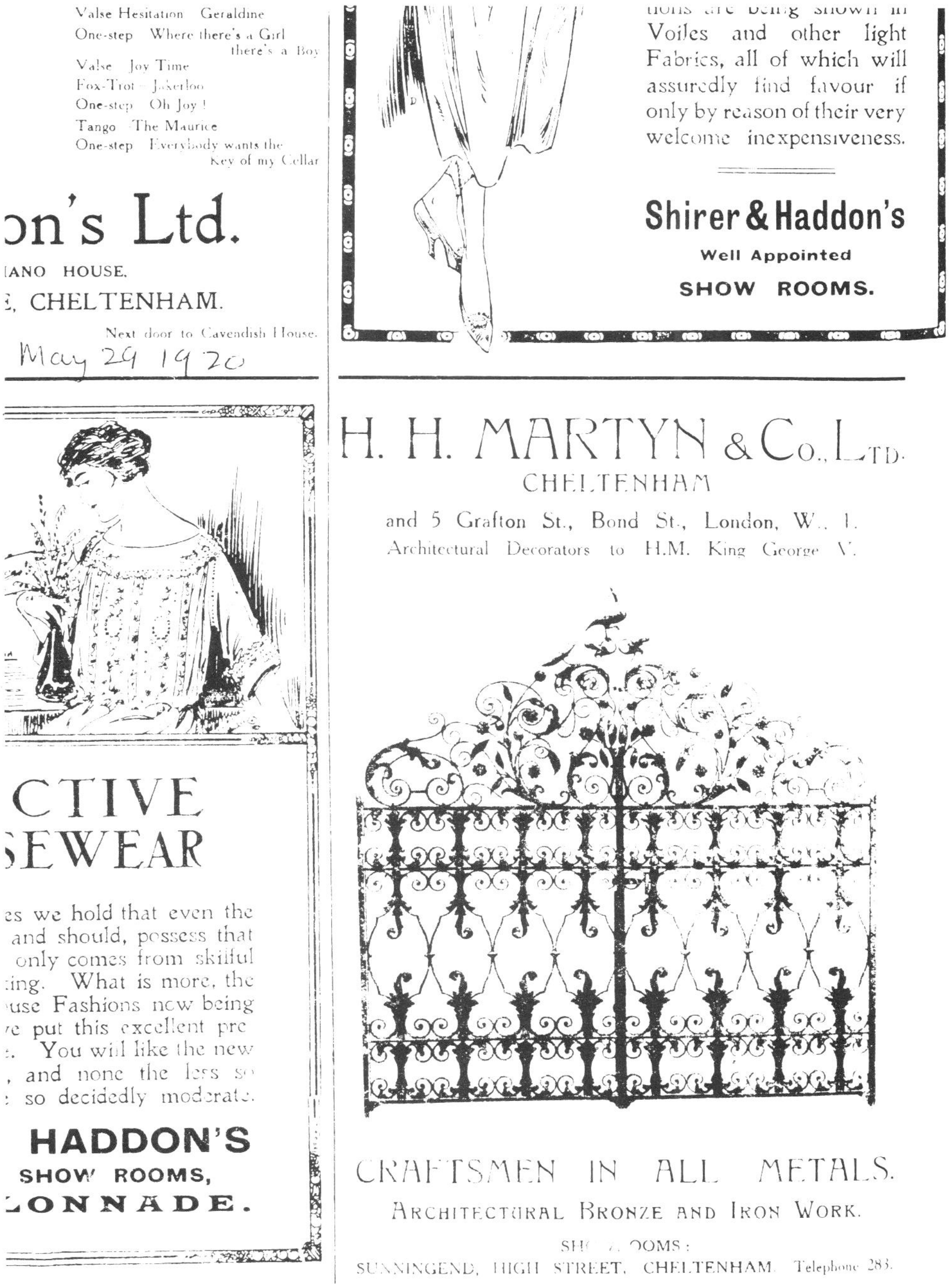

Valse Hesitation Geraldine
One-step Where there's a Girl there's a Boy
Valse Joy Time
Fox-Trot J-kerloo
One-step Oh Joy!
Tango The Maurice
One-step Everybody wants the Key of my Cellar

on's Ltd.
IANO HOUSE.
E, CHELTENHAM.
Next door to Cavendish House.

May 29 1920

tions are being shown in Voiles and other light Fabrics, all of which will assuredly find favour if only by reason of their very welcome inexpensiveness.

Shirer & Haddon's
Well Appointed
SHOW ROOMS.

CTIVE
SEWEAR

es we hold that even the and should, possess that only comes from skilful ting. What is more, the use Fashions now being ve put this excellent pre . You will like the new , and none the less so so decidedly moderate.

HADDON'S
SHOW ROOMS,
LONNADE.

H. H. MARTYN & Co., Ltd.
CHELTENHAM
and 5 Grafton St., Bond St., London, W. 1.
Architectural Decorators to H.M. King George V.

CRAFTSMEN IN ALL METALS.
ARCHITECTURAL BRONZE AND IRON WORK.
SHOW ROOMS:
SUNNINGEND, HIGH STREET, CHELTENHAM. Telephone 283.

29th May 1920.

THE ARCHITECTURAL REVIEW

MARTYNS'
CARVERS,
CHELTENHAM.

Also LONDON and GLASGOW.

Architectural Review, first advertisement, January 1904. The format remained in this form to January 1913.

Architectural Review 1913.

Architectural Review August 1914.

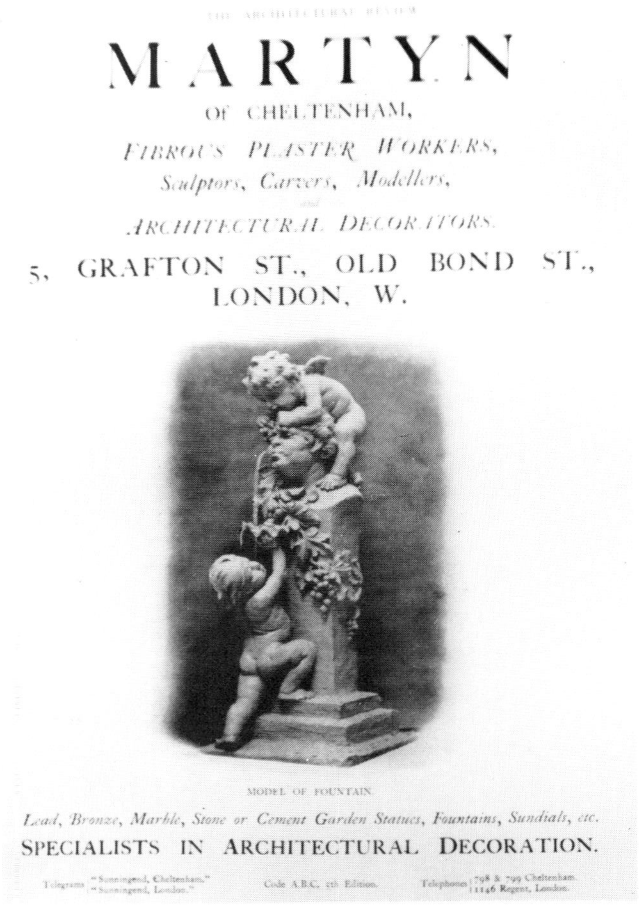

Architectural Review December 1914.

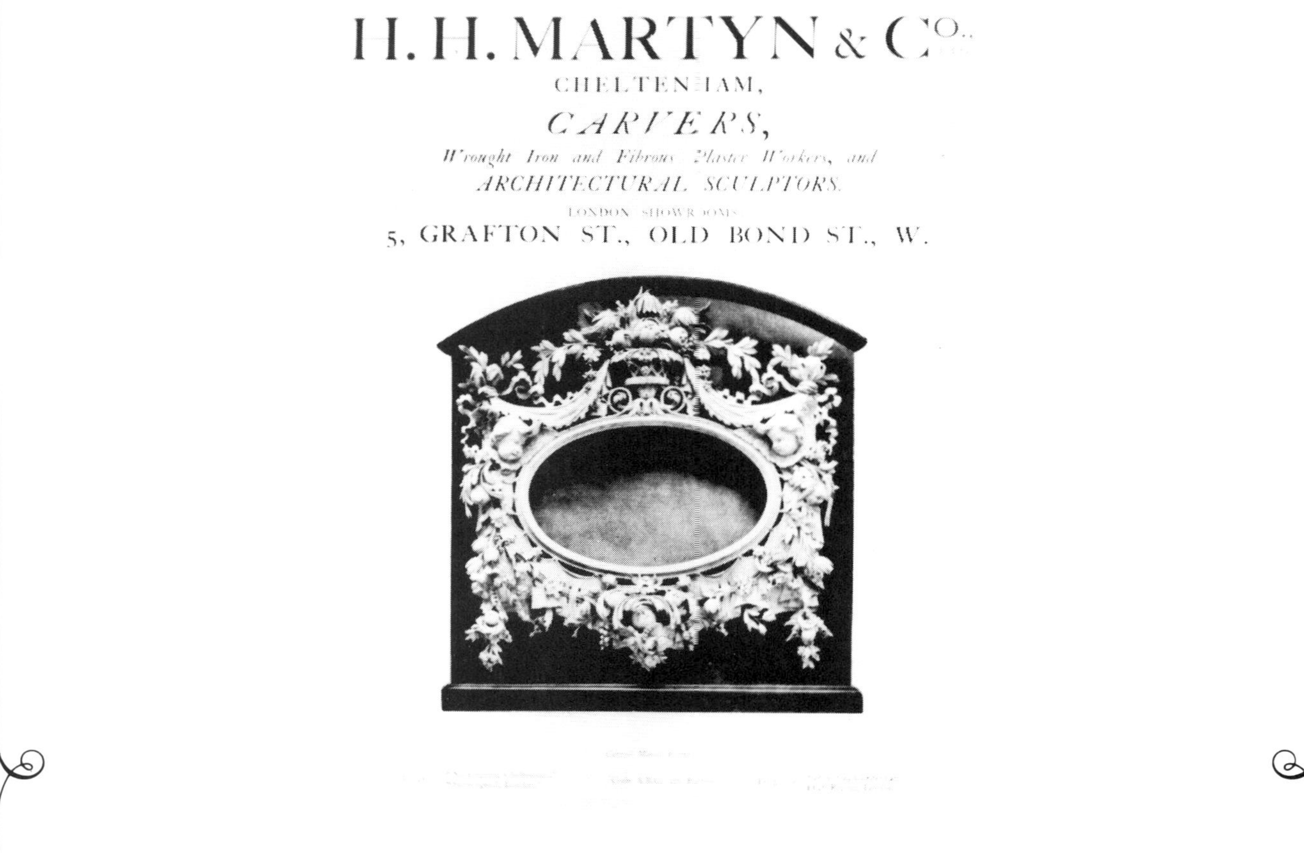

Architectural Review 1915. (All full page advertisements.)

H. H. MARTYN & Co., LTD.

CHELTENHAM,

ARCHITECTURAL DECORATORS

By Appointment

TO H.M. THE KING.

MEMORIAL SCULPTURE

STAINED GLASS

WOOD CARVING

DECORATIVE INTERIORS

BRONZE AND IRON FOUNDERS

READING DESK, WEST U.F. CHURCH, ABERDEEN. G. BENNETT MITCHELL, Esq., M.B.E., F.S.I., (Architect)

and

5 GRAFTON STREET, BOND STREET, LONDON, W.1

Scottish Agents: GALLOWAY GIBB & CO. LTD., 18 Blythswood Square, GLASGOW.

Telegrams { "Sunningend, Cheltenham." "Sunningend, London."

Photographs and Estimates on application.

Telephones { 1162-3-4 Cheltenham. 1148-9 Regent, London.

Telegrams:
"Sunningend, Cheltenham."
"Sunningend, London."

ARCHITECTURAL DECORATORS

BY APPOINTMENT

TO H.M. KING GEORGE V.

Telephones:
1162-3-4 Cheltenham.
1148-9 Regent, London.

H. H. MARTYN & Co. Ltd.

CHELTENHAM

And 5 Grafton Street, Bond Street, London, W.1

ARCHITECTURAL DECORATION IN ALL BRANCHES

KASHMIR STALL, BRITISH EMPIRE EXHIBITION. INTERIOR AND EXTERIOR BY H. H. MARTYN & CO., LTD.
Architect: PAGET L. BAXTER, Esq.

OTHER WORK EXECUTED BY H. H. MARTYN & CO. LTD. AT THE BRITISH EMPIRE EXHIBITION INCLUDES—

PORTIONS OF MALAYA SECTION
,, ,, LYONS GRAND RESTAURANT
,, ,, SARAWAK SECTION
,, ,, PALESTINE SECTION

Electrolier in Wrought and Hammered Bronze executed in our Works for Middlesex Guildhall

Architect: J. G. S. Gibson, Esq.

Telegrams:
"Sunningend, Cheltenham"
"Sunningend, London"

Telephones:
1161-2-3-4 Cheltenham
7355-6 Regent, London

ARCHITECTURAL DECORATORS — By Appointment — TO H.M. KING GEORGE V

H. H. MARTYN & Co. LTD.

Sunningend Works

CHELTENHAM

and

5 Grafton St., Bond St., London, W.1

ARCHITECTURAL DECORATORS
AND
ARTISTS & CRAFTSMEN IN ALL MATERIALS

WROUGHT AND CAST IRON BRONZE WORK · MODELLING SCULPTURE · WOOD CARVING FIBROUS PLASTER · FURNITURE AND FITTINGS . . .

PUBLIC BUILDINGS · THEATRES
and
SHIP INTERIOR DECORATION

Wrought Iron Balustrades and Lift Enclosures at Lazard's Bank, Old Broad Street (illustrated in this issue), executed by H. H. Martyn & Co. Ltd., Cheltenham and London.

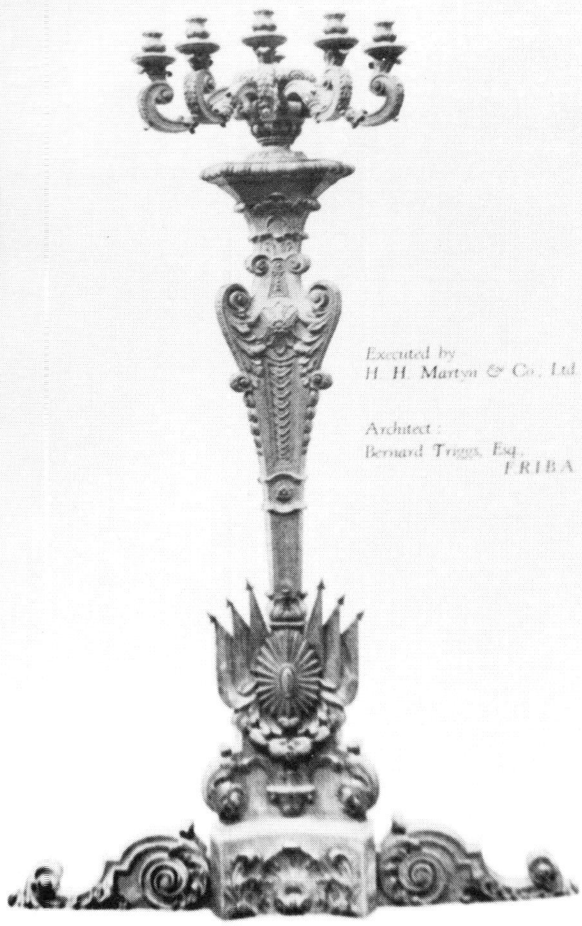

Executed by H. H. Martyn & Co. Ltd.

Architect: Bernard Triggs, Esq., F.R.I.B.A.

Torchère—Lal Bagh Palace—India

Architectural Review April 1926.

Telegrams
"Sunningend, Cheltenham"
"Sunningend, London"

ARCHITECTURAL DECORATORS

BY APPOINTMENT

TO H.M. KING GEORGE V.

Telephones:
1161-2-3-4 Cheltenham
7355-6 Regent, London

H.H.MARTYN & Co.Ltd.

CHELTENHAM

and 5 Grafton Street, Bond Street, London, W.1

ARCHITECTURAL DECORATORS AND CRAFTSMEN IN ALL MATERIALS

CARVED DROPS. Executed by H. H. Martyn & Co. Ltd.

ARCHITECTS' ENQUIRIES INVITED FOR INTERIOR AND EXTERIOR DECORATION

For many years H. H. Martyn & Co. have made a speciality of executing the most delicate carvings in Lime Wood, which are generally acknowledged to be second only to those by Grinling Gibbons, whose work they so closely resemble. Indeed, in some cases the modern productions may be said to surpass in delicacy of execution and fineness of detail the beautiful creations of the seventeenth-century master.

The Regent Cinema,
Bristol.

The illustration shows a portion of the Auditorium, the decorations of which were carried out by H. H. Martyn & Co., Ltd., to the designs of W. H. Watkins, Esq., F.R.I.B.A., Architect, Bristol.

H. H. Martyn & Co., Ltd., invite inquiries for Architectural Decorative Work. Studios at Cheltenham are equipped for Joinery, Woodcarving, Fibrous Plaster, Modelling, Sculpture, Wrot and Cast Metalwork, Furniture, Stonework, etc. etc.

H. H.
MARTYN
& CO., LIMITED
CHELTENHAM
and 5 Grafton Street, Bond Street, London, W.1

Telegrams:
"Sunningend, Cheltenham"
"Sunningend, London"

Telephones:
[illegible] Cheltenham
[illegible] Regent, London

Architectural Review December 1930.

H. H. MARTYN & CO., LTD., SPECIALISE IN ARCHITECTURAL WORK OF EVERY DESCRIPTION AND ARE THE ONLY FIRM IN GREAT BRITAIN EXECUTING THE ENTIRE RANGE OF DECORATIVE WORK IN THEIR OWN STUDIOS.

THE COMPANY HAS BEEN ENTRUSTED WITH IMPORTANT CONTRACTS IN ALL PARTS OF THE WORLD.

QUEEN VICTORIA MEMORIAL, CALCUTTA:
Wrought and Cast Bronzework. Marble Sculpture.

ROYAL COURTS OF JUSTICE, RANGOON:
Cast Bronzework.

NATIONAL BANK OF INDIA, RANGOON:
Wrought Bronzework.

JOHANNESBURG TOWN HALL:
Joinery and Woodcarving.

LAL BAGH PALACE, INDORE:
Fibrous Plasterwork, Joinery, Furniture and entire decorations. Wrought and Cast Bronzework. Cast Nickel Silverwork.

VANCOUVER HOTEL:
Joinery and Woodcarving.

SYDNEY MORNING HERALD:—
Cast Bronze Doors.

NORTHERN PARLIAMENT BUILDINGS, BELFAST:
Fibrous Plaster, Stone and Marble-carving. Wrought and Cast Bronzework.

ETC. ETC.

H. H. Martyn & Co., Ltd.,
have carried out decorative work to the following vessels:

MALOJA
VANDYCK
VAUBAN
LANCASTRIAN
CAMERONIA
MOLDAVIA
EMPRESS OF ASIA
EMPRESS OF RUSSIA
TELMA
ULNA
INDARRA
PRINCESS MARGUERITE
ORVIETO
OTRANTO
ORAMA
ORMONDE
ORONSAY
ORFORD

Figure Head on the Royal Barge, carried out by H. H. Martyn & Co., Ltd., for the Admiralty.

THE
PREMIER
ARCHITECTURAL
DECORATORS

H. H.
MARTYN
& CO. LIMITED
CHELTENHAM
and 5 Grafton Street, Bond Street, London, W.1

THE STUDIOS AT CHELTENHAM COVER FIVE ACRES OF WORKING FLOOR SPACE IN WHICH ARE CARRIED OUT UNDER EXPERT SUPERVISION:—

JOINERY
WOODCARVING
FURNITURE
FIBROUS PLASTER
MODELLING
STONE AND MARBLE-CARVING
SCULPTURE
WROUGHT METALWORK
CAST METALWORK

"but craftsmen are still here and splendid work is still being done . . . We knew this, of course, as a fact arising out of our experience, and the knowledge was doubly underlined on July 9th when a party of members visited the Sunningend Works of Messrs. H. H. Martyn & Co., Ltd., Cheltenham.

"The operations of Martyn's extend to all the building crafts that permit of artistic treatment. Woodwork, metalwork, stone and marble, plastering and painted decoration—and their staff of between 800 and 900 consists of skilled workers in the crafts mentioned. Almost all had work in which they could take an interest, that contented and satisfied the mind in a condition not typical of industry in our time." . . .

The Journal of the Incorporated Clerks of Works Association of Great Britain—September, 1931.

H. H. Martyn & Co., Ltd.,
have carried out decorative work to the following vessels:—

VULCANIA
TOLOA
PRINCESS KATHLEEN
DUCHESS OF BEDFORD
DUCHESS OF ATHOLL
DUCHESS OF RICHMOND
DUCHESS OF YORK
LADY NELSON
LADY DRAKE
LADY RODNEY
LADY HAWKINS
ORONTES
RANGITATA
RANGITANE
EMPRESS OF JAPAN
EMPRESS OF BRITAIN
MONARCH OF BERMUDA
Queen of Bermuda

Advertisement in the Cunard Christmas Number 1931.

at

DERRY & TOMS'

modern store, Kensington,

H. H. MARTYN & CO. LTD. executed FIBROUS PLASTER WORK, PAINTING AND DECORATING, JOINERY, INCLUDING DOORS AND SURROUNDS, LIFT FRONT SURROUNDS, DADO PANELLING AND MIRROR TREATMENT TO WALLS,
BRONZE FURNITURE TO DOORS, CASTING OF WINDOW GRILLES TO EXTERIOR ELEVATIONS.

Architect: Bernard George, Esq., A.R.I.B.A.

H. H.
MARTYN
& CO LIMITED
CHELTENHAM AND LONDON
5 Grafton Street Bond Street London W1

Architectural Review September 1933.

WROUGHT METALWORK—1. THE FORGE

Even in this machine age there are still some things which can be better made by hand. And there are still men to be found who are craftsmen in the highest sense of the word. We have many such men in our own works, though we, too, are far from despising the machine. Some people hold that to make by hand in these days is an anachronism; but others who require that indefinable "quality," which even to-day is appropriate to much building work, will agree that it can only be truly and honestly produced by the care and affection which the craftsman bestows upon his work.

Our activities are by no means limited to wrought metalwork; in fact, our works are equipped for all sorts of architectural work in which fine craftsmanship is involved: Joinery, Furniture, Fibrous Plaster, Cast Metalwork, Stone Carving, Wood Carving, and so on. We are, besides, the makers of "Maisteel" metal door frames.

We have draughtsmen who are expert in each of these various subjects, and our drawing office is at the disposal of architects who wish for help or advice.

H. H. MARTYN AND COMPANY, LIMITED, *Sunningend Works, Cheltenham, and 5, Grafton Street, London, W.1.*

Architectural Review. Arthur Smith featuring in the October 1935 issue.

H. H.

MARTYN

& CO., LIMITED

CHELTENHAM

and 5 Grafton Street, Bond Street, London, W.1

FOR FLATS, HOUSING SCHEMES, ETC.

"MARSTEEL" SLIDING WINDOWS

"Steel Trim" is assuming greater and greater importance in the world of building; for door frames, doors, skirtings, window sills and radiator casings it is coming to be used instead of timber, with which it competes in cost as well as in efficiency. We shall be glad to send full particulars or to give advice about it to those who are interested.

DOORS
WINDOWS
DOOR FRAMES
WALL SKIRTINGS
WINDOW SILLS
RADIATOR CASINGS
PICTURE RAILS
CORNICES, ETC.

CASTLE CIRCUS HOUSE, TORQUAY FOR WALTER W. JENKINS & CO., LTD.

STEWART LLOYD THOMSON, A.R.I.B.A. ARCHITECT, LONDON

The "Marsteel" sliding windows shown in the illustrations are electrically welded and zinc sprayed. Other work carried out on this building consists of roof railings, bronze on wood entrance doors, steel flagpole, bronze nameplates, etc.

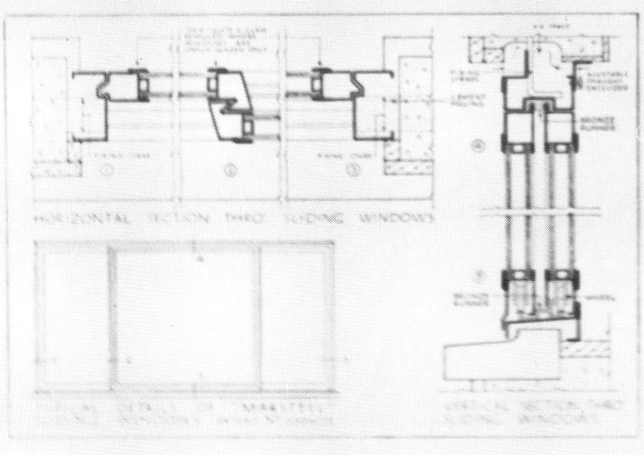

Architectural Review August 1936.

A selection of advertisements.

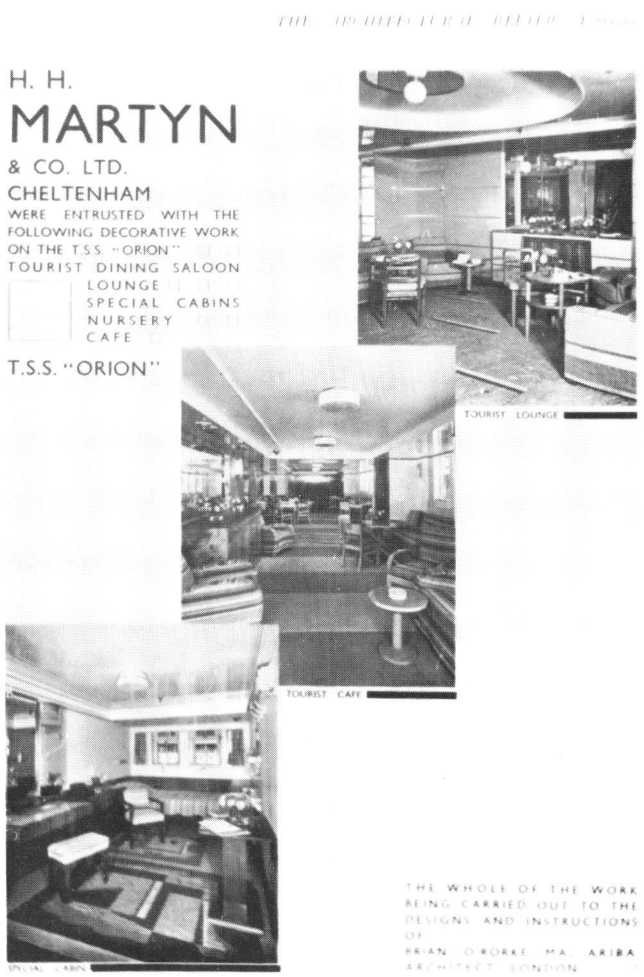

A selection of advertisements.

Architectural Review. The last advertisement to appear and showing a decline to wording only. 1939.

Architectural Review June 1913

H. H. Martyn & Co. Ltd.

(Associated Art Craftsmen)

STUDIOS:
SUNNINGEND.

ART JOINERY WORKS:
59 HIGH STREET.

Cheltenham.

Telegrams:
Martyn, Sunningend, Cheltenham.
Telephone No. 298.

Sculpture Carvings . .
Architectural Modellings
Fibrous Plaster and . .
Carton Pierre . . . .
Metal Work, &c. &c. .

Carved Mahogany Frieze, executed for and designed by Sir William B. Richmond, R.A.

SOME thirty years ago the Arts and Crafts of England stood on a considerably lower plane than they do to-day, the firms then doing good work could have been counted on the fingers of one hand, and notwithstanding that little good work was attempted, still less was accomplished.

Mr. H. H. Martyn, the original founder of the present Company, then started the present business, with the view of producing the *best*. Associates were selected and carefully trained; several of these early Students, now artists of considerable repute, are still assisting the Company, and it is with pleasure we feel that the ideal of thirty years since is now fully recognised.

The 1905 brochure which was interleaved with tissue and printed in two colours.

During these years the reputation won by good work has caused a continued and large development in the business, and to-day we are proud to think that our firm stands second to none in the Kingdom.

Corner of Wood-Carving Shop.

Some five years ago the increase of trade necessitated the formation of the business into a Limited Company; the original founder remained a Director, though the active management was placed in the hands of his son, Mr. A. W. Martyn, and Mr. H. A. Dutton, whose wide experience was found of great value. This gave the Firm the desired opportunity of associating their best craftsmen with them permanently, indeed, making the business as it was intended, an Association of Art Craftsmen, and by this means they were enabled to secure the best interests of the Artists, and to give better results at a given cost than the ordinary unassociated business.

Panel Chimney-Piece. J. J. Talbot, Esq., Architect, Liverpool.

The Shops were extended and a Plant of the most up-to-date machinery was laid down this being a necessity demanded by Clients who desired that such joinery work as might be connected with the carvings should be controlled and executed under the same supervision. Studios for Modelling and shops for the execution of high-class Fibrous Plaster Work have been fitted up, and at present there are some two hundred men employed in the various Studios, a large proportion of them being occupied in artistic work. Amongst the latter we would especially mention our chief Sculptor, who has repeatedly exhibited at the Royal Academy, and whose work at the Liverpool Walker Art Gallery induced the Liverpool Corporation to ask him to compete by sending in a design for the Queen Victoria Memorial to be erected there; and from something like a hundred designs sent in by various artists he received the first award

Panel in Marble for Chimney-Piece, Designed by J. J. Talbot, Esq., Architect, Liverpool.

View of Joinery Works, about 6,000 feet super.

of £100. An idea of this Model may be seen by reference to the illustration showing the Sculpture Studio. The Memorial is designed to be about 50 feet high, with a colossal central figure of Her late Majesty in white marble, standing under a canopy. Crowning the cupola is a figure of St. George slaying the Dragon. On the base are twelve life size Bronze Figures representing the Imperial Forces. On the Pediment are Sculptured Figures emblematical of Poetry, Music, Literature, Painting, Sculpture, and Architecture. Medallions of the Empress Frederick (Princess Royal), Duke of Coburg and Princess Alice are in bas-relief on the bronze pediments rising from the base.

Caryatide for Chimney Piece. G. H. Fellowes Prynne, Esq., Architect.

Cartouche for Chimney Piece. R. A. Briggs. Esq., Architect.

We have also had the honour of forwarding to several of the Colonies designs for Memorials to the late Queen, and are still being invited

Example of Fibrous Plaster Work.

to tender for further work in this connection.

We have also been honored with work for the Royal Family, the Colonial Government, etc., and the Company continue to receive the confidence of Clients, many of whom, high in the Architectural profession, we have worked under for many years.

Among works of public and general interest executed by us may be mentioned the interior carvings for the Assize Courts, Birmingham, under the direction of the well known Architect,

Aston Webb, Esq., A.R.A.; and the Reredos Altar (see Frontispiece) and Screen, etc., for Jesus Chapel, Worcester Cathedral, which is considered to be some of the finest work executed in the 19th century; this was designed by R. A. Briggs, Esq., F.R.I.B.A.

Late Extension of Joinery Works.

In fact the work both ecclesiastical and domestic, embracing the various styles of Architecture, to be seen in all parts of the Kingdom testifies to the confidence reposed in us by some of the ablest and best known Architects of our time.

Amongst other commissions executed and Clients worked for might be mentioned carving (wood and stone) for Hereford Cathedral and Malvern College Chapel, for Sir Arthur Blomfield & Sons; E. Goldie, Esq., under whose direction some exceedingly fine Gothic Canopies are now being erected by us at Hawkesyard Priory; G. H. Fellowes Prynne, Esq., F.R.I.B.A., Altar etc. at Holy Trinity Church, and Carvings at Gifford House, Roehampton, and numerous commissions of varying importance.

Figure of St. Patrick.

The various photos of our work represented in these pages will, we trust, do more than words to illustrate the class of work which it will be always our best effort to produce, and which we believe will cast no discredit on the advanced development of artistic craft work of the twentieth century.

As all our work is finished throughout under our own personal supervision we can guarantee absolute satisfaction, and the fact that we are constantly receiving testimonials from our customers in all parts of the country speaks of the confidence which is reposed in us.

Another Corner of Joinery Works.

Portion of the Wood Carving Studio.

View of Machine Shop.

Copy of Letter received referring to Portrait Panel.

Carved Walnut Panel in Overmantle at Tunstall Manor. L. Banks, Esq., Architect, London.

MESSRS. H. H. MARTYN & CO.,
CHELTENHAM.

Dear Sirs,

I have your favor enclosing photos of the three Panels which you have made for my Billiard Room Overmantels, and which I have pleasure in accepting. Regarding the manner in which you have carried out the work, I can only say that the centre panel (a likeness of my late Father) far exceeded my expectations, and unless I had had the actual experience I could scarcely have believed it possible to obtain such a perfect representation.

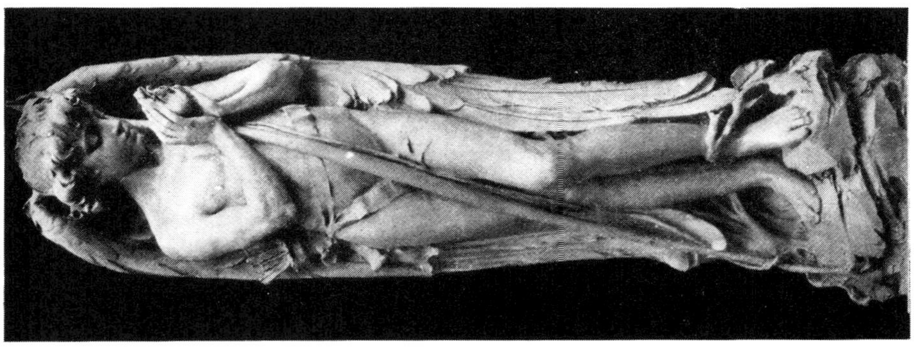

Figure for Niche, Gifford House. G. H. Fellowes Prynne, Esq. Architect, London. Exhibited Royal Academy, 1901.

The walnut panel above was carved by Harry Breckin.

Corner of the Sculpture Studio, showing Model for the Liverpool (competition) Queen Victoria Memorial.

Sketch Model of Chimney Piece, E. Goldie, Esq., Architect, London.

Example of "Grinling Gibbons" Carving. R. A. Briggs, Esq., Architect.

Altar Piece Waterloo, E. Kirby, Esq., Architect, Liverpool.

A Panel
for
Overmantle,
Tunstall
Manor.

Works executed for

HER LATE MAJESTY QUEEN VICTORIA

J. S. Alder, Esq.
McVicar Anderson, Esq.
J. Arnold, Esq.
Messrs. Boehmer & Gibbs.
Messrs. Buckland & Farmer.
Sir Arthur W. Blomfield & Sons.
R. A. Briggs, Esq.
Messrs. W. & C. A. Bassett-Smith.
Swindon Barter, Esq.
Messrs. Banister, Fletcher & Sons.
Messrs. Baines & Son.
W. H. Bidlake, Esq.
J. Banks, Esq.
Messrs. Carpenter & Ingelow.
Messrs. Cossins, Peacock & Bewlay.
G. Cuthbert, Esq.
Messrs. Cox & Silk.
Somers Clarke, Esq.
A. Conder, Esq.
E. Dunn, Esq.
Messrs. Douglas & Minchul.
Messrs. Essex, Nichol & Goodman.
R. Fowler, Esq.
E. Goldie, Esq.
Messrs. Gordon & Gunton.
G. H. Gaud, Esq.
H. S. Gamble, Esq.
H. B. Guest, Esq.
Messrs. Higgs & Rudkin.
Messrs. Henman & Cooper.
Messrs. W. Hale & Sons.
Messrs. T. H. & F. Healey.

Grill for Staircase. G. H. Fellowes Prynne, Esq., Architect.

Statue of
St. Peter.
Sir A.
Blomfield &
Sons,
Architects,
London.

Works executed for—*continued.*

Ralph Heaton, Esq.
J. J. Holding, Esq.
J. Hopkins, Esq.
Messrs. Ingoll & Son.
Messrs. Isaacs & Florence.
E. Kirby, Esq.
F. Kempson, Esq.
W. T. Lowdell, Esq.
Messrs. Martin & Martin.
Messrs. Newland & Higgs.
Messrs. Nevison & Newton.
T. Norton, Esq.
E. Nicholls, Esq.
Lloyd Oswell, Esq.
A. Beresford Pite, Esq.
G. H. Fellowes Prynne, Esq.
Messrs. Protheroe & Phillott.
Messrs. Potts, Son & Pickup.
C. E. Ponting, Esq.
J. A. Pippett, Esq.
Messrs. Pugin & Pugin.
Sir William B. Richmond, R.A.
E. R. Robson, Esq.
P. Robson, Esq.
Greenwood Stephenson, Esq.
G. H. Shepherd, Esq.
Messrs. Sinnott, Sinnott & Powell.
J. J. Talbot, Esq.
Messrs. Treadwell & Martin.
Bruce Vaughan, Esq.
Messrs. Waller & Son.
Aston Webb, Esq., A.R.A.
T. B. Whinney, Esq.
Messrs. Worthington & Son.

Works executed at

Canterbury Cathedral.
Worcester Cathedral.
Gloucester Cathedral.
Hereford Cathedral.
Tewkesbury Abbey.
Malvern Abbey.
All Souls College, Oxford.
Cheltenham College Chapel.
Cheltenham College.
Ladies' College, Cheltenham.
Malvern College.
St. Agatha's Church, Birmingham
Harborne Church, Birmingham.
Stirchley Church, Birmingham.
St. Edward's Church, Birmingham.

Works executed at—*continued.*

St. Simon's Church, Birmingham.
St. Oswald's Church, Birmingham.
St. Paul's Convent, Birmingham.
St. Patrick's Church, Walsall.
Parish Church, Stone, Kidderminster.
Parish Church, Bewdeley.
St. Simon's, Paddington, London
St. Lawrence's Church, Old Jewry.
St. Saviour's Church, Ealing.
Holy Trinity Church, Roehampton.
St. Peter's Church, South Tottenham.
St. James' Church, Muswell Hill.
Parish Church, Leamington.
Hawkesyard Priory, Rugeley.
St. Saviour's Home, Hendon.
Parish Church, Shenley, Bucks.
St. John's Church, Sidcup, Kent.
Trinity Church, Henley-on-Thames.
St. Mark's Church, Brighton.
St. Andrew's Church, Starbeck.
Lowe House, St. Helen's.
St. Nicholas Procathedral, Liverpool.
St. Thomas' Church, Waterloo, Liverpool.
St. Wilfrid's Church, Preston.
Parish Church, Chorley.
Roman Catholic Church, Chorley.
St. Werburgh's Church, Chester.
St. Peter's Church, Stalybridge.
St. Thomas' Church, Bedford Leigh.
Manafon Church.
Parish Church, Upton Bishop, Ross.
St. Mary's Church, Monmouth.
Parish Church, Ilfracombe.
St. James' Church, Devonport.
St. Neot's Church, Cornwall.
Sheviock Church, Cornwall.
St. John's Church, Penzance.
The Parish Church, Cheltenham.
Christ Church.
All Saints' Church.
St. Phillip's & St. James' Church.
St. Stephen's Church.
St. John's Church.
Church of the Holy Apostles.
St. Mark's Church.
Leckhampton Parish Church.
Cleeve Parish Church.
Prestbury Parish Church.
Ashorne Hill House.
Cowley Manor.
Thornton Manor.
Brockhampton Park.
Tunstall Manor.
Gifford House, Roehampton
Addersley Park.
Severn End, Worcester.
Battenhall Mount.
Sudeley Castle.
Madresfield Court.
Blakesware.
Berkeley Castle.
Pyports, Cobham.
Blackpool Town Hall.
Assize Courts, Birmingham.
New Library, Birmingham.
Kyrle Hall, Birmingham.
Christchurch Buildings, Birmingham.
London C. & M. Bank, Birmingham.
London C. & M. Bank, Chepstow.
London C. & M. Bank, Salisbury.
Manchester College, Oxford.
Metropolitan Fire Offices, Moorgate Street, London.
Lloyd's Advertising Offices, London.
Buildings, Oxford Street, London.
The Exchange (extension), London.
Queen Anne Schools, Caversham.
Lloyds Bank, Cheltenham.

Statuette of Sir Launcelote.

9 Hill Street, Mayfair, London W. Architect: R.L. Williams. Portion of Decorative Ceiling.

H.H. Martyn at 90.

A.W. Martyn.

Martyn family portrait. Ida, Cyril, Mrs. Ada Martyn, Madeline.

Chapter 18

FINAL REFLECTIONS

When I began writing this book, my intention was to produce a document of record, because I felt that the massive commitment of time and skill which had gone into Martyns over nearly a century should have a place, no matter how small, in the annals of this country.

In the course of my six years' research, I found that I had undertaken something much more than a simple accumulation of facts. After tracing and viewing thousands of works of art, ranging in scale from the miniature to the majestic, both in three dimensions and in illustrations; after I had read the memories, views and aspirations of the men involved; after I had met and talked with the survivors, none of them young and some well into their eighties and nineties; I found that I had opened the door into a treasure house of social history. I can also say that whatever effort and time I have put into this book, I have been rewarded tenfold by the pleasure and interest I have enjoyed.

In writing the story of Martyns, it is difficult to unravel the men from the work they produced, because in art, the work is the man and the man is the work. The gifted artists and craftsmen of Martyns are part of a tradition which commenced with the cave drawings of our distant ancestors and has been carried on down the ages by countless thousands of dedicated men. Their names have disappeared but their memorials are all around us. They represent civilisation, in the sense that their work is super-numerary to the crude and basic requirements of existence and appeals to the aesthetic and spiritual elements which are peculiar to the human animal.

What kind of men were these artists? They were privileged to be born with an uncommon gift which in some ways they had no choice but to express, and to which they were committed throughout their lives. In producing works of skill and beauty they added to, not subtracted from, the store of human good. Perfectionists in their trade, they were by and large honourable men in their lives, their gifts transcending the petty rivalries and greed of less fortunate souls.

In many ways their lot was harsh, especially by the pampered standards of today. They depended entirely on others to provide them with work, and when this was not available, they found themselves without income. After a lifetime of dedicated effort, they could expect no rich and easy retirement. Many of them suffered the vexation of an uneasy business takeover by a company which was clearly out of sympathy with the style and philosophy of Martyns.

All I can say, after my long search for the ghosts of the past and my many meetings with those that still survive, is that in the true sense of the word, these were great men.

What then of the founder of the business and his son? Outstanding as were the individual artists who served Martyns, their contribution was only made possible by the special qualities of H.H. and A.W. Martyn. Artists have always depended on patronage, and with the passing of the great courts and the decline in the power and influence of the Church, it has fallen in recent generations to men of business to organise, fund and support the arts.

Himself an artist in stone, H.H. Martyn recognised from his earliest years in business the need for a structure within which art could flourish. A humble and honest man, he brought into the business others of greater gifts, and so motivated and supported them that they were able to achieve astonishing success, both individually and as a corporate unit. Anyone who has undertaken quite simple tasks of organisation and planning involving the handling and delivery of materials will appreciate the staggering level of devotion and efficiency achieved in the complex fields mastered by the management and staff of Martyns over the years. The opportunities for error were infinite, and only quite exceptional care at every level could have created and maintained the company's reputation for such a long period.

The story of the two Martyns is an intensely human one. Both of them faced extreme problems and rose heroically to the occasion. Both had an instinctive recognition that the future lay with the young men, and that there was a profound obligation on the present generation to train the men of the next. Above all, both were generous in the broadest sense of that word — by no means sentimental, but prepared to give practical help both to their personal families and to the wider family of associates who toiled with them under the banner of Martyns.

The peculiar circumstances of the twentieth century saw to it that the influence of Martyns extended beyond the world of art. Twice within a generation Gloster Aircraft Co., lusty offshoot of a marriage of necessity, contributed towards the preservation of that civilisation without which the peaceable arts cannot flourish. This is yet another thread to the story — the courage, skill and flair of brave young men who lived dangerously both in peacetime and in war. Successors of those pioneers at Cheltenham and Hucclecote are responsible for artefacts in their own way as fine as any work of art, both technically and in the manner they have affected all our lives.

Great men have heart as well as intellect. No-one could fail to be moved by H.H. Martyn's recollections, at the age of 80, of his cruelly deprived childhood, his meeting with his childhood sweetheart, to whom he was happily married for so many years, and the story of his ultimate success. It is equally inspiring to read of his unselfish dedication to the welfare of those less fortunate than himself, whose problems and heartaches he could understand only too well from his own experience.

In A.W. we have a picture of the thrusting businessman, in day-to-day control of his burgeoning company and yet finding the time to plan ahead for a future with which he knew he would not be personally concerned.

No-one knows precisely the reason why he disengaged himself from the two companies which had been his life for nearly thirty years, but we can be sure it was a sensible decision based on objective thinking. It enabled him to start what amounted to a new career, the culmination of which was his association with George Dowty. His generosity to Dowty, including the fact that he refrained from taking control of Dowty's company when it was his for the asking, tells more about the man than volumes.

To sum up, none of us catches more than a glimpse of the enormous canvas that constitutes life on earth. In our short stay, we enjoy the beauty and gifts of nature, our association with our peers and the works of art, craft and skill which come about when the human brain is applied to the natural materials of our world. What is unique about Martyns is the way in which the human, the natural and the artefact combined to produce something of lasting greatness.

Finally, in H.H. Martyn's own modest words:

> *I do not want to seem boastful for I have personally done little beyond inciting far more clever craftsmen than myself, at any cost to do* **the best** *that was in them: this is the only and small success of which I can boast.*

INDEX

Notes to the Index:

1. Within the book there is a series of lists of work carried out by Martyns, venues, personnel, etc. Rather than itemise all the contents of these lists in the main index, it has been considered more convenient for readers to include a separate index of lists which follows the main index.

2. 'Macmillan' is spelt correctly in the index, incorrectly in the text.

Beck, Wallace, 188.

Whiteman, Thomas Weston, 16.
Whittle, Frank, 173.
Whyte, Robert, 228.
Wilcox, Sam, 146.
William III, 133.
Williams, Charles, 18.
Williams, T.O., 167.
Willis, Fred, 164.
Winchester College Chapel, 50.
Winchester College, 51.
Windsor Castle, 3, 56, 255.
Winter Gardens, Cheltenham, 47, 49, 153.
Winter, Fred, 31.
Wintle, C., 112.
Wolseley Car Co., 164.
Woolwich, 41, 57.
Worcester Cathedral, 13, 41, 57.
Working Men's College Magazine, 16.
Working Men's College, 15, 17, 21, 31, 38.
Working Men's Institute, 10.
Wren, 73.
Wykes, Henry, 133.
Y.M.C.A., 43.
Yeand, C.F., 47, 60.
Young, R., 194.
Young, R.W., 47.
Youngman, H.J., 74.

Robert Lindsey Clark R.S.B.S. Martyns head sculptor and art director.